D1499363

Careers of the Criminally Insane

Careers of the Criminally Insane

Excessive Social Control of Deviance

Henry J. Steadman

and

Joseph J. Cocozza

Lexington Books
D.C. Heath and Company
Lexington, Massachusetts
Toronto London

Library of Congress Cataloging in Publication Data

Steadman, Henry J.
Careers of the criminally insane.

1. Insane, Criminal and dangerous—United States. I. Cocozza, Joseph J., joint author. II. Title.
HV6791.S83 364.1 74-16930
ISBN 0-669-96503-0

Published simultaneously in Canada

Printed in the United States of America

International Standard Book Number: 0-669-96503-0

Library of Congress Catalog Card Number: 74-16930

Contents

List of Figures

List of Tables

Foreword

Jackson Toby
Rutgers University

Some phrases have the power to evoke fear out of proportion to the reality to which they refer. ''Drug addict'' is one such phrase; the ''criminally insane'' is another. The research reported in this book provides an opportunity to find out what the phrase ''criminally insane'' really means.

Who are the criminally insane? They are persons involuntarily held in special security hospitals (often operated by a correctional agency), hospitals more oriented to custody than to treatment. How are persons sent to hospital-prisons for the criminally insane? There are four paths, two important, two comparatively unimportant.

1. The least important path is the one that the general public thinks of first: adjudication in a criminal court as *not guilty* of some serious crime by reason of insanity. Only about 2 percent of persons incarcerated in hospitals for the criminally insane are sent there for this reason.

2. Another relatively unimportant path is the result of violent behavior in a civil psychiatric hospital. For these persons, the status of ''dangerously mentally ill'' is achieved, not by conviction of a criminal offense, but by *transfer* from a civil hospital to a hospital-prison for the criminally insane.

3. Incompetency to stand trial is a major path into hospitals for the criminally insane. The NIMH monograph, *Competency to Stand Trial and Mental Illness* (1973:2) estimated that in 1967 15,000 persons were committed to hospitals for the criminally insane for incompetency in the United States compared with 1,450 commitments resulting from verdicts of not guilty by reason of insanity.

4. Finally, some persons are incarcerated in hospitals for the criminally insane because they are first imprisoned for a criminal offense and then become mentally ill. This path is also a major one.

The research reported in this book was the incidental byproduct of a 1966 decision of the United States Supreme Court *Baxstrom* v. *Herold*. Johnnie Baxstrom, a mentally ill inmate, had been ''civilly committed at the expiration of his penal sentence without the jury review available to all other persons civilly committed in New York'' (U. S. Supreme Court, 1966). This was common practice not only in New York State but in the rest of the country. However, Chief Justice Earl Warren, speaking for the majority of the Court, held that such procedures were unfair; they failed to give mentally ill inmates equal protection of the laws in two respects. Most obviously, the mentally ill inmate did not have an opportunity for a jury trial, a right which a noncriminal could claim. Second, the mentally ill inmate being considered for continued incarceration in a hospital-prison for the criminally insane did not get a hearing to determine whether he was so *dangerous* to others as to justify being held in a *correctional* hospital rather than in the more *open civil* hospital. He was presumed dangerous merely because he had previously committed a crime (regardless of the nature of the crime of which he had been convicted).

The alleged dangerousness of the criminally insane (Morris, 1968) is one of the central issues of this book. When the Supreme Court held in 1966 that Johnnie Baxstrom was being unconstitutionally incarcerated, it set in motion a natural experiment. Not only Baxstrom but nearly a thousand other inmates of hospitals for the criminally insane were transferred to civil hospitals, and ultimately about half of them were released to the community. Thus, an unprecedented opportunity existed to discover whether long incarcerations—fifteen years on the average—were justified. Steadman and Cocozza capitalized on this research opportunity; they examined the behavior of the Baxstrom patients first in the civil hospitals and then in the free community. As you will see, their conclusion is that the psychiatrists in the hospitals for the criminally insane were too cautious and the protection of society does not require such lengthy incarceration of the so-called criminally insane. A comparison of Figures 1 and 2 elucidates their argument. Figure 1 portrays the assumptions of most laymen concerning the criminally insane; in it a *majority* of those simultaneously psychotic and criminal are dangerous. Figure 2 portrays the facts as the researchers uncovered them; only a small *minority* of the criminally insane constitute a serious threat to other people

In reading this important research report, keep in mind its limitations. The Baxstrom patients were quite old when they were finally released —over 50 on the average. Since the younger patients tended to be more aggressive in the community, it is likely that the conclusions of this research would be less applicable to younger inmates of hospitals for the criminally insane. Second, the Baxstrom cases ultimately transferred or released had been kept in hospitals for the criminally insane because psychiatrists were reluctant to transfer or release them, but they did not constitute *all* the criminally insane patients in these hospitals.

Nevertheless, the Steadman-Cocozza report cannot be dismissed lightly. It suggests that American society has been responding irrationally and punitively to a group at the social margin: mentally ill individuals whose behavior is alleged (or proven) to have violated our criminal laws. While some of them may indeed require prolonged incarceration, many do not; we have used a meat ax to kill a spider. If the test of the moral worth of a civilization is the way it treats its weakest members, the incredibly lengthy incarcerations of criminally insane persons is a blemish that requires correcting. Earlier release means a slight additional risk of criminal

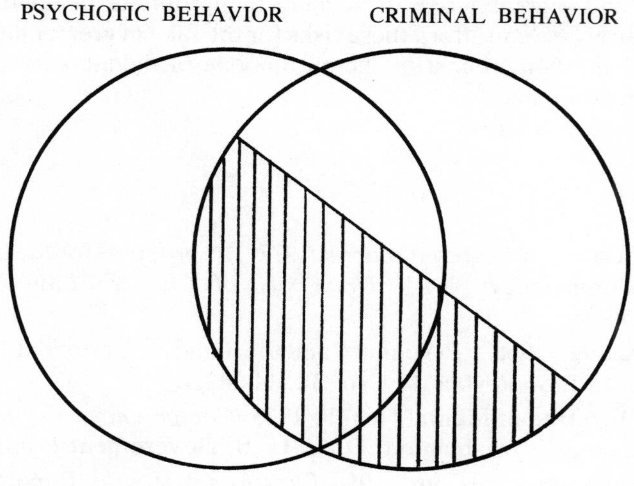

Figure 1. The Popular Stereotype of the Interrelation among Mental Illness, Criminality, and Dangerousness

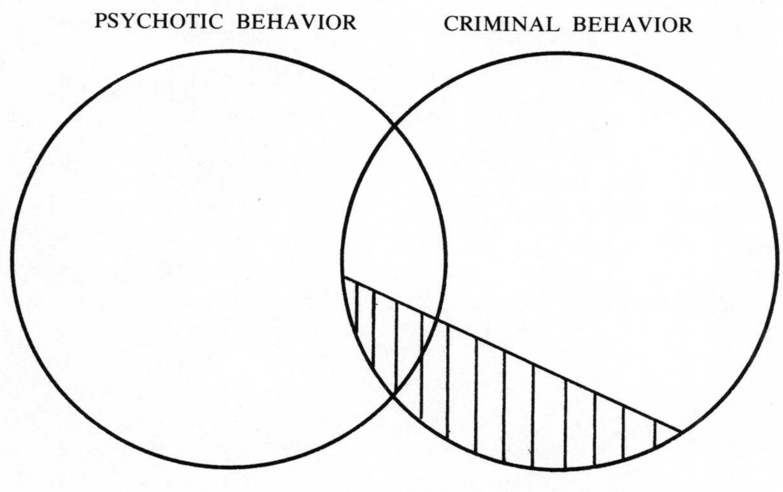

Figure 2. The Most Likely Empirical Interrelation among Mental Illness, Criminality, and Dangerousness.

violence and a greater risk of socially inappropriate behavior in public places. Surely we can afford these risks for the sake of greater justice just as we afford the human cost of the automobile (accidents) for the sake of greater convenience.

References

Burt, Robert A., and Norval Morris. 1972. "A proposal for the abolition of the incompetency plea." *University of Chicago Law Review* 40 (Fall):66-95.

Morris, Norval. 1968. "Psychiatry and the dangerous criminal." *Southern California Law Review* 41 (No. 3):514-547.

National Institute of Mental Health. 1973. *Competency to stand trial and mental illness*. Washington, D.C.: U. S. Government Printing Office.

United States Supreme Court. 1966. *Baxstrom* v. *Herold*. Reports 383:107.

Acknowledgments

The research that forms the core of this book was initiated by Elaine Cumming, then the Director of the Mental Health Research Unit, where this work was conceptualized and begun in 1969. It is to her that much of the credit must be given for seizing the opportunities offered by the sequelae of the *Baxstrom* decision. The guidance and stimulation she provided at the outset were invaluable.

The Baxstrom project reflects to a great extent the commitment to critical research by the New York State Department of Mental Hygiene. It provided the gamut of research aid, from office space to computer time and personnel. This interest in and commitment to research is also reflected in the complete cooperation of the directors of all the state hospitals who allowed us total access to their records. All of the case materials cited herein either use pseudonyms, if confidential records were the source, or are drawn from records in the public domain. All project work was in accord with the Use of Human Subjects' guidelines of the National Institute of Mental Health's Center for Studies of Crime and Delinquency, whose funds (MH 20367) supplemented those of New York State.

Portions of the analysis presented in Chapters 5 through 8 were conducted as part of Cocozza's doctoral dissertation work at Case Western Reserve University.

Two people who especially contributed to this research were Charles Eysaman and Margaret Perkins. Chuck, a contributor to all Unit projects, oversaw all facets of the data collection and early analyses, while Peggy gave many extra hours systematically organizing lists of patients that enabled us to obtain records on all 967 Baxstrom patients and all 359 of the Pre-Baxstrom patients. Also within the MHRU, Terry O'Brien and Gregg Bell were mainstays in data collection, coding, and analysis. Other researchers and clerks whose work was crucial were Arlene Halfon, Gary Keveles, who had prime responsibility for the community follow-up, Leah Arnold, Linda Heck, Paul Niedbolac, and Daniel Couture, a yeoman coder.

As the manuscript was readied for initial reading and final preparation, Mrs. Gail Bullis and the rest of the MHRU secretarial staff were truely indispensible and without exception met the tight deadlines we always seemed to set.

The current form of the book, with whatever deficiencies it may still have, is vastly improved over early drafts which were read and insightfully critiqued by Joseph Morrissey and Loren Roth, two excellent reviewers and esteemed friends. Jackson Toby, who has gifted us with the foreword, and Robert Burt also had comments which have been incorporated.

Another person whose contributions were somewhat less direct is Norvall Morris, one of the people who first recognized the importance of the *Baxstrom* decision and the value of a follow-up of the patients it affected. His interest had a great deal to do with our undertaking the manuscript.

Although acknowledging one's family often seems little more than a perfunctory routine, in our case it is not. Carolyn and Frances, our wives, aided us throughout the research itself and during the writing of this manuscript not by any single idea or phrase that you may read here, but by their confidence in our conviction about the importance of our endeavors. Our debt for this is as significant as any of these others.

In these few acknowledgments we have attempted to express our appreciation to those people and agencies who aided us. Hopefully their assistance which has resulted in this book will lead to some insights into Johnnie Baxstrom, the people who bear his name as the "Baxstrom patients," and to all those who are called criminally insane, of whom so little is known and of whom most often so little is desired to be known.

Permission to reprint materials under copyright is gratefully acknowledged from the following:

American Medical Association for quoting from Bernard Rubin, "The Prediction of Dangerousness in Mentally Ill Criminals," *Archives of General Psychiatry* 77 (September): 397-407. © 1972, American Medical Association;

American Psychiatric Association for quoting from J.J. Cocozza and H.J. Steadman, "Some Refinements in the Measurement and Prediction of Dangerous Behavior," *American Journal of Psychiatry* 131 (September, 1974): 1012-1014;

American Psychiatric Association for quoting from John Hess and Herbert Thomas, "Incompetency to Stand Trial: Procedures, Results, and Problems," *American Journal of Psychiatry* 119 (February, 1963): 713-720;

American Psychiatric Association for quoting from H.J. Steadman and G. Keveles, "The Community Adjustment and Criminal Activity of the Baxstrom Patients," *American Journal of Psychiatry* 129 (September, 1972): 304-311;

American Psychiatric Association for quoting from H.J. Steadman, "Follow-Up on Baxstrom Patients Returned to Hospitals for the Criminally Insane," *American Journal of Psychiatry* 130 (March, 1973): 317-319;

American Psychiatric Association, for quoting from Marc F. Abramson "The Criminalization of Mentally Disordered Behavior: Possible Side-Effect of a New Health Law," *Hospital & Community Psychiatry* 23 (April 1970): 101-105;

Journal of Legal Education for quoting from A.M. Dershowitz, "The Law of Dangerousness: Some Fictions About Prediction," 23 (1970): 24-56;

Social Psychiatry (Springer-Verlag) for quoting H.J. Steadman and J.J. Cocozza, "The Criminally Insane Patient: Who Gets Out?" 8, No. 4, (November, 1973): 230-238;

Society for Study of Social Problems for quoting from Kai Erickson, "Notes on the Sociology of Deviance," *Social Problems* 9, No. 4, (Spring, 1962): 307-314;

Society for Study of Social Problems for quoting from H.J. Steadman, "The Psychiatrist as a Conservative Agent of Social Control," *Social Problems* (Fall, 1972): 263-271;

The Psychiatric Quarterly for quoting from Newton Bigelow, "Editorial Comment," (October, 1967): 767.

Careers of the Criminally Insane

Memorandum to the Legislature of Massachusetts Presented by Dorothea L. Dix, 1843

I cannot but assert that most of the idiotic subjects in . . . prison . . . are unjustly committed, being wholly incapable of doing harm, and none manifesting any disposition either to injure others or to exercise mischievous propensities. I ask an investigation into this subject for the sake of many whose association with prisoners and criminals, and also with persons in almost every stage of insanity, is as useless and unnecessary as it is cruel and ill-judged. If it were proper, I might place in your hands a volume, rather than give a page illustrating these premises.

1 The Background and Foreground

Introduction

Most people know the names of Sirhan Sirhan, Jack Ruby, and Richard Speck. Each of these people attained instant notoriety either by killing a well-known figure or by committing mass murder. When these individuals were tried for their acts, a major portion of the prosecution and defense testimony was presented by psychiatrists. This testimony addressed such questions as whether the defendants knew what they did was wrong and, if they could distinguish right from wrong, whether they were unable to do what was right because of mental illness. These issues were raised by the possible verdict that the defendants were not guilty by reason of insanity (NGRI). In all three cases, however, the defendants were determined to have been responsible for their conduct at the time of the incident and were convicted.

Another widely publicized case was that of Garret Trapnell who hijacked a TWA jet over Iowa in January 1973. He attempted to obtain over $300,000, to talk to President Nixon, and to get the release of then imprisoned Angela Davis. However, he was shot and apprehended at John F. Kennedy Airport in New York while the hijacked plane was stopped for a crew change. He was then committed for psychiatric evaluation. The ensuing media coverage noted that Trapnell had been arrested at least 20 times between 1957 and 1972 for crimes ranging from larceny to robbery and had spent only two years incarcerated. He had consistently plead that his Mr. Hyde alter, "Greg Ross," had performed the criminal act and that he, Ross Trapnell, was not guilty. Most juries accepted this defense and found Trapnell not guilty by reason of insanity. However, after a hung jury in the hijacking case, Trapnell's NGRI defense failed, and in May 1973 he was found guilty of skyjacking.

Unfortunately, both public attention and understanding of the criminally insane are limited for the most part to media coverage of spectacular criminal trials of infamous assassins, hijackers, or mass murderers, in which the defense is not guilty by reason of insanity. However, NGRI cases make up an extremely small portion of all criminal cases and of all the criminally insane patients. Morris (1971) estimates that throughout the United States not more than 2 percent of all the criminal trials involve NGRI defenses and Arens (1969) determined that defendants found NGRI represented only 6 percent of all the completed criminal cases in Washington, D.C. between 1954 and 1966. In fact, in 1967, of all those individuals who were arrested and diverted from the criminal justice system for psychiatric examination or treatment, the NGRI cases accounted for only 4 percent (Scheidemndel and Kanno 1969).

All individuals diverted into the mental health system from the criminal justice system before, during, or after trial tend to become grouped under the term criminally insane. However, both public and professional knowledge of all the criminally insane tends to be incorrectly inferred from the atypical, but widely publicized NGRI cases. The other 96 percent of the people included among the criminally insane are primarily routine cases, involving lower-class individuals, that rarely command any press coverage. Thus, the criminally insane have become stereotyped as infamous assassins; fierce stranglers; black rapists; or decrepit child molesters. Such is not the case. Those people called criminally insane are predominantly non-violent individuals, charged with the few sex crimes who suffer the fate of many other stereotyped groups—that is, they are seriously handicapped in their apprehension, custody, treatment, and community reintegration by the ignorance and fear of others.

One of the most serious discrepancies between fact and stereotype is that *those labeled criminally insane are not necessarily criminals nor necessarily insane*. For example, some of the criminally insane are individuals who have no previous police records, who are only *charged* with crimes, and who are found incompetent to stand trial. At the same time, some of those found incompetent may be malingering defendants who see mental institutions as preferable to penal institutions because of greater personal freedoms and escape potential. Of course, some of the criminally insane are persons who become psychiatrically disordered while serving time after being convicted of serious, violent offenses. Most basically, the characteristic that is common to all the criminally insane is simply that *they are individuals who have been detained in a hospital for the criminally insane*.

This book is about the various types of people who have all been called criminally insane and specifically about one especially significant group of such patients. This study is an attempt to replace stereotypes with facts.

Impetus and Aims

The initial impetus for this book stemmed from our research on one group of criminally insane patients. These patients are called the Baxstrom patients. They are so called because they were generated by policy decisions following a 1966 U.S. Supreme Court decision, *Baxstrom v. Herold,* 383

U.S. 107, in which Johnnie K. Baxstrom petitioned New York's Dannemora State Hospital for the criminally insane for his release. Baxstrom had been convicted in 1956 of assault and sentenced to Attica State Prison. While serving his sentence, he was diagnosed as mentally ill and was transferred to Dannemora where mentally ill felons were treated by the Department of Correction. When Baxstrom's sentence expired in 1961, he was retained in Dannemora as mentally ill. Since he had become a civil patient, he subsequently petitioned local, state, and U.S. Supreme Courts for his release from this correctional hospital. In February 1966 the U.S. Supreme Court upheld Baxstrom's petition by stating that he had been denied equal protection under the Fourteenth Amendment in the review he had received at the expiration of his criminal sentance.

In evaluating the directives of this decision, which mandated—for Baxstrom and others in this class—review under existing civil procedures, including a jury trial on the question of mental illness, the New York State's Department of Mental Hygiene determined that there were 966 other patients for whom such review would be necessary. Rather than provide the reviews, all 967 patients from Dannemora and Matteawan, the state's other hospital for the criminally insane, were transfered to civil mental hospitals between March and August 1966. Because the Baxstrom patients were seen as dangerous, these transfers took place under great duress from the civil hospital staffs and the surrounding communities.

The Baxstrom patients are important in themselves from both clinical and substantive perspectives and in general because they were in 1966, and to a great extent remained in 1974, typical of patients in traditional hospitals for the criminally insane throughout the United States. For the most part, they were long-term, chronic patients who were greatly feared by the hospital staffs and the society that had warehoused them in hospital facilities. Their's was a custodial existence, with few overt or covert attempts at treatment. The Baxstrom group were atypical patients only in that they received the opportunity to move into less restrictive, more treatment-oriented situations and, for many, from there into the community. Because of their representativeness and because of the natural field experiment for questions pertaining to the dangerousness of the criminally insane that their careers provided, they are a very significant group of patients whom we studied for four years after the landmark court decision.

Thus, our initial interest in writing this book was our desire to report the data and findings on the Baxstrom patients. As we progressed, an important second aim emerged. We recognized that not only was there a necessity for much empirical research on numerous issues surrounding the criminally insane, but there also was a dire need for a general overview and introduction to the lives, legal predicaments, institutional experiences and community problems of these people. Our review of the existing literature indicated that basic information was glaringly absent and what was available had not been systematically integrated. Because of this, we decided to take as our goals for this book two that were distinct, yet highly dependent: (1) a general introduction and comprehensive view of what is now known about the people called criminally insane and the institutions that process them and (2) a detailed report on a group of criminally insane patients who were transferred from maximum security hospitals in 1966 due to a U.S. Supreme Court decision.

The selection of these two aims influenced another basic choice we had to make in preparing this book. In our review of the existing literature and in our efforts to arrive at an understanding of the criminally insane, we were constantly confronted with the unusually interdisciplinary nature of the area. While trained as sociologists, we found that to complete our research it was necessary to branch into other areas, particularly psychiatry and law, where much of the research and discussion of issues existed. As sociologists, our first inclination was to orient this book exclusively towards sociological concerns. For example, there is much in this book that bears directly on the topics of societal reaction theories of deviance, interorganizational analysis, occupational roles, mechanisms of social control, and so forth. Yet, we felt that the planned contents of the book were equally relevant to the other related fields. Thus, we decided to develop a more balanced work that did not focus on the major issues of a single field but rather touched upon and reflected the sociological, legal, and psychiatric issues surrounding the criminally insane.

Because of the interdisciplinary nature of these three areas and this book's forays into all of them, the amount of material in any one area is not as extensive as the reader who has been deeply involved in researching, treating, or advising the criminally insane might want. However, a primary thrust of this book is to introduce people in any of these fields to the current state of knowledge about the criminally insane in all of these disciplines, while also presenting empirical data that is important for even the most sophisticated in each field.

We have attempted to please all of the people some of the time. When we talk of "labeling theory" as a major theoretical framework, the sociologist familiar with this literature will feel that more could have been said. Likewise, when we trace the emerging trends in litigation and legislative action, the lawyer may feel that it is too sketchy. The psychiatrist will likely prefer more clinical detail and the criminologist might wish for additional information on the incidents in the patient's criminal history. However, the costs of taking an interdisciplinary approach we feel are more than offset by the awareness of how the many professions are involved with the criminally insane, the interrelatedness of these professions, and the need for each profession to develop skills in the others' areas.

Careers as a Framework

In accordance with our interdisciplinary intents with sociological overtones, the framework that we have employed both in our introductory materials to the criminally insane and for the analysis of the Baxstrom patient data is that of careers. Commonly and traditionally, career has related to the business or professional worlds and the advancement or strategies for advancement through various occupations. The early sociological uses of this concept by Hughes (1937) in these occupational contexts defined two major components of careers, the objective and the subjective. The first related to the educational pathways to jobs and the statuses and hierarchies through which a person moved as his/her career progressed. The subjective aspects of career involved the person's reactions to what happened in the objective sphere.

Through Hall's work (1948) on the stages of medical careers and through Becker's (1963) application of this concept to deviants, the concept of careers in the sociological literature moved away from a purely occupational context. Becker focused on both the formal structure and movements through the deviant systems with their career contingencies, "those factors on which movement from one position to another depends." Career has been used and popularized by Goffman (1961) and Spitzer and Denzin (1968) in the context of mental patients. In these contexts, there continues to be an emphasis on both the formal, structural aspects of career that relate to the organizational or institutional network and the subjective component relating to the individuals' reactions to the structures encountered. Thus, Spitzer and Denzin (1968, p. 191) note: "It is possible to conceptualize the experience of persons defined and treated as mentally ill as a temporal sequence of events or 'career.' The concept of career encompasses at least two notions. First, it refers to the sequence of movements from a position in any particular network by a given person, and second, the sequence of individual adjustment accompanying the movement." They proceed to delineate the three major segments of the mental patient career as the prepatient, inpatient, and postpatient phases.

In our overview of the careers of the criminally insane, we initially discuss the institutions and statuses through which they pass throughout their entire careers from the prepatient to the postpatient phases. We consider the prepatient period mainly through our examination and integration of previous research, although some pertinent prepatient information from the Baxstrom patients' hospital records is also weighed. However, in our major empirical analysis of the Baxstrom data, we concentrate on the formal structures and career contingencies of the inpatient and postpatient phases of their careers.

In addition, a primary emphasis of our Baxstrom data analysis is on the formal structure rather than on the subjective adaptations or coping behaviors of the Baxstrom patients. While we do look in some detail at their behaviors in the latter two patient phases, our aim is to explore the appropriateness of their institutional treatment rather than to understand their subjective responses to the formal structure. Thus, we concentrate on career contingencies as they relate to psychiatric and legal decision-making in the processing of the criminally insane.

Some of the Issues

In analyzing the careers of the criminally insane generally and the Baxstrom patients specifically, a number of important issues in sociology, law, and psychiatry arise. The major ones addressed in this book are (1) the centrality of the concept and prediction of dangerousness in decision-making about the criminally insane; (2) the conservatism of society and psychiatrists in dealing with the criminally insane; and (3) the importance of certain social factors relative to medical or legal influences for the careers contingencies of these patients as they move from the criminally insane hospitals to the civil hospitals and to the community.

Dangerousness

In a 1965 lower court hearing concerning the continued retention of Johnnie Baxstrom in Dannemora, one of the main points raised by the state was whether Baxstrom was dangerously mentally ill. This question was raised in the context of the state's Mental Hygiene Law that allowed the retention of patients under civil orders in hospitals for the criminally insane run by the Department of Correction, if the person was determined judicially to be dangerously mentally ill. This practice of detaining civil patients in maximum security hospitals if they are dangerous has been and continues to be common throughout the United States. The idea that dangerousness can be determined and is an appropriate reason for special security and differential treatment (or non-treatment) has general public, legislative, and medical support, despite the inherent difficulties of defining and predicting dangerousness.

One indication of just how basic the problems surrounding the use of dangerousness are is the lack of consensus on what it means. Katz and Goldstein (1960, p. 410), for example, have discussed the vagueness of the concept and its many uses in both research and legislation. They found it used to mean: (1) only the crime for which the insanity defense was successfully raised; (2) all crimes; (3) only felonious crimes (as opposed to misdemeanors); (4) only crimes for which a given maximum sentence or more is authorized; (5) only crimes categorized as violent; (6) only crimes categorized as harmful, physical or psychological, reparable or irreparable, to the victim; (7) any conduct, even if not labelled criminal, categorized as violent, harmful, or threatening; (8) any conduct which may provoke retaliatory acts; (9) any physical violence towards oneself; (10) any combination of these. With such diversity of intended or supposed meanings, it is not surprising that Rappeport and colleagues (1965) concluded that "there are no articles that would assist us to any great extent in determining who might be dangerous, particularly before he commits an offense" (p. 79).

Because so little is known about dangerousness and because estimations of dangerousness are such important contingencies in the careers of the criminally insane, a major thrust of our Baxstrom patient data analysis and inferences relate to considerations of dangerousness. As Halleck (1967) has noted, "Research in the area of dangerous behavior (other than generalizations from case material) is practically nonexistent" (p. 314). By examining such indicators in the Baxstrom patient data as institutional and community assaultiveness, rates of hospital discharge, level and type of subsequent criminal activity, and readmission statistics, some of the empirical void in evaluating the appropriateness and accuracy of psychiatric and judicial attributions of dangerousness can be filled.

Psychiatric Ideology and Social Control

The general tendency of psychiatrists to be very conservative in their decisions to release patients from mental hospitals and their inclination to attribute sickness whenever there is any doubt has been discussed by Scheff (1966). He notes the medical ideology that has been carried over into psychiatry discourages releasing sick patients (avoiding Type 1 errors) at the cost of hospitalizing any number of healthy people (Type 2 errors).

Many of the studies from which Scheff draws his inference examined involuntary civil commitments. Scheff (1964), Miller and Schwartz (1966), and Maisel (1970) all concluded that civil hearings were extremely terse, almost meaningless, and committed many people about whom the researchers felt there were serious questions as to the need for hospitalization. Zitrin and his co-workers (1969) and Wegner and Fletcher (1969) also studied civil commitment hearings and found that when lawyers were actively involved in the cases pre-hearing and/or were present at the hearings, psychiatrists were less likely to both recommend and obtain commitments.

There is very little research or theory on the issue of psychiatric conservatism in criminal cases. McGarry (1969), as part of an impressive five-year study of incompetent defendants in Massachusetts, did report that when there was any doubt at all as to the competency of the accused, psychiatrists recommended an incompetency finding to the court. McGarry (1971) and McGrath (1968) both discussed psychiatric decisions for patient release from hospitals for the criminally insane and both concluded that the psychiatric decisions were consistently in a conservative direction. McGrath felt that such conservative psychiatric decisions were caused mainly by political pressures from legislators and local communities that caused psychiatrists to "underwrite the political evasions."

As the historical views of psychiatry by Deutsch (1949) and Szasz (1970) have pointed out, there are a variety of political, cultural, and religious factors that must be considered when exploring the societal roles of psychiatry. The diagnosis of mental illness, the evaluations of need for treatment, and estimations of dangerousness are all segments of psychiatric role behavior that must be set within the broader social matrix to be understood. In such a macro perspective, psychiatric conservatism in ideology and in decision-making very much relates to the history of their participation in institutions of social control as mental hospitalization replaced burning at the stake and incarceration. As certain bizarre, violent, or otherwise unacceptable behavior became to be defined as mental illness rather than witchcraft and as these behaviors were cause for commitment, legislative acts authorized psychiatrists to make the evaluations and estimations of dangerousness for societal protection. Functioning as agents of social control to a certain extent, psychiatry developed a position of power that was diminished only when they incorrectly released rather than inappropriately detained patients.

Part of our interest in the Baxstrom patients was the opportunities they offered to determine just how conservative psychiatric evaluations of them had been. We develop this theme through a retrospective analysis of what happened to the Baxstrom patients after they were transferred to civil mental hospitals and from there to the community. In addition, we have some further data on a comparison population of all patients transferred from Dannemora and Matteawan to civil hospitals in the two years preceding the Baxstrom decision. The comparisons between these two patient groups allow some insight into which factors, such as age, race, criminal history, and so forth, were associated with psychiatric decisions to transfer some patients out of hospitals for the criminally insane while detaining others.

These two research populations are also compared to determine whether the detention of either group appeared warranted on the basis of their subsequent behavior. This question of how warranted their continued detentions were is especially important for the Baxstrom patients since their transfers to civil hospitals were never approved by psychiatrists. Rather, they were transferred under court orders *against* psychiatric advice. Thus, if these two groups, particularly the Baxstrom patients, show a low level of subsequent behavioral problems, there would be a basis for postulating a conservative bias in psychiatric evaluations of the criminally insane. Such findings would raise questions about the existence and validity of this type of preventive detention and controversial psychiatric involvement in these modes of social control. On the other hand, should the data reveal that these two patient groups fared poorly after their transfer, the reluctance to transfer these patients before the Supreme Court decision and the need for separate, secure facilities for the criminally insane would gain support.

Social Factors

Sociologists who have studied mental illness have consistently focused on the relevance of social factors for understanding who becomes mentally ill, who is hospitalized in mental institutions, and how well patients function after release.

Much of the early work in psychiatric sociology was characterized by epidemiological studies of the rates of mental illness and hospitalization. Through studies such as those by Faris and Durham (1939), Hollingshead and Redlich (1958), and Srole et al. (1962), the importance of socioeconomic status, social mobility, urbanization, and other social factors have been established. More recently, the problem of rehospitalization has been explored. Freeman and Simmons (1963) and Angrist et al. (1968), for example, examined the possible relationship between rehospitalization and variables such as the tolerance of deviant behavior by family members, role expectations, and role performance within the family. In addition, some attention has also been given to the question of who is released from mental hospitals (Sall et al. 1966). At least one study (Greenley 1972) found that family desires concerning release are highly related to the length of hospitalization experienced by patients.

A common theme underlying most sociological studies in this area is the notion that social contingencies may actually be as, if not more, important than the psychopathology of the individual. This social perspective on mental illness, in particular, and deviant behavior, in general, has been developed into a more systematic perspective by Lemert (1951, 1967),

Kitsuse (1962), Becker (1963), Scheff (1966) and others. Known as labeling theory or the societal reaction perspective, this theory posits mental illness as resulting not from anything internal to the individual but rather as the result of the reactions of others. Erickson (1962, p. 11), for example, states:

> Deviance is not a property inherent in certain forms of behavior; it is property conferred upon these forms by the audiences which directly or indirectly witness them. The critical variable in the study of deviance, then, is the social audience rather than the individual actor, since it is the audience which eventually determines whether or not any episode of behavior or any class of episodes is labeled deviant.

While the validity of this perspective has been questioned (Gibbs 1966; Schur 1969; Gove 1970a and 1970b; Gove and Howell 1974), it remains one of the most influential sociological approaches to the study of mental illness.

Accordingly, the relative importance of social factors for understanding the careers of the Baxstrom patients is one of the main issues addressed in this study. As we follow these patients from the criminally insane hospital, to the civil hospital, to the community and, in some cases, back again, we examine the extent to which their careers are influenced by social, career contingencies over which they have no control.

Overview

This chapter has attempted to sketch the twofold aims of the book, our framework of careers of the criminally insane, the situations surrounding the *Baxstrom* decision, and its resultant mass patient transfers in sufficient detail to alert the reader to the structure, content, and issues of this book. However, still requiring considerable explication are a number of specific features of the processes whereby persons under the jurisdiction of the criminal justice system are diverted to the mental health system and acquire the criminally insane label. These details are essential to a comprehensive understanding of (1) who the criminally insane are; (2) the implications of the *Baxstrom* decision; and (3) the pathways patients travel through the various institutional settings. These pathways and procedures are also important for the discontinuities they demonstrate in the institutional careers of the criminally insane and for pointing out the established, low visibility routes by which people are diverted from the criminal justice into the mental health system.

We turn to a very detailed explication of the pathways to the acquisition of the criminally insane label in Chapter 2. From a closer examination of the processing of the criminally insane and through a review of what is known about these people, a solid step can be taken towards a meaningful understanding of their custody, care, and predicaments. Having examined the pathways and background characteristics of the criminally insane as revealed in the extant literature, Chapter 3 discusses the details of the *Baxstrom v. Herold* case from Baxstrom's first habeas corpus brief in 1963 through the Supreme Court decision.

In Chapter 4, we discuss our research procedures. These discussions are unusually detailed because we feel that our experiences with the various techniques we employed in this research are among our most important findings.

The Baxstrom patient data analysis and discussions from the perspective of their inpatient and postpatient careers are developed in Chapters 5 through 8. Chapter 5 focuses on who the Baxstrom and pre-Baxstrom patients were and the inferences suggested by the different characteristics of the two groups. Chapter 6 documents the experiences of the Baxstrom patients in the civil hospital portion of their inpatient phase. Next, in Chapter 7, we examine the topic of patient release from the civil hospitals to the community and attempt to uncover the critical factors related to psychiatrists' decisions to release some patients while retaining others. In Chapter 8, we follow the postpatient experiences of those patients released into the community. In Chapter 9, we chronicle the important trends in court decisions and legislation dealing with the criminally insane since 1966 and present some discussion about trends in treatment programs for the criminally insane in the United States. Chapter 10 draws out the implications of our data for major substantive and policy issues.

An understanding of the careers of the criminally insane, drawn from the ideas and data of this book together with other related resources and the reader's own ideas, is valuable in a number of ways. First, it facilitates examination of how the criminal justice and mental health systems work to detain tens of thousands of individuals each year in ways that often appear to be something other than what they are—that is, custody where treatment is assumed or preventive detention under mental health aegis where criminal retribution is expected. Second, knowledge of the careers of the criminally insane provides opportunities to examine significant issues about emerging psychiatric roles, dangerousness, social factors related to medical/legal decision-making, and how the interaction of the medical, legal, and legislative processes can lead to unintended or uninformed consequences. Finally, data on the lives of the criminally insane can provide information by which the criminal justice and mental health systems may become more responsive to patient-inmate needs. Our data are intended to provide information about a group of people who are little known, but greatly feared and who are institutionalized through confused, obfuscatory procedures that require scrutiny.

2 What Do We Know About The Criminally Insane?

Most of what people know about the criminally insane is learned from the press, mass media, and novels. Stories under banner headlines or sensational titles are often vivid descriptions of bizarre behavior. Such accounts develop an image of the criminally insane that bears slight resemblance to the actual people who, as will be documented below, tend to be functionally inept and most often non-violent. Certainly, the characterizations offered in works such as Truman Capote's *In Cold Blood* are valid, useful portrayals of certain types of the criminally insane. However, the heavy dependence on a few sensational case studies and media reports for knowledge and attitudes about the criminally insane results in inaccurate depictions. It is not surprising that public knowledge of the criminally insane depends so greatly on these sources. There is a marked scarcity of factual data that systematically describe the criminally insane and the systems that process, detain, and treat them. In this chapter, as part of our analyses of the careers of the criminally insane and as an introduction to our Baxstrom data, we review the research that does exist about the wide variety of people who become known as criminally insane.

To review what is known about the criminally insane, it seems most productive to start with a brief history of the institutions for the criminally insane from the time they were first developed in New York in 1859 through 1966, the year of the *Baxstrom* decision. Having examined the evolution of hospitals for the criminally insane, we explicate the interrelationships of the four major types of institutions that process the criminally insane and detail the four major legal categories into which the criminally insane are best divided. Having looked at these objective features of the careers of the criminally insane, careful consideration is given to developing a systematic integration of the existing body of research on the dynamics of their legal/psychiatric processing, on the problems caused and encountered by the criminally insane upon return to the community, and to the personal characteristics of the people who become known as criminally insane.

A Brief History of Institutions for the Criminally Insane in New York

The data reported in this book deal with two groups of patients in New

York's two hospitals for the criminally insane in the mid-1960s. The particular court decision from which our research stemmed was handed down by the U.S. Supreme Court in February 1966. Between the founding of the first facility for the criminally insane in the United States at Auburn, New York in 1859 and this decision in 1966, there was much significant legislation pertaining to the criminally insane both in New York and in other parts of the United States. It seems useful to document the particular developments in New York, since for the most part they were landmarks and appear to have influenced, if not dictated, similar movements in other states. Another reason for limiting our historical survey of arrangements for the custody and care of the criminally insane to New York is that the issues raised by these historical developments and our research data subsequent to the 1966 Supreme Court decision concentrate on New York.

After the opening of the first U.S. mental hospital in Philadelphia in 1756, the first real move to separate the mentally ill who were charged with or convicted of crimes from strictly civil mental patients was in 1827. An "Act respecting Lunatics" was passed in New York that prevented the overseers of the poor, who were responsible for the mentally ill, from housing the mentally ill in jails or "in the same room with any person charged or convicted of an offense" (N.Y. Laws 1827, ch. 294 Sec. 2). This law was quickly repealed in the following year, but confinement of the mentally ill in any jail remained unacceptable. They could be kept only in poorhouses. When the state's first asylum for the mentally ill was opened in 1842 at Utica, its patients were not only civilly committed patients. The 1842 legislative provisions for Utica asylum allowed for mixing of mentally ill convicts, those confined under indictments or criminal charge, and those acquitted because of mental illness with patients committed under any civil process.

By 1855, there was movement again towards separating patients who were convicted or alleged criminals from civil patients. This movement culminated with the February 1859 opening of an Asylum for Insane Convicts at Auburn, the first institution of its kind in the United States. During its first year of operation, Auburn Asylum received 59 inmates from Auburn Prison, Sing Sing, and Clinton. Auburn was described by New York's Governor Morgan as an "experiment" when it opened in 1859, but in 1861 the state legislature directed that all mentally ill male prisoners be transferred from Utica to Auburn, which affirmed some permanancy to this noble experiment. A female section of Auburn was opened in 1867.

In 1869, the name of the Auburn institution was changed from "Insane Convicts" to "Insane Criminals." This change was necessitated by the fact that in addition to its original population of mentally ill prisoners, Auburn was thereafter to house those persons acquitted because of insanity as well as defendants charged with murder, attempted murder, or arson who became mentally ill prior to trial or sentencing. Thus, as of 1869, convicted and unconvicted patients were again confined in the same facility as they had been before Auburn Asylum was opened. In addition, as of 1874, Auburn was authorized to receive mentally ill inmates from county penetentiaries as well as state prisons. Again, in 1884, Auburn's functions were further broadened to include patients administratively transferred from the state reformatory at Elmira and any criminal order patients judicially transferred from a civil hospital.

Because of the continuing expansion of categories of patients at Auburn, its resident population, despite a high discharge rate during its first few years of operation, grew from a census of 59 in 1859 to 150 in 1882. Accordingly, a legislative commission was established in 1886 to locate additional farmland that could be used for an asylum for Auburn's residents. This search resulted in the selection of a centrally located site of 200 acres in Matteawan in Dutchess County, approximately 70 miles north of New York City and 80 miles south of Albany. One of the positive features envisoned for the new facility, besides its accessibility to "natural beauty" and New York City by train, was its size, which would again allow for the separation within a single facility of unconvicted patients awaiting trial from mentally ill convicts. As a *New York Times* article reporting the opening noted, "The two classes of patients differ widely, the criminals giving the officials much anxiety at times. They are frequently dangerous and destructive" (*New York Times* 3 November 1892, p. 9, col. 4).

As had happened with Auburn soon after its opening, the number of patients at Matteawan quickly increased following its inception in 1892. During its first fiscal year, the census rose from 348 to 411 patients. While the patient population continued to burgeon at Matteawan, pressure also built for the separation of the "convict insane" from the other criminally insane patients. The 1894 State Lunacy Commission describing the events surrounding the establishment of Auburn and Matteawan noted that separate institutions were beneficial because of the presence of insane convicts "was very objectionable to the ordinary inmates" (of state hospitals) (State Commission on Lunacy 1894, note 60). Because of such political pressures and the growing patient load, a new facility was planned in 1894 to house only "insane convicts."

This new facility, Dannemora State Hospital, opened in northern New York in January 1900. By this time Matteawan was overcrowded with 719 patients in a building whose capacity was considered 550. When the time came to transfer patients from Matteawan, there was a hospital "revolt" of the inmates when they learned of the large numbers going to Dannemora, which was approximately 250 miles further north of New York City, where about half of the patients lived. The final decision was to transfer to Dannemora only patients who had been convicted and had more than 6 months remaining on their criminal sentences. After the original transfer, all inmates in the state who were determined mentally ill after a felony conviction would be housed in Dannemora. All other convicted patients and pre-trial cases would go to Matteawan.

Between 1900 and 1966, the patient population at Matteawan and Dannemora climbed steadily with Matteawan reaching a patient census of over 2,000 in the early 1960s. At the same time Dannemora reached a peak of about 1,400 patients. However, in these 66 years little changed in either the statutes or these two facilities. In 1859, all classes of the criminally insane were separated from civil mental patients. Then in the late nineteenth century the convicted patients within Matteawan were differentiated from minor offenders, pre-trial defendants, and NGRI cases. Female patients all remained in Matteawan. On bases that appear related to moral rather than treatment or custody issues, during the latter part of the nineteenth century distinct facilities were established for mentally ill convicted felons who were seen as more dangerous than the unconvicted and convicted misdemeanants. Thus, separate, but unequal formulae for dealing with patients housed in these hospitals gradually evolved and became entrenched. In these administrative adaptations, the institutions became known as hospitals for the criminally insane.

Institutional Processing and Legal Statuses of the Criminally Insane

Current institutional arrangements for the apprehension, processing, and treatment of all groups of the criminally insane vary considerably by, and often within, county, state, and nation and have been changing rapidly in the last few years. However, to sort out these arrangements, it is convenient to think in terms of the institutions of the criminal justice and mental health systems. These are the jails and prisons on the one hand and special security and regular civil mental hospitals on the other. Each of these four types of institutions develops points of interchange with the others through which the criminally insane move and by which they acquire their label.

Figure 2-1 presents the interfaces of the criminal justice and mental health systems. The arrows indicate the usual locations and directions of patient-inmate movements into, through, and out of these institutions. The paths through any particular state's system are dependent on specific statutes and institutional arrangements. However, there are four distinct legal statuses of patients during the inpatient phases of the criminally insane career: (1) mentally ill inmates; (2) incompetent to stand trial defendants; (3) not guilty by reason of insanity patients; and (4) dangerously mentally ill patients. With the exception of the last group, all individuals

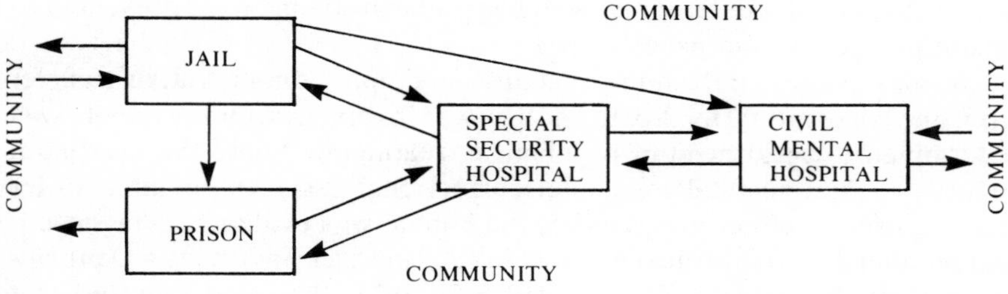

Figure 2-1. Typical Pathways Between Major Institutions of the Criminal Justice and Mental Health Systems.

who become residents of facilities for the criminally insane have their institutional career phases initiated by police apprehension and criminal charges. Only the dangerously mentally ill, a group of civilly detained individuals who in many states are housed with the other three types, do not necessarily have criminal convictions or charges. Let us turn to a detailed examination of each of these four legal statuses.

Mentally Ill Inmates

The processing of this type of patient is the most easily understood because it does not vary greatly from standard criminal justice system processing. This group makes up about 40 percent of all those individuals called criminally insane. This is also the group that was referred to as "insane convicts," in the early laws of New York. In the late nineteenth and early twentieth centuries, such patients were seen as especially inappropriate for care in institutions housing civil mental patients.

Members of this legal group have been first arrested, convicted, and sentenced. While serving time, they may be administratively transferred to special institutions for the criminally insane, if they are diagnosed by psychiatrists or other prison mental health professionals as mentally ill and administrative approval for transfer is granted. The processing of mentally ill inmates is quite clear cut. More difficult to describe and more important are the determinants of inmate access and acceptance by medical services in correctional facilities. Such access is crucial since it is through evaluation in these services that the pathways to mental hospitalization are opened. For example, Rundle (1972) has depicted the recent situation at San Quentin as one in which medical services were used by correction officers as manipulative, reward/punishment devices for control of the inmates. He argues that officers determined which medical problems were presented to prison physicians and psychiatrists.

In most states, until quite recently, a simple administrative transfer from one correctional facility to another was involved, after the inmate was determined to be in need of psychiatric treatment. Where the maximum security mental hospital was under correctional auspices, no court order was required to effect the transfer; the inmate was evaluated, diagnosed, and recommended for transfer. Then in 1969 in a case involving a Dannemora patient, *Schuster v. Herold*, 410 F.2d 1071, the court required that "before a prisoner may be transferred to a state institution for insane criminals, he must be afforded substantially the same procedural safeguards as are provided in civil commitment proceedings, including proper examination, a hearing upon notice, periodic review of the need for commitment, and trial by a jury." The court so ruled "in view of substantial deprivations, hardships and indignities transfer from prison to institution for the criminally insane may produce."

In those states where the maximum security mental hospital had been operated by departments of mental health, the transfer of a mentally ill inmate required judicial authorization, since the move was between systems. Even where such authorization was necessary, there was and is a strong tendency to rubber stamp such requests. This tendency is increased when the courts making these authorizations are those of the county in which the penal facility is located, which means that the court deals with the same types of cases and the same medical and administrative officers of the penal facility over and over again.

After transfer to a hospital for the criminally insane, the patient-inmate may remain, often without mandated psychiatric review, up to the maximum length of his current sentence. If the psychiatrists decide at any time before sentence expiration that the patient-inmate is not mentally ill, he is simply returned to prison to complete his sentence. The procedure for detaining patient-inmates who are still considered mentally ill at the expiration of their sentences varies. If continued involuntary retention is required, these retentions usually follow procedures for involuntary civil commitments. If such a civil retention is obtained, institutionalization will, with some exceptions, be in a regular civil hospital. One exception, for example, is the patient-inmate whose time has expired but who is considered dangerous. In this case, a special order may be sought for continued detention in a maximum security facility under the category "dangerously mentally ill." This latter status will be discussed below in greater detail.

The situation of the patient-inmate whose sentence expires while in a special security mental hospital is of special importance here because these were the circumstances of Johnnie Baxstrom whose case and its sequelae are a focus of this book. To help concretize the procedures associated with this legal status, let us look at the actual experiences of one of the mentally ill inmates who was among the patients transferred because of the *Baxstrom* decision.

Andrew Bowman,[a] a white male, was born in New York City in 1908. He stayed in school until he was 15 and had reached the eighth grade. He worked for a couple of years as an electrician's helper but was fired for unknown reasons. Shortly thereafter he joined the Navy, which he did not like. He received a medical discharge from the Navy, and in the two years following his tour, he lived the life of a New York City vagrant—stealing milk from bottles on doorsteps and sleeping in vacant buildings. His first encounter with the law was an arrest for grand larceny in Brooklyn in 1924. This charge was dismissed. Six months later, in April 1925, he was arrested for vagrancy and given a suspended sentence.

In August 1930, Bowman was arrested in Brooklyn for burglary of a store. In March 1931, he pleaded guilty to the reduced charge of unlawful entry. He served 6 months of his indefinite sentence in the N.Y. County Penitentiary. His records indicate then that "the prison physician reported that he was an imbicile—low grade moron and a chronic masturbator. He would sit for long periods of time in one position and would not eat or talk." Based on this, Bowman was transferred to Matteawan State Hospital for the Criminally Insane on September 28, 1931. The admitting psychiatrist there concluded that "this is undoubtably a case of 'Demetia Praecox' and in view of above noted symptoms is best described by a diagnosis of 'Hebephrenia.'"

Bowman's full term expired on January 9, 1934. He remained in Matteawan as mentally ill nevertheless until March 29, 1966, when after the *Baxstrom* decision he was transferred to a civil mental hospital in New York City. His condition at transfer was described by the Matteawan psychiatrists as unimproved, and the schizophrenia, hebephrenia diagnosis was retained. Upon admission to the civil hospital he was described as ". . . in very poor contact. He is quite deteriorated, and it is evident that he has no knowledge of his present whereabouts and lacks insight and judgement." Through 1970, the end of our follow-up period, Bowman remained quite stable in the civil hospital as a voluntary patient. His final ward note says: "Patient continues to work in kitchen, is clean, quiet, cooperative, and is not a management problem."

The institutional career of Andrew Bowman is typical of those patient-inmates who have made up the largest portion of the patients in traditional U.S. hospitals for the criminally insane from their beginnings in New York in the late nineteenth century. The Andrew Bowmans and Johnnie Baxtroms were those most affected by the Supreme Court decision that is

[a]This and all other names used in case histories in this chapter are pseudonyms.

central to our research reported in later chapters. These convicted patient-inmates are still numerous in U.S. mental institutions, although their numbers are steadily decreasing because of revised statutes and recent court decisions. However, mentally ill inmates continue to comprise about 40 percent of all such individuals labeled criminally insane in the United States today.[b]

We next move to the group of criminally insane patients that comprises the other large segment of individuals labelled criminally insane.

Defendants Incompetent to Stand Trial

Incompetent defendants also make up about 40 percent of the individuals in the United States called criminally insane. There is considerably more variation in statutes and procedures for determining and processing incompetent defendants than for mentally ill inmates. There are, again, however, some fairly general procedures and locations for processing common to most states, and these allow a tracing of the pathways through the criminal justice and mental health systems that result in judicial determinations of incompetent to stand trial. The incompetent defendant comes into contact with jails, special security hospitals, and civil mental hospitals. While mentally ill inmates usually encounter only "within system" transfers, the incompetent defendant experiences both within and between system interchanges.

Throughout the United States, the usual bases for determining competency to stand trial are the common-law criteria of whether an individual is of sufficiently sound mind to understand the court proceedings and charges against him and to cooperate with an attorney in his own defense. It is important to realize that competency does not imply that a defendant must be free of mental illness. According to these criteria, it is possible to be determined mentally ill *and* competent to stand trial. The legal questions relate to whether any diagnosed mental illness prevents an understanding of charges and cooperation with an attorney during court proceedings. The determination of competency in the United States is a judicial one, but it is

[b]It should be noted that in most states there is a subtype of mentally ill inmates called Criminal Sexual Psychopaths (CSP) or some variation of a similar label. This group includes individuals convicted of certain crimes that should be of a sexual nature by the label but occasionally are not because of vague statutory language that inappropriately includes non-sexual offenses (c.f. Allen et al. 1973). These convicted individuals are often institutionalized under lengthy or indeterminant sentences for special treatment. Whether one chooses to include this group of individuals under the criminally insane label depends on one's orientation and the statutes of the particular area being considered. Since this category is small and has very distinctive patient-inmate careers, we will not include them in most of our discussions. They will be included primarily in the review of what is known about the criminally insane, since one of the better pieces of research about the people who are processed by criminal justice/mental health mechanisms centers on CSPs.

heavily dependent on psychiatric testimony, which is a much debated point. Many lawyers argue that it should be their decision whether they can work with a given defendant and not a psychiatric decision dependent on medical criteria. Currently, however, it does remain the court's decision, which depends greatly on psychiatric recommendations.

The early stages of the incompetent defendant's criminal/psychiatric processing are areas in which little is documented. Exactly when, by whom, and for what reasons (i.e., are they strictly medical concerns or dispositional ploys) the question of competency is raised are areas in which little is known. The only point that is clear is that the early processing of incompetent defendants begins with arrest. Just about anyone can request a competency evaluation, including the arresting officer, the defendant's family, or the defense or prosecution attorney. Most often it seems the request for psychiatric evaluation is made by the arresting officer, the defense attorney, or arraigning judge. The location of the ensuing evaluation may be in the local jail, in a special psychiatric ward of the jail, in a special prison ward at a general hospital, or even an outpatient clinic, if the defendant is out on bail. The particular arrangements depend on state statutes and local policies. Less often, but with some frequency, the question of competency is raised before sentencing following a conviction. The location of examination, criteria employed, and institutionalization would be the same as with pre-trial competency evaluation. If competency is the finding, sentencing occurs in the usual manner.

One interesting note about defendants evaluated for competency is how these evaluations may be used by defense attorneys who are intending to use an NGRI defense. Some attorneys see it to their advantage to have the question of competency raised and to obtain a trial delay from an incompetency determination to strengthen an NGRI defense. Thus, there is considerable screening done by psychiatrists on special prison wards used for pre-trial evaluations, so that defendants are not admitted who are obviously competent. In many such cases, simply having a client admitted for evaluation may have been the intent of the defense attorney.

If the examining psychiatrists—usually two—feel that the defendant is incompetent to stand trial, there is a hearing for a judicial determination of competency. These hearings are intended as non-adversary proceedings where the judge listens to medical findings, talks with defendant and counsel, and makes a decision as to whether the defendant is able to proceed with a trial with whatever delays exist for criminal trial in that area. As we discuss later in this chapter, when we consider the dynamics of those hearings, they frequently develop into adversary proceedings with the defendant who wants to stand trial contravening the medical testimony with the assistance of counsel, usually assigned by the court. The psychiatrist thus becomes the hearing ally of the district attorney who may want a defendant found incompetent. Occasionally, the reverse occurs where the defendant accepts the psychiatric finding of incompetency, but the district attorney wants a determination of competency so that he can proceed with a criminal trial.

After a competency hearing, if the defendant is determined to be competent, he is returned to await trial. Such a transfer, does not preclude the question of competency being raised at a later point during the same retention. Should there be a long trial delay during which the defendant deteriorates, the question of competency could again be raised. However, the defendant found competent usually proceeds through the criminal justice system in the regular manner.

If the defendant is found incompetent, he will be returned to the pre-trial psychiatric ward or local jail for a short time while administrative details of transfer to a special security mental hospital are effected. The special security hospitals to which incompetent defendants are transferred come in many forms. They may be administered by a corrections or a mental health department. There may be one hospital to serve all legal categories of criminally insane from the whole state. Alternately, there may be multiple hospitals with either homogeneous or heterogeneous legal statuses among the patients. All convicted mentally ill inmates from the entire state may be in one facility and all other types of criminally insane in another hospital or all types of patient-inmates from one portion of state may go to one facility while other portions of the state may be served by another facility.

Thus, the incompetent defendant moves from a jail situation of some type to a special security hospital for periods that vary between states. It may be 30, 60, 90 days or a year. If, during these maximum periods before mandated judicial review, the defendant becomes competent, he is returned to jail to await trial with subsequent movement determined by criminal justice processes.

If the defendant is considered still incompetent at the conclusion of the criminal order of commitment, another order may be sought for continued detention in the special security hospital. A range of other options in the institutional careers of incompetent defendants develop at this point, however. In many states, arrangements may be worked out for voluntary stay in the special security hospital or a regular civil hospital. If the special security hospital is run by a department of mental health, it is also possible to retain a patient under civil orders for involuntary commitment. This latter procedure is often the most desirable retention from the hospital's standpoint because it may not require examination by psychiatrists other than those from the hospital or from that area's community mental health center. It also may mean that the court deciding on the retention will be the local county's where judges and legal aid attorneys are familiar with the hospital staff. Continued detention under renewed criminal commitment orders as incompetent would require a hearing in the county where the individual was indicted, where judges are unknown, and where the special security hospital psychiatrists may have to travel long distances to testify.

Another possibility for the incompetent defendant who is considered still unable to proceed with his trial at the expiration of the first criminal commitment order is transfer to a regular civil hospital under a voluntary or involuntary order. This course would be taken with extreme caution and only in cases that involved non-violent charges and in which the district attorney has little interest in prosecuting. In some states, including New York, this latter route is a very frequent one for incompetent defendants.

One recourse, which the incompetent defendant has, for returning to trial is a *habeas corpus* brief. This same device is available to all patients in the special security mental hospitals. This procedure and formulae vary by state but basically involve a court hearing where the psychiatrist is required to justify continued hospitalization. Our impressions are that this procedure has infrequent success partly because it is extremely technical to initiate and because these hearings occur in the local court of the hospital where judicial decisions almost always mirror medical recommendations.

It is possible for incompetent defendants to reach the street directly from special security hospitals without again coming in contact with the criminal justice system. The most direct route is discharge from the special security hospital to the community. This occurs at or after the expiration of the original criminal order of commitment, when the defendant is seen as not requiring mental treatment *and* when either (1) charges have been dropped, (2) in a felony case an indictment has not been obtained, or (3) the district attorney allows the the defendant out on his own recognizance while criminal processing continues.

The second route to the street from special security hospitals is like the first except that the regular civil hospital is an intermediate point. After treatment in the regular security civil hospital, if charges have been dropped or the defendant is permitted out while processing occurs, an incompetent defendant may be back in the community without again coming into contact with the criminal justice system. This latter possibility does not imply in any way that the defendant does not spend considerable lengths of time involuntarily confined after arrest before returning to the community (c.f. Hess and Thomas 1963; McGarry 1971). In New York, for example, a defendant can be detained on successive criminal court orders of commitment for up to two-thirds of the maximum sentence for the crime that he is alleged to have committed. In fact, frequently defendants diverted into the mental health system as incompetent to stand trial never come back into contact with criminal justice agents before reaching the street because the prosecutor sees hospitalization as a substitute for incarceration (Steadman and Braff 1973).

To get a better understanding of what takes place under this legal designation of incompetent defendant, let us examine the patient career of one Baxstrom patient who was found incompetent to stand trial.

Fred Ross was born in Italy in 1898. His schooling was preparation for the priesthood, but deciding against this vocation, he dropped out of school at the age of 14. In 1915, he came to the United States where he worked as a bartender and porter. In 1927, he entered a common-law marriage arrangement with a widow with whom he had no children. He drank quite heavily throughout this period and was arrested in 1922 for intoxication (fined $200) and in 1929 for involvement in a stabbing fray (charges dismissed).

The incident that led to his police apprehension occurred in August 1934 at the age of 36. It is described in his hospital records as follows: "On August 16, 1934 there was nothing out of the ordinary in the daily routine. The wife was preparing soup for the next meal and had been out in the dooryard and as she stepped inside to see about the soup, the patient was pacing the floor; he immediately grabbed her by the hair of the head and rushed [*sic*] her against the wall, pounding her and then began slashing her with his jackknife. She shouted for help and fought the knife off but he managed to cut five deep, long gashes in her neck. He also slashed her hand. She sank to the floor in a semi-conscious condition. The neighbors rushed in and found the patient in the kitchen washing the knife."

On September 17, 1934, Ross was admitted from jail to a state hospital under a 60-day order of examination. Six weeks later he was diagnosed as "suffering from a schizophrenic psychosis, probably of the paranoid type." He was found incompetent to stand trial and sent to Matteawan State Hospital in December 1934 with a charge of assault, first degree pending. This indictment was dismissed in June 1943, but Ross remained in Matteawan for a total of 32 years, until the *Baxstrom* decision resulted in his transfer back to a state hospital in July 1966.

When returned to the hospital, Ross' mental condition was summarized as one of "confusion, disorientation, delapidation (suggesting) a diagnosis of *Schizophrenia, Paranoid*. The patient's previous diagnosis is maintained despite the fact a certain amount of cerebral arteriosclerosis has entered the picture." Almost three years later, in April 1969, Ross was placed by the hospital in a family care situation where he remained at the close of our research. At that time, he was "making an adequate adjustment to the family care home. He socializes little and only speaks when spoken to. He is cooperative and pleasant when approached but basically he is quite seclusive. For the most part he sits and reads his newspaper and watches TV. Has to be encouraged to go outside. Has memory defects but is sociable when approached. Patient quite apathetic. He claims he receives satisfactory care; however, he is not overly joyed with being on family care nor does he request return to the hospital."

The long-term hospitalization of Ross under a determination of incompetent to stand trial reflects the conditions of such defendants in most of the United States before 1966. Since that time, more regular judicial and psychiatric review has been mandated and maximum lengths of confinement relative to potential sentences have become more common. In addition, more incompetent defendants are now returning directly to the community after mental hospitalization without or during criminal processing. Thus, the incompetent defendant frequently comes into contact with all four facilities involved with the interfaces of the criminal justice and mental health systems: jails, prisons (if subsequently convicted), special security mental hospitals, and regular civil mental hospitals.

Not Guilty by Reason of Insanity

Despite the popular conception that tends to equate those people found NGRI with the total criminally insane population, such cases comprise only about 4 percent of the total. The processing of this legal category, as with the two previously discussed, begins with arrest. The next step is arraignment and plea, where the defense enters a NGRI plea. The case rests on questions of the defendant's mental condition at the time of the alleged incident. The commission of the alleged incident is not contested. Although criteria vary among several jurisdictions, the most frequent considerations are whether the defendant could tell the difference between right and wrong and had the ability to control the commission of the criminal act, or, under the former Durham ruling, whether the act was a result of mental disease or defect.

The psychiatric evaluation in NGRI cases, as with questions of incompetency, occurs during pre-trial detention. When the insanity defense is raised, it is not uncommon to have the defendant evaluated by several psychiatrists for both the defense and prosecution. At the trial, this often results in what is referred to as the "battle of the experts," since conflicting medical testimony often occurs between the defense and prosecution psychiatrists. Should the defendant be found sane at the time of the act, the defendant will be found guilty, since the NGRI defense does not contest the defendant's having committed the act. Because the NGRI defense just about precludes plea bargaining and because of the admissions necessary for the plea, it is infrequently used. It attains its high visibility from its disproportionate frequency in trials of political assassins and mass murderers.

When a defendant is determined by the court to be not guilty by reason of insanity, there usually follows an indefinite commitment to a regular security civil hospital. Where a state administers its special security hospital through a mental health department, which thus makes it a *civil* institution, the NGRI defendant can be sent there. In most cases, only the criminal court, which made the NGRI finding and authorized this indefinite commitment, can release the NGRI individual to the community. This release authorization would follow upon the request of the director of the mental hospital when the staff feels the patient is no longer mentally ill or dangerous. Once in the mental hospital, the NGRI individual's release thus rests both with the medical decisions of the hospital staff *and* the criminal court's where he was found "not guilty."

For the NGRI individual, like the mentally ill inmate and the incompetent defendant, legal/mental health processing begins with arrest, and commitment is under a criminal court order for mental hospitalization. Unlike cases involving the other two groups, however, the mental condition on which the court must decide from psychiatric testimony concerns the defendant's mental state at the time of the commission of the criminal act rather than his current one. The legal and psychiatric writing about this defense has far outstripped the volume of court cases involving it, partly because NGRI determinations are so challenging and debatable and partly because such determinations focus on many broader issues surrounding the interfaces of the criminal justice and mental health systems.

The kinds of difficulties and the intriguing issues that NGRI cases pose are exemplified in a recent New York case. Bruce Burman, was arrested on December 1, 1971 and charged with the first degree murder of his estranged wife. At the time of his arrest he was 30 years old. His police record began at the age of 18 when he was adjudicated a youthful offender for stealing a car. In May 1961, at age 20, he was arrested for assault, third degree, but charges were dismissed. His first incarceration resulted from a "drunken rampage" with 7 other people in September 1961, which resulted in convictions for burglary, assault, and malicious mischief. After this incarceration, Burman had four other arrests before that for the murder of his wife.

In 1970, for unexplained reasons, Burman had been shot by his father, which resulted in his being paraplegic. Consequently, Burman began to drink heavily and brood over the hostility he had towards his father. On the afternoon of December 1, 1971 Burman loaded himself and his wheelchair into his car and drove to the trailer where his wife was living with their 11-year-old daughter. He parked outside the trailer to await her arrival from work. When she got out of her car, Burman shot her five times with a .30-06 rifle. She died almost immediately. Several hours later there was a complaint that someone was firing shots into the trailer home of Burman's parents. His mother called the sheriff who, upon arriving, spotted and apprehended Burman 300 yards from the trailer. Found in Burman's car were around 110 live rounds of ammunition; a semi-automatic .30-06 rifle; a bolt action .243 rifle with telescope sight; 30-40 spent cartridges of both calibers; and a half consumed quart of liquor.

In May 1972, at his trial, Burman was found not guilty by reason of insanity on the basis of concurring reports of psychiatrists for both the defense and prosecution. As the judge concluded, "Although . . . I would ordinarily have found the guilt of the defendant beyond a reasonable doubt, I was compelled, because of the uncontroverted medical testimony, to deliver a verdict of acquital by reason of insanity."

The more difficult issues in Burman's case arose when the civil hospital to which the court committed him requested his release less than 3 months after his trial. The hospital's release committee in July 1972 concluded that Burman showed "no evidence of being mentally ill or in need of continued hospital care." Subsequently, two court appointed psychiatrists agreed with the hospital release committee. In addition, these psychiatric examiners concluded that Burman had an "explosive personality," which could be set off by his drinking, and there was no way they could assure the court that he might not under such influences attempt to kill his father. However, he had no treatable mental illness.

In 1974, Burman's case remained in the state courts because the trial judge, believing Burman to be dangerous, refused to approve his release from the civil hospital. The judge did demand that the hospital establish some community treatment program for Burman that would make him unlikely to attempt to kill his father or anyone else. However, since Burman would not be on parole under such an arrangement, there was no sanction that the court could employ to make him stay in such a program, and Burman refused to agree to outpatient treatment. Thus, he remained in a civil mental hospital because the judge decided that the hospital was obliged to protect the community from this dangerous person by retaining him even though he did not have treatable mental illness.

The numerous provocative issues raised by cases such as Bruce Burman's indicate why NGRI cases receive so much legal, psychiatric, and public attention. These are controversial, wide-ranging issues, and there is usually extensive local media coverage. So while NGRI defendants make up a very small proportion of all criminal cases and of the criminally insane, they nevertheless hold much fascination and will continue to in spite of their small numbers.

Dangerously Mentally Ill

The legal status, designated as "dangerously mentally ill," is quite different from the previous three. It involves a *civil* commitment to a hospital for the *criminally* insane because of behavior while hospitalized in a civil mental hospital. The types and uses of statutes dealing with this portion of the criminally insane vary widely by state. Much of the special security that violent mental patients receive occurs within civil hospitals through closed wards and other special precautions employed in the day-to-day operations of the hospitals. However, there is some provision in most mental health laws for the extremely difficult or violent patient to be transferred to special security hospitals that are often under correctional departments' control. Thus, for this type of criminally insane patient, there is no criminal conviction, but the label is acquired by transfer to an institution for the criminally insane.

Certainly, many of the acts leading to patients being determined dangerously mentally ill, had they occurred in the community, would be considered criminal. In fact, the New York Mental Hygiene Law has defined a dangerously mentally ill situation as one in which the "patient has committed or is liable to commit an act which, if committed by a person criminally responsible for his conduct, would constitute homicide or felonious assault or is so dangerously mentally disabled that his presence in the department hospital or school is dangerous to the safety of other patients therein, to the officers or employees thereof, or to the community."[c]

The patient pathways through the mental health and criminal justice systems under this legal status are usually between the civil mental hospital and the special security hospital. This movement is often between the mental health and criminal justice systems since the special security hospitals are often under correctional auspices. Movement proceeds in both directions between these two facilities. Special security hospitals are usually hesitant to take the responsibility for direct discharges of patients who have been determined dangerously mentally ill. Thus, patients are usually returned to the civil hospital from which they may return to the community.

The final case we present as an example of what these statuses actually represent is that of a pre-Baxstrom patient. John Biddle, born in 1902, had a normal childhood and school record, until he quit school in the seventh grade at age 15. He held a variety of odd jobs and eventually became a "tester of electric motors." His difficulties began at age 18 when he got into a violent argument with an uncle who knocked him down with his fist. Within 6 months, Biddle had his first epileptic seizure, which led to his dismissal from his job. In September 1925, he was admitted on a voluntary basis to a state school because of periods of unconsciousness during attacks.

During Biddle's first institutionalization, he was brought for special evaluation to a nearby neurological institute where some treatment was

[c]This New York law was declared unconstitutional in November, 1973 by the State Court of Appeals because of the inappropriateness of committing a civil patient to a correctional institution.

administered, but with little significant change. During Biddle's stay in the state school, it was felt he developed a psychosis associated with his epilepsy. Because of his record of several disturbances, he was transferred to a regular civil hospital in 1943. He continued to have seizures and to fight with other patients even when not experiencing seizures. In 1945, the hospital records indicate that "he frequently became involved in altercations with other patients. Since his altercations became more frequent, patient (Biddle) had to be kept in camisole for extended periods of time." Finally, in January 1950, Biddle was declared dangerously mentally ill and transferred to Matteawan, New York's hospital for the criminally insane under the direction of the Correction Department.

Biddle showed little change physically or mentally in Matteawan between 1950 and 1966. As his hospital records for this period indicates, "his psychosis is characterized by deterioration, irritability, assaultiveness, seclusiveness and rather marked mental tension defects. He has shown no improvement during the many years he has been in institutions." Just prior to the *Baxstrom* decision, in February 1966, Biddle was transferred back to the civil hospital where he had resided between 1943 and 1950. He was admitted in a "mute and semiconscious" condition. His seizures still occurred and on November 10, 1966 he died in the hospital infirmary. His death was due to Status Epilepticus.

The dangerously mentally ill, like the NGRI, make up a relatively small proportion—under 10 percent—of all the criminally insane. Unlike the NGRI, the dangerously mentally ill get little attention, and popular conceptions of the criminally insane do not even recognize them as included among the criminally insane. They are, however, solely by reason of the facilities within which they are detained.

These, then, are the four classifications of the criminally insane: mentally ill inmates, incompetent defendants, not guilty by reason of insanity patients, and dangerously mentally ill patients. The precise terminology and, more importantly, the specific procedures vary widely both between and within states. However, each of these groups is discernible among the patient populations of special security mental hospitals and among those people passing between the criminal justice and mental health systems. By far, the two largest segments of the criminally insane are mentally ill inmates and incompetent defendants. These two groups also make up almost all of the two research populations of this book, because the Baxstrom patients were a group generated by a court decision dealing with maximum incarceration/hospitalization time, which was not relevant to either the NGRI or dangerously mentally ill who do not have determinant sentences. The pre-Baxstrom patients to be studied as a comparison group include a few dangerously mentally ill patients, approximately in proportion to their representativeness among the criminally insane as a whole. Since NGRI cases in New York must go to civil facilities, there were none in our research populations, all of whom were patients who at one point were in special security hospitals for the criminally insane and subsequently transferred to regular civil hospitals.

These are the outlines of the criminal justice and mental health system interfaces and the four major careers of the criminally insane through them. We now move to review and integrate the research on the dynamics of how these systems of legal/psychiatric processing actually function.

The Dynamics of Legal/Psychiatric Processing

As is evident from much of the preceeding material, there are vast differences in the pathways by which people become labeled criminally insane. However, as with our discussion of the legal statuses, there are certain processing points through which all of the criminally insane at some time pass. These are police apprehension (with the exception of the few dangerously mentally ill), courts, and mental hospitals. Courts, for example, relate to the careers of incompetent defendants immediately after arrest for arraignment and for competency hearings, and they relate to dangerously mentally ill patients involved in civil proceedings at the time of transfer from a regular to special security mental hospital. The dynamics of the legal/psychiatric processing at each major point appear most comprehensible by an approach that focuses on each processing point rather than on the statuses resulting from the processing. In doing this, we analyze what happens at four major career contingency points: (1) courts before hospitalization; (2) special security hospitals; (3) criminal trials after hospitalization; and (4) the community after release.

Courts before Hospitalization

At the outset, two distinctions are needed. First, this section includes data dealing only with court processing of the criminally insane, which results in this label being applied, rather than with criminal trials after hospitalization. Second, we begin our review of the literature of legal/psychiatric processing with prehospitalization courts because to our knowledge there are no published data specifically dealing with police apprehension of the criminally insane. Part of the reason for this is that mentally ill inmates' careers from arrest to criminal convictions are like those of anyone else processed through the criminal justice system. The same would be the case of NGRI individuals who would have been so adjudged at criminal trials.

The dangerously mentally ill would not have their criminally insane processing begun with police apprehension, since their inclusion is the result of behavior while already hospitalized. These factors do not, however, explain why there are such empirical lacunae on the police apprehension of incompetent defendants or what differences might exist during arrest and incarceration for mentally ill inmates and inmates never diverted from the criminal justice system. Thus, research on the dynamics of the legal/psychiatric processing of the criminally insane begins with materials dealing with prehospitalization court hearings.

Psychiatric evaluation, which necessarily preceeds any court hearings, may involve either questions of competency or criminal responsibility. In the case of incompetency, this evaluation occurs pre-trial or pre-sentence. For criminal responsibility, it would be before or during a criminal trial. Most of the published works on the pre-trial evaluation phase are essays dealing with the questions of which issues are being and should be raised and what are appropriate roles for the psychiatric and legal participants. Much of what actually happens to defendants being evaluated for competency in terms of institutional experiences, lengths of evaluation confinements, lengths and types of psychiatric examinations, characteristics of patients determined competent pre-hearing, and procedures for obtaining a hearing completely lack research data. About the only facet of the processes of pre-trial competency evaluation that has been explored is the distribution of offenses of defendants referred. As Cook et al. (1973) point out, most of these data are not particularly useful, however, in that they are not base rates relative to state crime statistics. Data for questions about the dynamics of psychiatric evaluations for NGRI cases are similarly absent.

There are a few helpful studies on competency evaluation procedures such as Vann (1965), Pfeiffer et al. (1967), Cooke (1969), Laczko et al. (1970), and McGarry (1973). All found a fairly consistent percentage of evaluated patients being found incompetent by psychiatrists. In these studies, the percentage found incompetent by examining psychiatrists ranged from 22 percent to 49 percent. Very importantly, McGarry (1965) noted that when psychiatric clinic screening recommendations rather than those of the court were used before referral for intensive evaluations, the percentage incompetent rose dramatically to 65 percent. However, this latter procedure is utilized in very few locales, and the figure of 25 percent of those evaluated being found incompetent noted in a recent report of New York City procedures (Resnik and Schack 1972) appears to be more typical and in line with the research cited above.

Once the examining psychiatrists find a defendant incompetent there is little likelihood that the court will disagree. Vann found a 100 percent agreement rate, and Pfeiffer, 90 percent between psychiatric recommendations of incompetency and court decisions. This latter figure is almost exactly identical with our preliminary findings obtained from 178 competency hearings in New York City in 1971 and 1972, which show an 89 percent concurrence rate on decisions of incompetency and 87 percent on those of dangerousness. These rates are also very similar to those summarized by Gove (1970) for involuntary civil commitment hearings. Gove's work and that of others on civil proceedings (Scheff 1964; Miller and Schwartz 1966; Maisel 1970) suggest strongly that the dynamics of competency hearings for the criminal defendants are very similar to those of civil commitment with regard to the existence of confused or questionable psychiatric and judicial roles and a very high concurrence of the courts with medical testimony.

There is no comparable literature on NGRI evaluations or the dynamics of trials in which this offense is raised. Some useful material on NGRI processing in Washington, D.C. is presented by Arens (1969) who noted the inappropriateness of much of the psychiatric testimony and the confusion of the juries on the central points. However, the atypicalness of Washington to situations elsewhere in the United States greatly constricts the use of this single empirical work in this area. One reason for the dearth of NGRI research data is the infrequency of these cases, as mentioned previously. For example, only .53 percent of the 36,643 felony dispositions in California in 1965 involved NGRI pleas. Of 515 homocide indictments in Detroit between 1959 and 1963, only one was decided by an NGRI verdict. The jurisdiction where NGRI cases are most frequent is Washington, D.C. In 1954, there were three cases in that city, while in 1962, 66 defendants were found NGRI, which is still only 5.1 percent of all felony cases and 13.8 percent of all felony cases tried (Matthews 1967). The paucity of empirical research on NGRI cases reflects accurately the frequency of these cases on criminal court calendars.

One facet of competency hearings that draws heavy criticism from a number of studies is the confusion caused by insufficient knowledge of issues and procedures by legal, psychiatric, and judicial participants. Hess and Thomas' (1963) study of 119 patients at Ionia State Hospital in Michigan, Rosenberg and McGarry's (1972) examination of 48 cases from Bridgewater State Hospital in Massachusetts, and our work in progress all support the following conclusion:

> The confused statutes regarding incompetency to stand trial and its distorted application by both physician and lawyer tends to subvert the social and legal principle inherent in the concept of competency and in doing so to sacrifice the professional identity of both lawyer and physicians as well as their appropriate functions as assigned by society and which their client has the right to expect (Hess and Thomas 1963, p. 718).

Mentally ill inmates also come in contact with courts before their hospitalization. There is no reason to expect that these hearings are any different from those of civil commitment, incompetency, and commitment of the dangerously mentally ill (i.e., hearings that are exceedingly terse and usually in concurrence with medical recommendations). However, there is no research dealing specifically with these hearings.

In sum, the courts come into play *before* hospitalization of the criminally insane: (1) in pre-trial and pre-sentence decisions of competency, (2) in criminal trials and subsequent commitment proceedings, (3) in some jurisdiction for NGRI cases, (4) in the civil commitments of the dangerously mentally ill, and (5) in the transfer of mentally ill inmates. There is little published data on the dynamics of the court proceedings except for the first type. The work on incompetency determinations indicates little about the evaluation phase but presents a strong consensus that between 60 and 75 percent of all patients evaluated for competency are found able to stand trial, that there is a psychiatric-judicial concurrence rate on findings of competency of about 90 percent and that competency hearings are characterized by legal and psychiatric confusion.

Special Security Mental Hospitals

There are three general themes running through the research literature on the special security hospitalization of the criminally insane: (1) excessive detention; (2) lack of treatment; and (3) a strong psychiatric conservatism to release these patients. Research dealing with incompetent defendants (Hess and Thomas 1963; Tuteur 1969; McGarry 1969; McGarry and Bendt 1969) and with NGRI patients (Lewin 1968; Morrow and Peterson 1966) provides much data on the lengthy confinement of the criminally insane. Eight of the patients Tuteur studied who became competent after transfer from the special security hospital in Illinois to the state hospital had spent from 2 to 11 years in special security. In McGarry and Bendt's study, the 6 males who were criminally committed spent an average of 4.5 years hospitalized.

In McGarry's other study (1969), of 219 patients his group examined for competency from Bridgewater State Hospital (Massachusetts' special security facility), the 56 men they returned as competent had spent an average of 4.3 years in special security, while those not found ready to return to trial had spent an average of 14.9 years in Bridgewater. This latter figure was similar to that of a group of NGRI patients studied by Lewin who had no benefit of private attorneys after commitment. These 10 patients spent an average of 12 years hospitalized. The 13 patients with private attorneys had an average stay of 1 year, 10 months.

Morrow and Peterson found their NGRI patients had been hospitalized for an average of 32 months and the criminal sexual psychopaths for 29 months. These two averages are deceptive because the standard deviation of 31 and 25.5 indicates that one-third of their sample were hospitalized either 1 month or less or over 5 years. Rubin (1972) has discussed 17 patients in Illinois ("The Menard 17")—8 who were NGRI; 8, incompetent; and 1 who was unable to be executed—all of whom through administrative error were inappropriately detained for an average of 25 years. Thus, many of all types of criminally detained mental patients are hospitalized much longer than they would have been incarcerated for their alleged offenses. The situation may not be quite as serious as this conclusion by Hess and Thomas (1963, p. 716): "In essence, the result of the Michigan management of the problem of incompetency is the incarceration, often for life, of persons without benefit of trial or the safeguards of civil commitment procedures." Nevertheless, the literature we reviewed has the constant theme of inordinate detention of all the criminally insane.

The excessive confinement of the criminally insane is further demonstrated by the frequency with which these long-term patients are returned to trial and the community when some type of outside treatment or research program is instituted for them. When McGarry's (1969) research group selected and evaluated 219 incompetent defendants at Bridgewater State Hospital for return to trial, they found 56 (25.6 percent) competent. In addition, after the 219 were originally selected for research, Bridgewater returned as competent another 15 (6.8 percent) to court. Thus, 32.4 percent of the group evaluated under the impetus of a demonstration and research grant from the National Institute of Mental Health were found competent. A remarkably similar percentage of incompetent defendants were returned to trial when they received special research attention at Elgin State Hospital in Illinois (Tuteur 1969). Of the 36 patients transferred there from Illinois Special Security Hospital, 8 (22.2 percent) were returned as competent after 1 to 12 months special treatment and another 3 (8.3 percent) were discharged to the community after their charges were dropped. Thus, 30.5 percent were removed from the special security and regular hospital after some special attention was afforded them. Tuteur also studied another group of 36 patients admitted directly from court as incompetent. After 2 to 23 months of treatment, 11 individuals (30.6 percent) were returned for trial and 3 (8.3 percent) had charges dropped and were returned to the community, which made a total of 38.9 percent who were discharged as competent.

This consistent percentage of patients, both short-term and long-term, who were returned to trial when given special evaluations or intensive treatment is further confirmed by two other reports. In McGarry's and Bendt's (1971) study of civil versus criminal commitments, of the 10 males civilly committed, all 10 were released during the seven-year follow-up period. Of the 6 criminal commitments, only 2 were discharged. In the second report, Hess and Thomas (1963) inferred that a major problem for hospitalized incompetent defendants was ". . . that the goals of treatment were vague and inconsistent. In an attempt to combat this, the [hospital] staff apparently bypassed entirely the legal intent behind the incompetency principle and sought to perceive and manage the incompetent patient as they would patients committed for other reasons" (pp. 716-7). These conclusions are supported by the Tuteur and the McGarry and Bendt studies referred to above in which about one-third of the incompetent patients who are systematically treated or evaluated under proper guidelines were removed from mental hospitals.

In all studies of criminally insane patients in special security hospitals, there is the implication of inactive and ineffective treatment programs, confusion and conservatism on the part of the medical staffs, and detentions much longer than are necessary. When these studies took a special interest in a group of patients through either research or special treatment and evaluation programs, a significant number of even long-term patients were returned to court and the community. When special interest or active legal assistance was present, significantly shorter periods of confinement occurred, which were entirely unrelated to offenses, previous mental conditions, or estimations of dangerousness. In fact, active legal assistance for Lewin's NGRI murderers shortened their confinements by an average of 5 years and 9 months compared to those patients without private counsel. Unfortunately, continuous legal assistance, active treatment programs, and openness by institutional medical personnel to release the criminally insane to alternative environments are rare.

Criminal Trial after Hospitalization

This segment of the processing of the criminally insane is relevant only to incompetent defendants. NGRI cases have been "acquitted" before hospitalization. Mentally ill inmates have been convicted before being defined as mentally ill, and the dangerously mentally ill are not liable for any type of criminal prosecution, since their's is a civil order of commitment. Incompetent defendants, however, have charges pending while hospitalized.

From the four studies that have examined this portion of the processing of incompetent defendants, it is difficult to find any consistencies. A Massachusetts study (McGarry 1971) found that of 71 incompetent felony defendants returned to trial after an average of 14 years and 9 months in Bridgewater State Hospital, 46 percent (33) were convicted and 20 percent (14) were found NGRI. The remaining, 34 percent (24) were not prosecuted.

In one New York study (Vann 1965) of 27 defendants from Erie County who were incompetent felony defendants, 19 were discharged from Matteawan State Hospital for the criminally insane between 1950 and 1960. Only 5 of the 19 were convicted and the other 14 (74 percent) had their indictments dismissed.

The 5 patients convicted were returned to trial after an average hospitalization of 9 months. For those 10 patients whose indictments were dismissed while still hospitalized, the average was 1 year and 1 month in Matteawan. For those committed, released, and whose indictments were than dismissed (4 patients), the average was 2 years and 5 months. There were an additional 7 individuals among the 17 committed to Matteawan who were indicted and still detained in Matteawan at the conclusion of Vann's research. Their average hospitalization to that point was 6 years and 2 months and their charges included 2 murders, 1 assault, 1 robbery, 1 child molestation, 1 burglary, and 1 illegal possession of a machine gun. The more serious the offense, the longer the stay in Matteawan, but as this occurred, there was an increased likelihood that the indictment would be dismissed.

A Detroit study (Matthews 1970) involved only homocide offenders between 1959 and 1963. Of these 21, 18 (86 percent) had their charges dismissed, 2 were guilty of manslaughter, and 1 was NGRI. The author does not give their lengths of hospitalization, but he says they were "long."

The second New York study completed by the New York City Bar Association (1968) was the largest of the four. It determined the dispositions for all cases (235) returned to court from New York's Matteawan State Hospital in fiscal 1964. In marked contrast to the Erie County and Detroit findings, only 8.9 percent (21) of all those returned to court throughout New York State in this period had their charges dismissed. This was after an average of 4 years in Matteawan. The most frequent outcome was a guilty plea (67 percent of the cases), usually to a reduced charge (58 percent), and a sentence of time served.

The one thread of consistency among these four studies is Vann's (1965) conclusion that ". . . in the majority of cases the court has allowed the confinement to a criminal mental hospital to serve as compensation to society for a prison sentence" (p. 31). Where length of hospitalization was long, the conviction rate was low. When hospitalization was short, the conviction rate increased. In addition, the seriousness of the charge was postively related to longer hospitalization and therefore lower conviction rates.

On the one hand, it seems as though the criminal system is not overly punitive to these individuals when they are returned. Even with very serious offenses, significant numbers had their charges dismissed. On the other hand, for violent offenses against persons, there was much more apt to be lengthy pre-trial hospitalization and the possibility of continued involuntary detention in civil mental hospitals after a subsequent finding of NGRI.

Return to the Community

It is difficult to determine how well the criminally insane do upon return to the community. Many mentally ill inmates eventually return to the community after transfer to prison, and therefore their recidivism and adjustment data are included in correctional statistics. The dangerously mentally ill, the NGRI, and even incompetent defendants often return to the street by way of regular civil mental hospitals, which keep few records on patient community adjustment, especially involving criminal recidivism, unless rehospitalization is involved. Three studies that do provide data on the criminally insane in the community report lower recidivism rates for them than for comparable criminal populations. These data further question the validity of psychiatric conservatism towards their release.

Apparently the first follow-up study of the criminally insane in the community examined patients released from Illinois Security Hospital (Zeidler et al. 1955). By reworking the figures they provide, it seems that of the 63 patients in their research sample of 180 who were discharged to the community, 19 (30.2 percent) were rearrested over a five-year period. Three individuals (4.8 percent) were recommitted to mental hospitals which leaves 41 of the 63 (65.1 percent) defined as having had "good adjustment" in the community. There were an additional 15 patients for whom no information could be obtained. Since there was little likelihood that these individuals had been rearrested (the agency records utilized would have shown this), the criminal recidivism rate of the 78 released patients would be 24.4 percent (19/78).

Zeidler's sample included only discharged incompetent defendants, but a large number of these—43 of 121 (35.5 percent), which is atypical of most groups of criminally insane patients—were charged with sex offenses. McGarry's (1971) group of psychotic offenders returned to trial from Bridgewater is more typical with 11 (15.5 percent) sexual charges among 71 cases. Of the 71 returned to trial, 50 reached the community during the follow-up period. Of these 50, 24 (48.0 percent) were arrested at some time. McGarry feels this recidivism rate of 48 percent compared favorably with a four-year follow-up of paroled felons from Massachusetts' state prisons, a group whose recidivism rate was 59.8 percent.

Similarly favorable comparisons of recidivism rates of the criminally insane were obtained in Morrow and Peterson's study (1966) in both their NGRI and criminal sexual psychopath subgroups. Over a three-year period, 37 percent of the NGRI cases criminally recidivated and 25 percent of the CSPs did. These rates compare with Glaser's (1964) federal prison system's rate of 35 percent and California's prison sex offender's recidivism rate of 26.6 percent. Morrow and Peterson's recidivism figures are considerably lower than McGarry's because they used felony *convictions* as the indicator of failure, while McGarry employed arrest. In either case, the figures provide useful data in that baseline rates of penal recidivism rates from the same states demonstrate that the records of criminally insane patients returned to the community are better than or equal to that of paroled offenders.

In the research literature on the mechanisms that process the criminally insane reviewed in this section, there are some consistencies such as the recidivism rate comparisons just discussed. However, such consistencies and even studies that allow such comparisons do not dominate the area. Rather, non-cumulative studies, which barely begin to meet the needs in these problem areas, are the norm. Unfortunately, even less adequate data is available on the personal characteristics of those people who pass through these processing points. We now turn to the information that is available.

Personal Characteristics

In searching for data about who the criminally insane are, there are two major problems. First, much of the literature that does exist deals mainly with the issues at the socio-legal-medical level in essays from personal, clinical, or court experiences or from philosophical positions applied to specific situations such as competency hearings, insanity defenses, and the like. Very few people have bothered to go out and collect detailed information about the people in hospitals for the criminally insane.

The second problem is the frequent omission of descriptive details about the research subjects in published research reports. The reader is told, for instance, that a group of 75 incompetent male defendants are under study, and data on their evaluations and hearings for competency are then discussed. However, details about the basic characteristics of the group—such as their ages, racial characteristics, education, criminal records, and so forth—are simply not mentioned. Articles by Hess and Thomas (1963), Pfeiffer et al. (1967), and by Laczko et al. (1970) clearly demonstrate these difficulties. Hess and Thomas, in what is otherwise an extremely useful report, describe their sampling of the 1,484 patients in Ionia State Hospital in Michigan to arrive at 119 subjects representing 4 patient subgroups. After some information about the records used, the authors present conclusions about due process of competency hearings, excessive hospitalization, and inappropriate psychiatric roles. Nothing concrete is offered about the subjects themselves.

Both Pfeiffer et al. and Laczko et al. deal with defendants evaluated for competency, and both do describe their total samples of 85 and 453 subjects in useful detail. However, neither report distinguishes the characteristics of those people found incompetent from those competent, which is potentially a very significant difference. Consequently, nothing is added to what is known of the people who become labeled criminally insane. Certainly where a group is 91 percent white, like Pfeiffer's, the incompetent defendants will be mostly white. However, in most groups, description of the entire research population is inadequate.

The best description of criminally insane research subjects is provided by Morrow and Peterson (1966) in their follow-up study of 44 NGRI cases and 43 criminal sexual psychopaths. On incompetent defendants, Cooke (1969), Tuteur (1969), and Zeidler et al. (1955) provide some useful data. Lanzkron (1963) presents further data on 150 incompetent murder defendants. Unfortunately, on most characteristics, these studies are not directly comparable. For example, Morrow and Peterson, as well as Cooke, report average ages, while Tuteur reports only the age range of his subjects. There is, however, some consistency among the studies. All subjects, either by sample design or by the actual characteristics of the population sampled are predominantly male. In addition, all groups of incompetent defendants are predominantly white, in their early to mid-thirties at admission, and with a very low percentage of sex crime charges (except, of course, the CSP group of Morrow and Peterson). Very few of these people ever held jobs above unskilled levels, and most are not married. These are primarily marginal individuals with weak social ties and few community roots. They do vary from one research population to another in offense distribution. However, in the two studies that used appropriate base-rate statistics, the most frequent offenses reported are for violent crimes against persons, followed by sex offenses, with property and drug offenses the least frequent (Cooke et al. 1973; Steadman and Braff 1973).

Beyond these few studies there is little in the literature about the people who are called criminally insane. There are some clues such as offered by McGarry and Bendt (1969) who conclude their study of court procedures in Massachusetts by noting that the courts ". . . tended to commit the very old and the very young, alcoholic, and the nonpsychotic in a civil status. Men in their middle years with large numbers of previous misdemeanors arrests—classifiable perhaps as public nuisances—tended to be hospitalized in a criminal status" (p. 96).

These studies, then, constitute the body of descriptive literature available on the criminally insane in the United States. It is sketchy and non-cumulative. Researchers who have ventured into these areas have been more concerned with legal processing than with depicting the people who are processed. The same can be said of what research exists on the criminally insane outside of the United States. The only descriptive data that we could find were part of four studies of various criminally insane groups in Britain (Tong and MacKay 1959; Rollin 1965; McKerracher et al. 1966; Gathercole 1968). It is very difficult to compare or contrast the findings of these studies with U.S. data both because of fundamental differences in the criminal justice and mental health systems in the two countries and because the reports tend to focus on subgroups that do not exist, as such, in the United States. Thus, diagnostic categories are intermingled; age distributions and means vary widely both within and between groups; racial characteristics are unreported; and arrest rates and offenses are quite different, all of which severely limit the use of these data in clarifying the picture of who the people are in the United States that we call criminally insane. We currently know very little about those people who are so facilely called criminally insane.

Summary

What we most clearly know about the criminally insane are the four major legal classifications included under this designation. These are (1) the mentally ill inmates, with the subtype criminal sexual psychopath; (2) incompetent defendants; (3) those not guilty by reason of insanity; and (4) the dangerously mentally ill. The processing that results in individuals becoming called criminally insane depends on various state statutes involving four types of institutions for detention and sometimes treatment. These are jails and prisons (criminal justice system), and special and regular security mental hospitals (mental health system). The particular arrangements for the processing and treatment of the criminally insane in each state and locality depends on which of these types of facilities are available, which state departments operate which types of facilities, and widely varying statutes.

There are very few indications in the literature on the personal characteristics of the criminally insane. This void is a function both of the absence of research on most aspects of the criminally insane and of the omission of details that should be provided in published research reports. The vague picture that can be constructed from available accounts depicts the criminally insane as extremely marginal individuals with few work skills and weak family ties. Most are white and in their mid-thirties. Most frequently their criminal charges or offenses are for violent crimes against persons.

Property offenses were the least frequent and sex charges or offenses, while considerably less frequent than violent crimes, tended to be overrepresented among the criminally insane compared to state arrest statistics.

While there is a scarcity of data about most aspects of the people and the processes leading to the criminally insane label, there is more material dealing with certain segments of the actual processing of the criminally insane than with the people processed. With the exception of the dangerously mentally ill, processing of the criminally insane begins with police apprehension. Empirical data on this particular point is practically nonexistent. The data on the evaluation phase of processing (which may occur pre-trial, pre-sentence, or after conviction) document much confusion about the meaning of incompetence and its legal procedures. There is also the fairly consistent finding that about 25 percent of all cases in which competency is questioned result in an incompetency determination. The NGRI defense is infrequent, and little research addresses the dynamics of its procedures. As with the police apprehension stage, there is no data published considering the dynamics of the evaluation period in the processing of mentally ill inmates.

The type of judicial processing at the prehospital stage varies. Competency hearings are confused affairs with extremely high concurrence between psychiatric recommendations and judicial determinations. NGRI cases involve regular criminal trials. An NGRI determination usually means acquital and indeterminant mental hospitalization, with release dependent on court authorization. The dangerously mentally ill at this stage would be involved in involuntary civil hearings for transfer to a special security hospital, or, depending on state statutes, might be simply administratively transferred. The mentally ill inmate may require either an administrative transfer or a judicial hearing before hospitalization.

Hospitalization in most facilities for the criminally insane, the second processing point, is associated with lengthy confinements, (often more than if conviction had occurred), minimal treatment, a strong conservatism by institutional psychiatrists to discharge these individuals regardless of legal situations.

Most incompetent defendants are liable for criminal trials after hospitalization. For the other categories of criminally insane, a hearing would follow hospitalization usually only if a *habeas corpus* writ is involved. Around one quarter of incompetent defendants returned to trial have their charges dropped by the district attorney or trial judge. Also, those that are convicted often are given sentences of time served.

Upon return to the street, the criminally insane appear to fare as well as or better than released or paroled inmates in the same areas. However, there are no comparable data for released mental patients to indicate what sorts of adjustment problems the criminally insane encounter and how these may be associated with either criminal recidivism or rehospitalization.

These then are the legal classifications, the people, institutions, and processes associated with the label "criminally insane." It is in this context that the landmark *Baxstrom v. Herold* decision of the U.S. Supreme Court was handed down in February 1966. This decision resulted in the transfer of 967 patients from New York's two hospitals for the criminally insane to 18 regular security civil mental hospitals. In the two years immediately preceding this decision, under regular processing, 359 patients had been transferred from these same two facilities for the criminally insane to state mental hospitals, the latter's with psychiatric approval and the former's against it. By studying who these two groups were and what happened to them after their transfers, it is possible to develop some understanding about who the criminally insane are, what happens to them, and how they function when returned to the community. Through an intense examination of the court decision, the people it affected, and their subsequent behaviors, the importance of Baxstrom and pre-Baxstrom patients for the processing, custody, and treatment of the criminally insane become evident. It is to the *Baxstrom* decision and the people it affected, to which we now turn.

3 The Baxstrom v. Herold Decision

The two persons named in the *Baxstrom v. Herold* decision are Johnnie K. Baxstrom and Dr. Ross Herold. Baxstrom was a mentally ill inmate in Dannemora State Hospital. Dr. Herold was the director of that facility. Dannemora, as mentioned in Chapter 1, was from 1900 to 1972 the New York state hospital for male, convicted felons who became mentally ill while serving time. Contiguous with Clinton State Prison, it is located in Dannemora, New York, about 20 miles south of the Canadian border in the northeastern portion of the state. The population of the hospital at the time of the court decision in February 1966 was around 1,100 patients. Baxstrom was admitted to Dannemora from Attica State Prison on June 1, 1961 and remained there until a month after this decision.

Johnnie K. Baxstrom and His Case

Johnnie Baxstrom was a black male, born on August 12, 1918 in Greensboro, North Carolina. He was the youngest of 9 children. He quit school when he was 17, while he was in the eleventh grade. As described by his hospital notes, throughout his childhood "he had what he termed 'fainting headaches.' He said it felt as though someone were beating on the side of his temple and that he would black out in school. He was hospitalized from May 29, 1956 to June 8, 1956 for head injury. Diagnosis: Idiopathic Epilepsy and residuals from Bilateral Subdural Hematoma, following skull fracture."

Baxstrom had a very irregular job record showing that he worked only for short times at a variety of unskilled positions. He did have a good military record; he entered the Armed Forces in September 1943 and received an honorable discharge in March 1946. He was married three times. His first marriage was in 1939 to a woman who bore him four children. She died giving birth to their fifth child. Baxstrom remarried in late 1946. No children resulted from this marriage, and they separated after a brief time. He then entered a common-law arrangement with a third woman with whom he had five children. He left this woman in 1951.

Baxstrom's criminal record is a lengthy list of drinking and property offenses. However, his first offense did not occur until he was 30, which was two years after his getting out of the military service and while he was living with his second wife. It occurred on February 23, 1948 in Greensboro. He was charged with assaulting a female with a dangerous weapon, but the case was never disposed of in the courts. Again in 1950, he was arrested on two counts of assault and one of larceny in Baltimore, where his sister lived. He was found not guilty of all charges. His first conviction occurred 6 months later, June 1950, in Greensboro where he received a 12-month sentence on the road gang for an "affray assault on a female." He was discharged on March 26, 1951.

Over the next few years, Baxstrom appears to have taken up a wandering life style involving no work. Between 1951 and 1958, when he was sentenced to Attica, Baxstrom was arrested 12 times in Kannapolis, N.C.; Spartanburg, S.C.; Greensboro, N.C.; Raleigh, N.C.; Jessups, Md.; Baltimore, Md.; Rochester, N.Y. (September 1955); Syracuse, N.Y.; and Jamesville, N.Y. for such things as trespassing on Southern Railway property, drunkenness, vagrancy, disorderly conduct, intoxication, and one time for robbery for which he received and served a one-year sentence in the Maryland House of Corrections.

On October 21, 1958, Baxstrom was arrested in Rochester, N.Y. for attacking a police officer with an ice pick. According to hospital records, he stabbed the officer in the face, forehead, and collarbone. Little else about the incident is found in the hospital record. However, in a personal communication, Dr. A. L. Halpern, who examined Baxstrom extensively in 1966, reports Baxstrom's account of the incident, which is corroborated by the police report. Apparently Baxstrom was drinking in a bar where he got into a fight with another patron. During the fight Baxstrom pulled a knife or ice pick and stabbed the other combatant. This other combatant turned out to be a police officer in civilian clothes. For this act, he received a two-and-a-half to three-year sentence in the Monroe County Court on April 9, 1959. The conviction was for assault, second degree. He was admitted to Attica State Prison on the same day with his full sentence to expire on December 18, 1961.

While in Attica, Baxstrom was reported to "often have epileptic fits during which he was aggressive, assaultive [*sic*] towards guards and inmates. He also used obscene language." Because of this, he was transferred to Dannemora on June 1, 1961.

Baxstrom's record at Dannemora was marked by a number of reported incidents. He was first examined for possible transfer to a civil hospital on November 27, 1961 when his full term sentence was about to expire. At that time, he was deemed inappropriate for transfer. The hospital record reports that "since that time patient has been involved in many assaults and altercations. On January 14, 1963, he struck a blind patient, knocking him to the floor. On July 22, 1965, it is reported that he tried to rally other patients against officers and was placed in restraint. A similar incident is reported on September 2, 1965. In Dannemora, this man was considered unpredictable and dangerous and was not suited for transfer to a civil state hospital.''

During the period in which these various incidents were reported, Baxstrom had instituted a number of legal proceedings that may have been related to his organizing patients. The first of these proceedings was a Surrogate Court hearing on December 6, 1961, after the expiration of his full term. This followed the psychiatric examination mentioned above. The purpose of this hearing was to detain Baxstrom involuntarily under Section 384 of the Correction Law by showing that he was still mentally ill and should be detained in Dannemora rather than freed or transferred to a civil hospital. The court approved his retention under Section 384 and returned Baxstrom to Dannemora.

Shortly after this hearing and again in 1963, Baxstrom entered writs of *habeas corpus* in a state court to obtain his release to the community as free from any mental illness necessitating involuntary hospitalization of any type. In both instances the writs were dismissed by the court. The 1963 writ was appealed to the Appelate Division of the New York State Court, the state's highest court, and was dismissed. A further appeal resulted in the *Baxstrom v. Herold* decision of the U.S. Supreme Court (383 U.S. 107). Considerable legal ability was necessary to develop the various writs, file them at the appropriate times, and know the proper locations for filing. Surprisingly, Baxstrom himself was capable of such action. Apparently, again according to Dr. A. L. Halpern, while Baxstrom was growing up, an uncle, who was a lawyer, lived with his family. This uncle moved to Chicago while Baxstrom was in high school but left a cache of legal books in the attic. Baxstrom said that he studied these books every day after school, and from this work he acquired sufficient legal expertise to develop his own case right up to presentation before the U.S. Supreme Court. Only at the time of actual presentation to the Supreme Court was Baxstrom represented by counsel. Just how efficient Baxstrom was in his legal endeavors and the role that counsel played in the *Baxstrom* decision is seen in the reflections of his counsel, Louis B. Polsky, who recounted them in a personal communication in July 1973.

In February 1965 I was the attorney in charge of the Criminal Appeals Bureau of The Legal Aid Society of New York. In that capacity, I often received unsolicited letters and material from prisoners in various institutions complaining about their particular situation or seeking advice and/or legal counsel. It had always been my practice to personally answer each of these letters.

On February 4th I received a handwritten letter from Baxstrom—who previously was completely unknown to me—requesting that I forward to his sister copies of papers he had enclosed. I do not recall whether his letter was addressed to me personally or merely to ''The Legal Aid Society,'' and I had not the slightest idea why the papers were sent to me rather than directly to his sister.

In any event, the papers he had enclosed were a five- or six-page handwritten application to the Supreme Court of the United States for, I think, a writ of mandamus, together with a copy of the brief filed by the New York Attorney General in the Appellate Division, Third Department. After reading through the papers I realized, to my amazement, that Baxstrom, supposedly insane, had managed to meet all of the highly technical procedural steps for timely getting his case from the County Court, to the Appellate Division, to the Court of Appeals, to the U.S. Supreme Court. Also the issues involved seemed similar to those raised several years earlier in *Carroll v. McNeill*—a case I had worked on while a law clerk at the Second Circuit Court of Appeals. I recall telephoning Anthony Lokot, the Assistant Attorney General who handled the case in the Appellate Division to confirm factual details regarding the dates of various actions and possibly to obtain the citations to the Appellate Division and Court of Appeals action on the case.

I then wrote the enclosed letter to the Clerk of the Supreme Court intending that it be considered as an unofficial amicus brief in support of Baxstrom's application. I then promptly forgot about the whole thing. Sometime in late June the Clerk of the Supreme Court called to tell me he had some bad news and some good news. The bad news was that I had lost a case on the retroactivity of *Mapp v. Ohio* and the good news was that certiorari had been granted in *Baxstrom v. Herold* and Court had "requested" that I "continue" to act as counsel.

The argument of the case in the Supreme Court was as unusual as was the manner in which the case got there. I recall that after all the briefs were in, I was so convinced we had won that I was concerned that oral argument could only detract from our position. On the morning of argument, I decided that the best things to do was to say as little as possible and wait for some reaction from the Court before attacking the case.

After ten minutes of my allotted thirty minutes for argument I had not received a single question from the Court nor had anyone seemed at all interested in the case. At that point I decided to sit down and reserve my remaining twenty minutes for rebuttal to the Attorney General's argument. When the Assistant Attorney General stood up to argue, the Court suddenly began bombarding him with questions. One observer (now an Associate Justice of the Court) said it was like a firing squad being called to attention. By the time the State had finished its argument it was abundantly clear that Baxstrom had won and the best thing I could do would be to keep my mouth shut (quite a trick for a litigator) and waive oral argument.

The U.S. Supreme Court Decision

The decision that resulted was written by then Chief Justice of the Court, Earl Warren, and was a concise, incisive review of Baxstrom's legal predicaments, his unequal judicial reviews, and many of the crucial issues about mentally ill inmates, in particular, and the criminally insane in general. Because of the significance of this decision to all these issues as well as to our research it is included below in its entirety as handed down on February 15, 1966:

Mr. Chief Justice Warren delivered the opinion of the Court.

We granted certiorari in this case to consider the constitutional validity of the statutory procedure under which petitioner was committed to a mental institution at the expiration of his criminal sentence in a state prison.

Petitioner, Johnnie K. Baxstrom, was convicted of second degree assault in April 1959 and was sentenced to a term of two and one-half to three years in a New York prison. On June 1, 1961, he was certified as insane by a prison physician. He was then transferred from prison to Dannemora State Hospital, an institution under the jurisdiction and control of the New York Department of Correction and used for the purpose of confining and caring for male prisoners declared mentally ill while serving a criminal sentence. In November, 1961, the director of Dannemora filed a petition in the Surrogate's Court of Clinton County stating that Baxstrom's penal sentence was about to terminate and requesting that he be civilly committed pursuant to Section 384 of the New York Correction Law.

On December 6, 1961, a proceeding was held in the Surrogate's chambers. Medical certificates were submitted by the State which stated that, in the opinion of two of its examining physicians, Baxstrom was still mentally ill and in need of hospital and institutional care. Respondent, then assistant director at Dannemora, testified that in his opinion Baxstrom was still mentally ill. Baxstrom appearing alone, was accorded a brief opportunity to ask questions.[1] Respondent and the Surrogate both stated that they had no objection to his being transferred from Dannemora to a civil hospital under the jurisdiction of the Department of Mental Hygiene. But the Surrogate pointed out that he had no jurisdiction to determine that question—that under Section 384 the decision was entirely up to the Department of Mental Hygiene. The Surrogate then signed a certificate which indicated he was satisfied that Baxstrom "may require mental care and treatment" in an institution for the mentally ill. The Department of Mental Hygiene had already determined ex parte that Baxstrom was not suitable for care in a civil hospital. Thus, on December 18, 1961, the date upon which Baxstrom's penal sentence expired, custody over him shifted from the Department of Correction to the Department of Mental Hygiene, but he was retained at Dannemora and has remained there to this date.

Thereafter, Baxstrom sought a writ of habeas corpus in a state court. An examination was ordered and a hearing was held at which the examining psychiatrist testified that in his opinion, Baxstrom was still mentally ill. The writ was dismissed. In 1963, Baxstrom applied again for a writ of habeas corpus, alleging that his constitutional rights had been violated and that he was then sane, or if insane, he should be transferred to a civil mental hospital. Due to his indigence and his incarceration in Dannemora, Baxstrom could not produce psychiatric testimony to disprove the testimony adduced at the prior hearing. The writ was therefore dismissed. Baxstrom's alternative request for transfer to a civil mental hospital was again denied as being beyond the power of the court despite a statement by the State's attorney that he wished that Baxstrom would be transferred to a civil mental hospital. On appeal to the Appellate Division, Third Department, the dismissal of the writ was affirmed without opinion. 21 App Div 2d 754. A motion for leave to appeal to the Court of Appeals was denied. 14 NY 2d 490. We granted certiorari. 381 US 849, 14 L el 2d 723, 85 S Ct 1810.

---

[1]The state apparently permits counsel to be retained in such proceedings where the person can afford to hire his own attorney despite the fact that Section 384 makes no provision for counsel to be present. See 1961 Op NY Atty Gen 180, 1S1. Baxstrom is indigent, however, and had no counsel at this hearing.

(1) We hold that the petitioner was denied equal protection of the laws by the statutory procedure under which a person may be civilly committed at the expiration of his penal sentence without the jury review available to all other persons civilly committed in New York. Petitioner was further denied equal protection of the laws by his civil commitment to an institution maintained by the Department of Correction beyond the expiration of his prison term without a judicial determination that he is dangerously mentally ill such as that afforded to all so committed except those, like Baxstrom, nearing the expiration of a penal sentence.

(2) Section 384 of the New York Correction Law prescribes the procedure for civil commitment upon the expiration of the prison term of a mentally ill person confined in Dannemora.[2] Similar procedures are prescribed for civil commitment of all other allegedly mentally ill persons. N.Y. Mental Hygiene Law Sections 70, 72. All persons civilly committed, however, other than those committed at the expiration of a penal term, are expressly granted the right to de novo review by jury trial of the question of their sanity under Section 74 of the Mental Hygiene Law. Under this procedure any person dissatisfied with an order certifying him as mentally ill may demand full review by a jury of the prior determination as to his competency. If the jury returns a verdict that the person is sane, he must be immediately discharged. It follows that the State, having made this substantial review proceeding generally available on this issue, may not, consistent with the Equal Protection Clause of the Fourteenth Amendment, arbitrarily withhold it from some.

(3) The director contends that the State has created a reasonable classification differentiating the civilly insane from the "criminally insane," which he defines as those with dangerous or criminal propensities. Equal protection does not require that all persons be dealt with identically, but it does require that a distinction made have some relevance to the purpose for which the classification is made. *Walters v. City of St. Louis,* 347 US 231, 237, 98 L ed 660, 665, 74 S Ct 505. Classification of mentally ill persons as either insane or dangerously insane of course may be a reasonable distinction for purposes of determining the type of custodial or medical care to be given, but it has no relevance whatever in the context of the opportunity to show whether a person is mentally ill at all. For purposes of granting judicial review before a jury of the question whether a person is mentally ill and in need of institutionalization, there is no conceivable basis for distinguishing the commitment of a person who is nearing the end of a penal term from all other civil commitments.

(4) The statutory procedure provided in Section 384 of the New York Correction Law denied Baxstrom the equal protection of the laws in another respect as well. Under Section 384 the judge need only satisfy himself that the person "may require care and treatment in an institution for the mentally ill." Having made such a finding, the decision whether to commit that person to a hospital maintained by the Department of Correction or to a civil hospital is completely in the hands of

[2]As it appeared when applied to petitioner in 1961, NY Correction Law Section 384 provided in part: 1: Within thirty days prior to the expiration of the term of a prisoner confined in the Dannemora State Hospital, when in the opinion of the director such prisoner continues insane, the director shall apply to a judge of a court of record for the certification of such person as provided in the mental hygiene law for the certification of a person not in confinement on a criminal charge. The court in which such proceedings are instituted shall if satisfied that such person may require care and treatment in an institution for the mentally ill, issue an order directing that such person be committed to the custody of the commissioner of mental hygiene to be placed in an appropriate state institution of the department of mental hygiene or of the department of correction as may be designated for the custody of such person by agreement between the heads of the two departments.

administrative officials.[3] Except for persons committed to Dannemora upon expiration of sentence under Section 384, all others civilly committed to hospitals maintained by the Department of Correction are committed only after judicial proceedings have been held in which it is determined that the person is so dangerously mentally ill that his presence in a civil hospital is dangerous to the safety of other patients or employees, or to the community.[4]

(5) This statutory classification cannot be justified by the contention that Dannemora is substantially similar to other mental hospitals in the State and that commitment to one hospital or another is simply an administrative matter affecting no fundamental rights. The parties have described various characteristics of Dannemora to show its similarities and dissimilarities to civil hospitals in New York. As striking as the dissimilarities are, we need not make any factual determination as to the nature of Dannemora; the New York State Legislature has already made that determination. By statute, the hospital is under the jurisdiction of the Department of Correction and is used for the purpose of confining prisoners and persons, like Baxstrom, committed at the expiration of a penal term. N.Y. Correction Law Section 375. Civil mental hospitals in New York, on the other hand, are under the jurisdiction and control of the Department of Mental Hygiene. Certain privileges of patients at Dannemora are restricted by statute. N.Y. Correction Law Section 388. Moreover, as has been noted, specialized statutory procedures are prescribed for commitment to hospitals under the jurisdiction of the Department of Correction. While we may assume that transfer among like mental hospitals is a purely administrative function, where, as here, the State has created functionally distinct institutions, classification of patients for involuntary commitment to one of these institutions may not be wholly arbitrary.

The director argues that it is reasonable to classify persons in Baxstrom's class together with those found to be dangerously insane since such persons are not only insane but have proven criminal tendencies as shown by their past criminal records.

[3]In this case, the administrative decision to retain Baxstrom in Dannemora was made before any hearing was afforded to Baxstrom and was made despite the otherwise unanimous conclusion by testifying psychiatrists, including an independent examining psychiatrist and respondent himself, that there was no reason why Baxstrom could not be transferred to a civil institution. The following is a portion of the transcript of the hearing before the Surrogate: The COURT: (Addressing Dr. Herold) Have you any objection if this man is transferred to a civil hospital if the Department of Mental Hygiene so decrees? Dr. HEROLD: None whatever. The COURT: And I, sir, agree with you. I have no objection to his transfer if the Department of Mental Hygiene so finds. I hope that you will be transferred to a civil hospital. Good luck. And at the first habeas corpus hearing: Q. Do you feel, Doctor, from your examination and examining the records of this man, he needs additional care? Is that correct? A. (Dr. Kerr) Yes, sir. May I say something at this point, sir? Q. Surely. A. Since Mr. Baxstrom's sentence has actually expired, sir, I would like to say that in my opinion there is no reason why he could not be treated in a civil mental hospital. I would simply like to say that for the record, sir. The COURT: All right.

[4]New York Mental Hygiene Law Section 85, 135. See also NY Code Crim Proc Section 662-b (3) (b), 872 (1) (b), as amended, NY Laws 1965, c 540, Sections 1, 2. Former Section 412 of Correction Law, permitting commitment to Matteawan State Hospital of any patient who had previously been sentenced to a term of imprisonment, without the benefit of the proceeding accorded others under Section 85 of the Mental Hygiene Law, was held unconstitutional as a denial of equal protection in *United States ex rel. Carroll v. McNeill,* 294 F.2d 117 (CA2d Cir 1961), probable jurisdiction noted, 368 US 951, 7 ed 2d 385, 82 S Ct 393, vacated and dismissed as moot 369 US 149, 7 L ed 2d 782, S Ct 685 and was repealed by NY Laws 65, c 524. Even that provision required showing that the persons still manifested minimal tendencies.

He points to decisions of the New York Court of Appeals supporting this view. *People ex rel. Kamisaroff v. Johnson,* 13 NY2d 66, 192 NE2d 11; *People ex rel. Brunson v. Johnson,* 15 NY2d 647, 204 NE2d 200.

(6) We find this contention untenable. Where the State has provided for a judicial proceeding to determine the dangerous propensities of all others civilly committed to an institution of the Department of Correction, it may not deny this right to a person in Baxstrom's position solely on the grounds that he was nearing the expiration of a prison term.[5] It may or may not be that Baxstrom is presently mentally ill and such a danger to others that the strict security of a Department of Correction is warranted. All others receive a judicial hearing on this issue. Equal protection demands that Baxstrom receive the same.

The capriciousness of the classification employed by the State is thrown sharply into focus by the fact that the full benefit of a judicial hearing to determine dangerous tendencies is withheld only in the case of civil commitment of one awaiting expiration of penal sentence. A person with a past criminal record is presently entitled to a hearing on the question whether he is dangerously mentally ill so long as he is not in prison at the time civil commitment proceedings are instituted. Given this distinction, all semblance of rationality of the classification, purportedly based upon criminal propensities, disappears.

In order to accord to petitioner the equal protection of the laws, he was and is entitled to a review of the determination as to his sanity in conformity with proceedings granted all others civilly committed under Section 74 of the New York Mental Hygiene Law. He is also entitled to a hearing under the procedure granted all others by Section 85 of the New York Mental Hygiene Law to determine whether he is so dangerously mentally ill that he must remain in a hospital maintained by the Department of Correction. The judgement of the Appellate Division of the Supreme Court, in the Third Judicial Department of New York is reversed and the case is remanded to that court for further proceedings not inconsistent with this opinion.

It is so ordered.

Mr. Justice Black concurs in the result.

The decision of the court rested on the principle of equal protection under the Fourteenth Amendment. In Baxstrom's case—the case of a mentally ill inmate in a correctional department hospital at the expiration of his sentence—there were two distinct questions related to this doctrine. The first was the comparability of civil commitment procedures under Section 74 of the New York Mental Hygiene Law with those for mentally ill inmates under the Penal Law. The court stated that since a jury trial was allowed under civil proceedings to determine whether an individual is

---

[5]In oral argument, counsel for respondent suggested that the determination by the Department of Mental Hygiene to retain a person in Dannemora must be based not only on his past criminal record, but also on evidence that he is currently dangerous. Far from supporting the validity of the procedure, this only serves to further accent the arbitrary nature of the classification. Under this procedure, all civil commitments to an institution under the control of the Department of Correction require a determination that the person is presently dangerous; all persons so committed are entitled to a judicial proceeding to determine this fact except those awaiting expiration of sentence. Their fate is decided by unreviewable determinations of the Department of Mental Hygiene.

mentally ill, Baxstrom should have been given access to similar procedures, since with the expiration of his sentence he was no longer committed as a criminal patient. He was at that time a civil patient under the custody of the Department of Mental Hygiene.

The case's second question of equal protection related to the question of dangerousness. For civil patients, the only way in which they could be detained in Matteawan or Dannemora, the state's two hospitals for the criminally insane run by the Department of Correction, was for them to have been determined dangerously mentally ill. This procedure was spelled out in Section 85 of the MHL, discussed in Chapter 2. If an individual in a civil mental hospital was seen as dangerous by civil hospital psychiatrists, this patient had to have a court hearing to judicially determine dangerousness before or immediately after transfer to Matteawan. In the case of convicted Dannemora or Matteawan patients who were being reviewed for continued retention as mentally ill at the expiration of a sentence, the assumption implicit in Section 384 of the New York Correction Law was that if a patient were determined mentally ill, he was also, necessarily, dangerous. The U.S. Supreme Court's decision declared that this was not a legitimate assumption. Since Dannemora was definitely a facility distinct from civil hospitals, the court ruled that there should be judicial review of the question of dangerousness before retention in a hospital for the criminally insane was permissable. No longer could time-expired, mentally ill inmates be the only patients in New York who did not have access to jury review on the question of mental illness and dangerousness.

The U.S. Supreme Court's decision in Johnnie Baxstrom's case written by Chief Justice Warren highlights two main themes of this book —questions about psychiatric abilities to predict dangerousness and the conservative tendencies of mental health agents in detaining and treating the criminally insane. In footnote 5 of the *Baxstrom* decision, Justice Warren noted that a finding of dangerousness reached solely by psychiatrists to determine continued detention in a hospital for the criminally insane was "arbitrary." He notes that all persons, except mentally ill inmates at the expiration of their sentences received judicial review on the question of dangerousness in addition to the psychiatric evaluations from the Department of Mental Hygiene. The court rejected the Dannemora director's argument that previous criminal tendencies coupled with proven mental illness necessarily made these inmates dangerously mentally ill without specific review of the question of dangerousness.

The second theme highlighted in the court decision is the conservatism in medical decisions to release the criminally insane. In this particular case, conservatism was evident in the Department of Mental Hygiene's unwillingness to accept Johnnie Baxstrom in a regular civil facility despite the testimony of Dr. Herold and other psychiatrists at Dannemora. Footnote 3 of the *Baxstrom* decision relates the medical testimony of Dannemora psychiatrists at the 1961 Surrogate Court hearing and at the first *habeas corpus* proceeding in 1963 that indicates they were willing to transfer Baxstrom to a civil hospital, although the DMH refused to accept him. This DMH decision was legally correct under Section 384, since a person could be kept in any state institution for the mentally ill designated by the DMH. As we will see below, there were 650 patients in Dannemora and Matteawan being detained under Section 384. Such detainment was seen by DMH administrators and civil hospital psychiatrists as necessary because of the danger such patients would pose in regular civil facilities. The inaccuracy of this thinking will become evident from the data in subsequent chapters that shows how well Baxstrom and the other transferred patients fared in the civil hospitals and the community.

Results of the Decision

The first result of the *Baxstrom v. Herold* decision was the transfer of Johnnie Baxstrom from Dannemora to Marcy State Hospital in Utica, New York on March 15, 1966. Between this date and August 31, 1966, the New York State Department of Mental Hygiene transferred 966 other patients from Dannemora and Matteawan to 18 civil hospitals. The 967 patients transferred represented a number of legal categories other than mentally ill inmates who were in a correctional mental hospital at the expiration of their sentence. Dr. Robert C. Hunt, the psychiatrist in charge of the DMH planning for these transfers, and E. David Wiley, counsel for the DMH, in a one-year report on "Baxstrom" transfers (Hunt and Wiley 1968) noted that there were about 400 time-expired male felons in Dannemora plus about 200 time-expired male misdemeanants, and 47 females in Matteawan. To this group of 650 patients, 100 transfers were added due to a revised state statute that went into effect on July 1, 1966 that allowed patients in Dannemora and Matteawan to earn time off for good behavior just as they could had they been detained in prisons.

In addition to this total group of 750, there were approximately 175 incompetent defendants included from Matteawan. These individuals had been in Matteawan far beyond the maximum sentence for the crime(s) with which they had been charged, as was Fred Ross whose case was presented in Chapter 2 and who had been in Matteawan for 32 years for a charge of assault, first degree, for which the maximum sentence was 15 years. The final group included in the 967 Baxstrom patient transfers were approximately 50 patients detained in Matteawan under a section of the Correction Law that had been repealed in 1965, Section 412. This section permitted the simple administrative transfers of civil mental hospital patients who had ever been incarcerated to correctional hospitals for the criminally insane without judicial review. Even though this section had been repealed in 1965, there were 50 or so patients remaining in Matteawan who were included as part of the Baxstrom patient transfers. There were no NGRI cases and no dangerously mentally ill patients among the Baxstrom patients.

Because of the *Baxstrom v. Herold* decision of the U.S. Supreme Court and New York's response to it, 967 patients from two hospitals for the criminally insane were transferred between March 15, 1966 and August 31, 1966 to 18 regular security civil hospitals across the state. These Baxstrom patients were long-term patients who were seen as among the "most dangerous" patients in the state and were widely feared by the hospital staffs and communities that were required to accept them. Without this judicial intervention, most of these patients, who had been passed over for transfer for an average of 8 years beyond the expiration of their maximum actual or possible criminal sentences, would have remained in hospitals for the criminally insane. On the basis of this Supreme Court decision, these 967 people were transferred against psychiatric advice to the type of civil facilities from which the criminally insane had been separated by law since the late nineteenth century. If the Baxstrom patients did well in these facilities and in the community, it certainly would suggest that many patients in traditional state hospitals for the criminally insane in the United States are inappropriately detained. The research reported in this book was initiated to probe such questions and to explore the substantive issues of psychiatric conservatism, social factors related to community release, and dangerousness.

4 Research Procedures

The amount of detail in this chapter is unusual in comparison to most research reports. We have purposely included much that at first appearance may seem to be minutiae superfluous to the findings of the next four chapters. However, they are not. Throughout our research on the Baxstrom patients, we relied almost exclusively for direction on past experiences of research carried out within the Mental Health Research Unit (MHRU) of the Department of Mental Hygiene where our project was located. We did this both because these experiences were solid bases on which to proceed and because there was a dearth of assistance to be found in published research. The research methods chapters in many of these reports appeared to be simply formal matters to which authors felt they had to give standard mention before they could provide their own findings. Also, the reports on similar research projects with the mentally ill or criminals as subjects were not strictly applicable to our research on the criminally insane.

Our feeling when writing this chapter was that some of our most important findings related to the using of psychiatric records as secondary data sources, to the techniques for abstracting patient hospital records, to the approaches in locating and interviewing released criminally insane patients in the community, and the like. Accordingly, we have tried to report the procedures of our research in a very specific fashion so that others might find our work more useful than we found most sources we searched in our early research stages. We have attempted to discuss all of the factors, planned and serendipitous, that influenced the manner in which our research proceeded. Thus, for example, a major factor on the actual procedures was the application for grant support and the agency's handling of that application, so this is discussed. We have included such details because they are at the heart of the research endeavor to a much greater extent than many reports, which simply acknowledge their support sources, would indicate. This chapter may be as important as any in this book.

Research Rationale and Impetus

Our research interest in the Baxstrom patients began primarily because of the opportunities this group offered to develop some empirical data on the questions of predicting dangerousness. When our planning for a grant proposal was undertaken in the spring of 1969, there were strong indications in the work of Hunt and Wiley (1968) and White et al. (1969) that the Baxstrom patients had been much less trouble (i.e., less dangerous) in the civil hospitals to which they had been transferred than had been anticipated. Hunt and Wiley indicated that after one year the Baxstrom patients were being treated like any other civil patients and that an unexpectedly high number of them had been released to the community. Of all those released, only one was reported subsequently arrested within the first year, for larceny. White and co-workers examined the behavior and treatment of the Baxstrom patients transferred to Central Islip State Hospital and concurred with the positive findings of Hunt and Wiley. The Baxstrom patients had caused very little trouble.

Based on this earlier work, we set out to develop a number of indicators for studying "dangerousness" on a longitudinal basis among the entire Baxstrom patient population, especially for those who were released into the community. We focused on both hospital and community violence as necessary parts of any estimations and evaluation of the Baxstrom patients' dangerousness. We were interested in not only arrest records but also conviction records and actual incidents that were reflected in such statistics.

The importance of obtaining hospital and community adjustment data for a longer period was highlighted by the conflicting findings of three previous studies on the arrest records of ex-mental patients. Two studies by Rappeport and Lassen (1965, 1966) found that the first year after discharge was the peak period for rearrest for released mental patients. However, McGarry (1971) in a 37-month follow-up study of psychotic offenders returned to trial in Massachusetts found that only 20 percent of all the arrests occurred during the first year. So, when Hunt and Wiley report that only 1 of the 209 Baxstrom patients released to the community at some time during the first year after their transfer was arrested, the following two factors must be taken into account: (1) many of these people were released for only a small portion of that year, and (2) among other things, since the Baxstrom patients were a different legal category than the research subjects in the previous studies of arrest rates, there was no reason to expect they would follow one pattern or the other. The conflicting research on the most probable periods for arrests of ex-mental patients indicated that a longer follow-up period was needed to adequately evaluate the subsequent criminal activity as well as dangerousness of the Baxstrom patients.

Because of the importance of the Baxstrom patients for questions both of dangerousness and of methods of care and custody for the criminally insane, a research grant application was submitted in the spring of 1969, which proposed a three-year follow-up study of them. As frequently happens, the final shape of the research project was dictated by a number of chance occurrences. The first was that the grant submitted for more rapid review under the Small Grants Program was included in the granting agency's regular review process, which meant a delay in approval that went six months past the intended starting date. Next, the funding was delayed an additional three months past the approved starting date. In this time span, one of the original researchers returned to his academic post, which resulted in a project staff that had not been involved in the original application. Thus, by the time the preliminary pilot work had been completed —early 1970—it was decided that a four- to five-year follow-up was feasible and more desirable. The final fortuitous situation that most significantly influenced the actual research design was the large amount of state money that was available to supplement the small original award.

This study was originally intended to be a three-year follow-up that would allow three months for data collection and a few more for analysis. It became a four-and-a-half-year follow-up that required three and a half years to complete, seven full time staff members, and an unplanned follow-up of some Baxstrom patients through direct community interviewing.

Preliminary Work

From the Hunt and Wiley report, it was thought that there were 969 Baxstrom patients, of whom 755 were in state hospitals, 190 were in the community or correctional facilities, and 24 had died. Because so many subjects were institutionalized, the initial research strategies were based on the expectation that most of the data on patient backgrounds, hospital behavior, and discharge criteria would be available in the central office files of the DMH. With our research operation located in the central office, we would have easy data access, and little federal support would be needed either for data collection or staff, since most information could be generated from the DMH data processing system. However, these initial strategies were quite different from those actually employed.

Because the Baxstrom patients had been of interest from both program and research perspectives, they had been specially identified within the DMH's central data processing system from the times of their transfers. Thus, our first step was to obtain a card deck of Baxstrom patients and, subsequently, to generate from the computerized patient records all institutional moves during the follow-up period, plus some descriptive facts such as age and race. Having secured the "Baxstrom deck" and computer printout of patient transactions, it became evident that the designated 969 patients were not all Baxstrom patients nor were all the Baxstrom patients included. The original deck included about 20 patients who had been transferred before March 15, 1966, the date of Johnnie Baxstrom's transfer and the date used to specify the Baxstrom patients. In addition, there were about 18 patients who were not included in the original deck but who were transferred from Matteawan and Dannemora within the designated period and under the relevant legal statutes. Thus, the final working deck included 967 patients officially labelled as Baxstrom patients.

While cleaning up the Baxstrom population deck, it became clear that the central office files were entirely insufficient to answer the questions that had been posed. First, all clinical data concerning hospital behavior were not included in these files. These files had material related to admission and discharge—such as admission dates, date of birth, diagnosis—all of which were important data but inadequate in themselves to address the full range of questions we had raised. The second problem of the central office records was that they were kept only on current patients or those released within the previous year. Thus, with many Baxstrom patients having moved quickly into the community and with the expected death rate, there would be a considerable number for whom there would have been no information.

After two months of this preliminary work, we traveled to one of the civil state hospitals to examine their records and to determine what revised strategies would be necessary. This job was complicated by the lack of concern in the social science research literature for institutional records as data sources. In textbook after textbook, one finds numerous discussions about interviewing, instrument formation, pre-testing, and the like, but no mention of using secondary sources, specifically in our case, institutional records. About the only discussions of the pitfalls and advantages of institutional records are those of Madge (1965) and Webb et al. (1966), but both are sketchy and deal primarily with documents and records of other types, so they provided minimal guidelines for our endeavors.[a] Without such guidelines we approached these patient records with an eye to abstracting whatever portions dealt with patient histories, hospital behaviors, and any other facets related to dangerous or violent behavior.

After obtaining 15 patient folders, it became clear that there were some very distinct portions of the patient records that contained most of the information we needed. What was especially surprising about the patient records was their extent. Although a few were of barely measureable thickness, most were up to four and five inches thick. However, of the

[a]Subsequent to our study we encountered an excellent discussion of psychiatric record for research in an article by James Otis Smith, Gideon Sjoberg, and Virginia Austin Phillips, "The Use and Meaning of Psychiatric Records: A Research Note," *International Journal of Social Psychiatry* XV (Spring 1969): 129-35.

many entries in these folders, we obtained all the information we required from just a few. Upon admission a ''Summary'' was always done, which capsulized the psychiatric admission interview and the most salient facts from any previous institutional records available at the time of admission. This summary was often typed weeks after admission but did consistently contain fairly comprehensive background data. This summary also provided current diagnosis. Because all Baxstrom patients had been in hospitals for the criminally insane, most records also contained their New York State Identification and Intelligence System (NYSIIS) histories of all reported criminal activity.

The quality and amount of records on hospital behavior varied considerably between hospitals. In most instances irregular reports—''Progress Notes''—were kept on the wards and eventually filed in the record rooms. These notes were reported at various times—at a minimum of every 6 months when psychiatric review was legally mandated or often more frequently. Any serious acting out was recorded in these progress notes or in special reports. For patients released, but administratively on the books (i.e., convalescent care and family care), and those utilizing aftercare clinics, these notes would contain the reports of social workers who visited the patients after placement. Accident reports occasionally provided additional information on behavior of interest. If readmission occurred, ''Interval Histories,'' part of the summaries mentioned above, proved to be a source of much useful information about community behaviors.

From these first excursions, two definite impressions were developed about mental hospital patient records as data resources: (1) there was an unanticipated volume of records, and (2) there was a relatively small and definite set of records that usually contained all types of information needed to answer the questions we wished to address. At this same point in research, after a printout of all the patient transactions between 1966 and 1970 had been obtained, it was evident that more than the 18 civil hospitals to which the Baxstrom patients were originally transferred were going to be involved in the collection of patient records. When we arrived at a working deck of 967 Baxstrom patients—a deck that subsequently was changed, but with equal numbers of additions and deletions—we found that as of January 1970 the Baxstrom patients had been in 26 of the 27 state civil hospitals. In addition, a few had been returned to Matteawan and Dannemora. This complicated our data collection, because the practice was to forward the major segment of a patient's hospital file to the hospital of most recent admission. Also, since we wanted all information for as long a period as possible, it meant that the record collection would have to be done at 26 hospitals spread across the entire state. The number of records at these 26 facilities ranged from 157 to 1. In addition, because these patients were still being admitted and discharged, frequently a computer printout of most recent institutionalizations would be outdated by information obtained upon arrival at a hospital.

It quickly became clear what a small portion of each patient's record was actually needed and that much discrimination of materials within each record was required before data could be abstracted and coded. Thus, we decided to photocopy these portions of the records required and to compile at the MHRU a record folder for each Baxstrom patient from which coding would be done. Having decided what portions of the records were needed, having compiled what we thought to be an accurate list of the patient transfers, and having determined where the Baxstrom patients were located, in January 1970 we began going to the 26 hospitals to gather our data.

Data Collection

In January 1970, the patient record data collection was begun. We began with the hospital that had received the largest group of patients —160—during the transfers, because of the large number of cases, because their records were said to be among the best kept in the state, and because this is where our pilot work had been done. The record pulling and photocopying work went exceedingly well with what we thought were all the records being abstracted and copied in one week. In February 1970, records were gathered from Matteawan to determine how comparable their records would be for those patients returned to Matteawan and Dannemora. They were comparable in every regard. A three-month break in the data collection then occurred due to travel difficulties and staff unavailability during a period of major staff changes in the project. During this hiatus in data collection, the first stages of code book development were initiated.

The second stage of data collection began in May 1970 and lasted through October 1970, during which all 967 records were abstracted. Early in this phase of data collection, a number of unanticipated problems arose that slowed progress considerably. The first set of difficulties related to computer output errors from faulty inputs. This resulted in serious errors in items such as ID number, admission dates, institution of last residence, and multiple administrative numbers for different admissions all of which were crucial for locating the necessary records. Many of these problems were the usual difficulties of any patient data system caused by both inaccurate reporting and the absence of corrections when the data are not used in any corroborative way after input.

To overcome these and other data collection problems, it became necessary for us to develop a detailed understanding of all the administrative language associated with the patient record data. For instance, many hospitals kept all their records by the DMH patient ID number. This number was supposed to be unique to each patient and retained across all admissions. Among the Baxstrom patients, the use of aliases exacerbated this problem since a person who had multiple admissions under different names was assigned multiple ID numbers, which caused his records to be in separate locations. The other side of the same problem involved patients with a common name, such as James Washington, who had been assigned different numbers on each admission without sufficient record searches to verify their identity. For example, on our first trip to a hospital, the record of a James Washington, 060-73-7564, was abstracted and checked off as being completed. After the coding began, unexplainable voids appeared in his record. Through further computer runs and on subsequent hospital trips, other James Washingtons were checked by race, birthdate, and so forth and a second, entirely separate record for our subject was often located.

Another side of the ID number problem was that many hospitals did not use the DMH unique number for filing patient records, but used a consecutive admission number relating only to the most recent admission. On past admissions a previous number had been assigned to the same patients resulting in a substantial portion of needed records being missed. After this problem was recognized, we took all of these consecutive numbers from the data processing system when we first went to a hospital. Unfortunately, the difficulties of consecutive numbers was not recognized until a few hospitals had been done which necessitated return trips in the fall of 1970.

Utilizing two full-time assistants who worked meticulously in the office between trips preparing work sheets and updating computer errors, we completed record folders on all the 967 Baxstrom patients in October 1970. Our research in evaluating, planning, and abstracting these institutional records was an excellent learning experience about a data source little used by social scientists despite the considerable possibilities such a source offers.

Coding and Baxstrom Patient Sample

The development of code books and actual coding began while the record collection was in progress. The type of research population and questions under consideration led us to code variables that had been previously employed in studies of both mental patients and criminals. These included the usual array of background characteristics, birthdate, marital status, and race, plus factors such as previous hospitalizations, psychiatric diagnosis, criminal history, and current offense. Our work was complicated by our desire to have a longitudinal picture of hospital behavior after transfer. This intent led us to develop a series of 7 items (most "dangerous" behavior;

patient administrative status; medication; allocation of institutional privileges; most "dangerous" sexual behavior; other management problems) that were coded by six-month periods after transfer to a civil hospital. These items proved to be less useful than anticipated, and we relied mainly on a number of more static items on subsequent behavior that were also developed. Among these were subsequent criminal activity, community adjustment, and rehospitalizations.

During the time we were developing the items and categories for coding, we decided to alter our initial plans to study a limited number of variables in a straightforward coding format for all 967 Baxstrom patients. It was decided that due to many pilot features of our research, it would be preferable to do a more in-depth analysis of a wider range of variables. Thus, while the records of all 967 patients were being abstracted and photocopied, we decided that with our resources we could work intensively only with a smaller group of about 250 patients.

Since there were only 47 females among the 967 Baxstrom patients, all were included in the sample. Their records were abstracted, photocopied, coded, and analyzed in the preliminary data runs. However, it soon became apparent that because of their small numbers, the 47 Baxstrom women could not be analyzed with the same statistical controls as the men. Thus, after some very basic, descriptive work with the female data, which have been reported elsewhere (Halfon et al. 1971), we concentrated on more detailed examinations of the males, which is reported in Chapters 5 through 8.

As a manageable number, we selected a 20 percent random sample with replacement of the Baxstrom male patients. To draw this sample, we randomly selected with replacement two, single digits. We included in the patient sample all those patients whose DMH ID number ended in either digit. This ID number, is unique to each patient and is supposed to be constant across admissions. The only non-random feature of the ID number is that it is assigned in order of admission to the DMH. The number 020-20-20, for example, would have been admitted for the first time to a DMH facility in the early 1930s, while number 100-10-59 would have been admitted in the late 1950s. Thus, by using the last digit of this ID number, we were able to get a random selection. Using this particular sampling method, we drew 199 male Baxstrom patients. These 199 represented 21.6 percent of all the males and together with the 47 females gave us a total of 246 subjects whose records we coded.

Working with the records of these 246 patients, we began coding in August 1970 after one false start. We had thought two weeks earlier that we were ready, only to find after 5 to 10 cases that the code book needed more development. With two coders working practically full-time, it took from August 21 to November 13, 1970 to code, verify, and reconcile all 246 cases. Our coding procedures had one coder read each record entirely and then reread it while coding each item on a block code sheet. Subsequently, an independent coder again read the entire record and verified the first coding. Any differences were then reconciled by the two coders or a third party, when necessary. On the average about 6 out of every 90 items required reconciliation.

The problems recently discussed by Crittenden and Hill (1971) on coding reliability and validity were especially relevant to this coding operation. They noted that on purely factual data, even if on summary face sheets and even among well-trained coders, some coding unreliability could be expected. They further noted a distressing increase in errors when the coding decisions involved abstracting facts from a larger record or when coder judgement was involved. Our approach to minimize these errors was to read the entire patient record for factual information even when available on the summary sheets. Quite frequently, typographical or other errors had occurred on a prior admission, which were carried through record summaries on subsequent admissions. By reading the entire record and circling all data to be coded, we attempted to minimize these errors. Also, there were usually NYSIIS sheets in the records that provided race and birthdate and, thus, an across agency information check. Also, since all records were coded or verified by the project director and one of three other coders, there was systematic monitering and consistent interpretation.

Comparison Sample

As we coded the Baxstrom patient data and began to more firmly plan our analysis, it became evident that one of the major problems we would encounter was the inability to say how well the Baxstrom patients fared, in any relative sense, especially as compared to other patients who had been in hospitals for the criminally insane. To permit some comparisons, we decided to select an additional group of research subjects. On the one hand, whatever group we would choose had to be available inexpensively since our funds had been allocated almost completely for the Baxstrom portion of the research. On the other hand, we felt that if we were to generate a comparison group at all, it was important to obtain one which would allow meaningful comparisons with the Baxstrom patients. The resolution of these competing pressures led to the drawing of a comparison group we called the "pre-Baxstrom patients."

The pre-Baxstrom patients were defined as all those patients transferred from Matteawan and Dannemora, the same hospitals in which the Baxstrom patients had resided, to civil mental hospitals in the two years immediately preceding the Baxstrom patient transfers. These patients were of critical substantive interest in that they were psychiatrically approved for transfer, while the Baxstrom patients had been passed over as unfit for transfer. Since the medical staffs of Dannemora and Matteawan varied little in this time period, it meant that the variables surrounding other factors would be reasonably constant. Because the pre-Baxstrom patients were approved for transfer, it meant that they would provide a comparison group to determine which factors were associated with psychiatric approval. The criteria associated with these transfer decisions were significant partly because it was documented in Johnnie Baxstrom's court records that a major factor in the continued detention of patients in Matteawan and Dannemora was the estimation of their dangerousness. Thus, by defining the pre-Baxstrom patients as we did, we would be able to study which criteria were associated with psychiatric estimations of dangerousness.

In addition to these substantative reasons, by specifying the time period of April 1, 1964 through March 8, 1966 as the span that would define the pre-Baxstrom patient transfers, we were able to remain within our resources. This was the case since the department's central data processing system's tapes of patient transactions had been reformated as of April 1, 1964 and was adaptable to data outputs from the same programs that had been used to generate the Baxstrom patient lists. Also, this period conveniently produced a group of workable size—312 male patients and 47 females, which was about the maximum size that we felt manageable to duplicate our work with the Baxstroms' institutional records and their coding.

The procedures used and the data collected for the pre-Baxstrom patients were practically the same as those of the Baxstrom patients. As with the Baxstrom records, pre-Baxstrom records were located in 26 of the then 29 state hospitals. Similar listings were obtained from the department's data processing system which indicated institution of last residence as well as some identifying information and ID numbers. Photocopying the records began in March 1971 and was completed in July 1971. Exactly the same institutional records were copied for the pre-Baxstrom as for the Baxstrom patients. Also, as with the Baxstroms, after very preliminary analyses, we stopped work on the data of the 47 pre-Baxstrom females because of the limits its size placed on adequate analyses.

The most significant change in procedures between the two research groups was in the items that were abstracted and the coding categories used. Since the Baxstrom data analyses were simultaneous to the pre-Baxstrom coding, some indications of the most useful items and categories evolved that led us to make a number of coding changes on both substantive and time bases. For example, the data that had been coded by six-month time periods on the medication levels of the Baxstrom patients was found to have little usefulness and was omitted from the pre-Baxstrom data. Similarly, summary scale scores for institutional violence and criminal histories, which had been developed from the Baxstrom data, were coded. Despite the experience gained from the Baxstrom records, coding the 359 pre-Baxstrom records took 12 weeks, which was 30 to 45 minutes per record plus equal time to verify, with an additional average of 5 minutes per record for reconciliation of coding differences.

Baxstrom Patient Community Follow-Up

The original intent of our Baxstrom research was to develop materials from patient and criminal records exclusively. However, during the final stages of our analysis of the Baxstrom and pre-Baxstrom data, we felt there were a number of significant questions that were totally unaddressable unless we obtained some data on how these people did when they returned to the community. Because of the *ad hoc* nature of these plans, we did not have the resources to attempt a community follow-up of both groups. Thus, we decided to concentrate on the Baxstrom patients, since they were the primary research subjects.

Some preliminary computer runs on the available data indicated that of the 246 Baxstrom patients in our sample (199 males and 47 females), 121 had been released at some time between 1966 and our follow-up cutoff date of October 30, 1970. Of these 121 individuals, 85 were completely out of contact in 1970. This was the group that we decided to seek for information about their community adjustment. The data from this follow-up reported in Chapter 8 deal only with the male sample. The combined data appear in a previous article (Steadman and Keveles 1972), and below we describe the techniques utilized for the entire male and female group sought in the community.

As we planned our follow-up strategies, it became evident at an early stage that there were few guides in the literature.[b] Eckland (1968) did cite 8 studies that maintained contact with and reinterviewed from 88 percent to 100 percent of their cases in longitudinal designs over 2 to 25 year periods. However, all of these were educational studies whose subjects were almost all high school or college graduates. In reinterviewing more mobile and more marginal cases prospectively, Eckland noted that "no systematic treatment of the problem, to our knowledge, has ever appeared. We rely, instead, upon folklore." The problems in locating subjects like the Baxstrom patients were among the most severe. First, our research being

[b]Two recent discussions of this problem are quite useful: "Panel Studies: Some Practical Problems," by Donald M. Crider, Fern Willits, and Robert Bealer in *Sociological Methods and Research* 2 (August 1973): 3-19 and "Evolution of a Strategy for the Retrial of Cases in Longitudinal Survey Research," by Ronald McAllister, Edgar Butler, and Stevin Goe in *Sociology and Social Research* 58 (October 1973).

retrospective meant that no anchoring data had been obtained at a previous collection point. Second, we were searching for people we had never met, who had been confined for an average of 14 years in hospitals for the criminally insane and who had been released from civil mental hospitals up to 4 years before our research was undertaken. Finally, the Baxstrom patients were marginal in every sense of that term. Few were married or still had primary families. Job skills were minimal. Whatever most had had in the way of permanent residences in the community were gone. Also, the largest percentage of patients had been released in New York City, a locale offering maximum opportunities for minimum visibility.

In planning our strategies, we were able to find only three follow-up studies of criminally insane patients in the United States and two of somewhat comparable populations in England. The success of locating these released patients in the U.S. studies was highly variable. Morrow and Peterson (1966) located all 44 of their NGRI subjects and all 43 of their criminal sexual psychopaths. They defined a location as a personal reply, postal receipt, or any formal contact with any state agency during their follow-up period. They used only agency files and mailings to locate their subjects. Zeidler et al. (1955) had "positive contact" with 78 of the 180 male discharges from Illinois maximum security hospitals. They utilized only mailings. The group with the fewest research resources (Colorado State Hospital 1966) also had the lowest location rate—40 percent (32 of 79 patients released from Pueblo State Hospital). They provide no information about follow-up tactics.

The two English studies had quite similar experiences that resulted in a 72 percent contact rate by using only readmission and arrest statistics (Tong and MacKay 1955) and a 52 percent location rate by using mailed questionnaires to other state hospitals (Gathercole 1968). Our impression from these studies was that success was directly related to the amount of resources the research team had, the variety of techniques employed, and the liberalness with which a "location" was defined. Since our resources were quite limited by this stage of the research and since we wished to obtain specific information about the current situations of the subjects, we were not very optimistic about our chances for a high location and completion rate.

This pessimism was reinforced by the little help found in the literature on follow-ups of former civil mental patients. The major studies (Freeman and Simmons 1963; Angrist et al. 1968; Michaux et al. 1969; Cunningham 1969; Myers and Bean 1968) all concentrated on white, middle-class ex-patients. Tracing such individuals with some firm community roots at some time during their lives offered very little that was useful in locating our predominantly non-white, lower-class, highly transient group of former criminally insane patients. Probably the most detailed and relevant discussion of possible techniques was Robins' (1966) 30-year follow-up of a group of juveniles that had been seen in juvenile court clinics in St. Louis during the 1930s. With unusual thoroughness and comprehensiveness, she details the wide range of strategies her research group used to locate an amazing 92 percent of their subjects (572 of 624) and to obtain interviews with 82 percent. The special difficulties of our subjects are demonstrated partially by the two sources Robins noted as most fruitful, the Social Security Administration and the Department of Motor Vehicles. Because of their length of confinements, criminal records, and minimal job histories, very few of the Baxstrom patients had Social Security cards or had them under their current names. Even fewer had drivers licenses because of their institutional records, the rarity of automobiles when many of them were originally institutionalized, and the fact that many came from New York City where public transportation and high insurance rates make private cars much less common than in most urban areas.

Faced with such problems and having gleaned what we could from the materials available we began our community follow-up of the Baxstrom patients in January 1971. Our first step was to survey existing resources from which we hoped to develop others.

Existing Intra-Departmental Information

As part of the work before the follow-up had begun, we had established the residences for 65 percent of the sample as of the date, October 30, 1970. The data banks of the DMH indicated that 117 patients were hospitalized and 10 were being treated in the community under the control of DMH. The remaining 5 were found to be incarcerated in Matteawan or Dannemora. Consequently, there were 85 of the sampled Baxstrom patients whose residencies were unknown.

To develop leads on the 85 missing Baxstrom patients, two major sources were initially used: (1) patient hospital records to obtain clues to their whereabouts, and (2) continual investigation of our own state hospital system's transactions to find returnees. The largest payoff resulted from the Baxstrom patient hospital and aftercare records. As we had the photocopies of these records in our office, they were the primary source for possible community residence information for the Baxstrom patients. A secondary hospital source was the civil state hospital visitor records. Also, these folders contained patients' letters. The reason for our strong stress on information supplied by hospital files was the assumption that those persons, places, agencies and institutions with which these patients had contact in the past and were mentioned in the hospital records were those contacts most likely to be re-established upon release. The assumption proved accurate as 85 percent of all information producing leads was derived from these hospital sources.

Our high success rate from these records was obtained only by utilizing all aspects of the hospital files. For example, only 16 percent of all leads of this kind were found by using the last address that the patient left in the records upon release. A rather large proportion (approximately 75 percent) were found scattered somewhere else in the records. The remainder were found on visitor sheets and correspondence.

Other State Agencies

In the very early stages of our follow-up, we used the records of three other state agencies. Because the mean ages of the Baxstrom patients in 1970 were 52 for males and 54 for females, our first work with other agencies' records were death records of the New York State and New York City Departments of Health. In these records we found that 4 of the 85 patients we sought had died in New York after their releases.

The other state agency whose records were a major resource was the New York State Identification and Intelligence System (NYSIIS). Some major obstacles were encountered in developing a liaison with this agency, which were similar to those Morrow and Peterson (1966) report with regard to the FBI. Since the Department of Mental Hygiene was not one of the agencies that had been legislatively mandated to receive such arrest and conviction data, it first appeared that we could get no data with any identifying information on it. However, since all the Baxstrom patients had been fingerprinted upon admission to Matteawan and Dannemora and had been in civil mental hospitals, our department did receive reports on such individuals whenever a NYSIIS update occurred. Thus, throughout our research, we had these crime records to aid our search. With them, we found 7 of the 85 Baxstrom patients who were re-arrested during our follow-up.

One characteristic of 60 percent of the Baxstrom population was a non-New York birthplace. One possibility suggested by this factor was that these persons may have returned to other states after release and may have entered local state hospitals. Accordingly, we contacted a number of state hospital systems. We sent lists of our unknown Baxstrom patients to be checked against patient admissions files. We contacted 9 state hospital systems (California, Connecticut, Florida, Maine, Massachusetts, New Jersey, Pennsylvania, Rhode Island, and Vermont—states adjacent to New York—plus California and Florida where patients were thought to be), but none had admitted any Baxstrom patients.

The final agency source of information was a continuing check of

DMH's statistical unit's current administrative patient updates. These reports come out every three months and show all patient institutional movements within this period. Also, a review of updated statistical information proved very profitable in correcting a previous report's inaccurate or misleading information. We located 4 additional patients in this manner.

Attempted Contacts With Subjects

Three basic kinds of follow-up tools were employed: (1) letters; (2) phone; and (3) field investigation. At no time, except during the first few weeks, was any procedure used alone. From the previous research literature, letters were expected to be a low-cost tool of questionable effectiveness. They were first used in March 1971. Finding this technique rather ineffective, we began using the telephone, which produced impressive results. Because field investigations would be the most expensive, they were used sparingly, but productively at the end of the follow-up.

Letters. The first mailing in March 1971 included a cover letter and a two-page questionnaire with 25 open-ended and checklist questions. The questionnaire was directed at either the patient or someone who had the desired information. We had first constructed one questionnaire form that relied mainly on open-ended responses and one utilizing more checklist items. Both questionnaires were pre-tested with a group of outpatients at a nearby psychiatric clinic. The patients' responses suggested using a combination of open-ended and checklist items for simplicity and interest. The various cover letters for the patient, for relatives, for employees, and for landlords all contained the same basic information including a telephone number to call collect if the respondent wished.

Initially, we used the hospital records and aftercare notes for last known addresses. If there were none, which occurred frequently, we then attempted to locate relatives listed in the last few pages of the hospital record or aftercare notes. In almost all files, there was one or both. Our mailing contained the questionnaire, the cover letter, and a self-addressed stamped envelope.

During the first four weeks, we received only 9 responses. Of these 9, 5 gave adequate information. The remaining 4 were from relatives who stated that they either had no idea where the patient was or what he was doing. Fifty letters were returned unopened because the person had moved and left no forwarding address or the addressee was unknown.

The poor response rate from this first mailing necessitated a further examination of hospital records and aftercare notes for more clues. We then investigated *all* such records in our files. More names and addresses were found. A second wave of letters was sent to those who had not previously responded, to those whose letters were not returned by the post office, and to newly discovered names and addresses. Further, three letters with one dollar per requested address were mailed to customer service units of general post offices asking them for available forwarding addresses.

After two more weeks, we received 8 letters with completed questionnaires and 10 letters offering some newer information on the subjects. Thirty "addressee unknown" letters were returned by the post office. At this time, we also wrote letters to the 9 state hospital systems mentioned above. In addition, at this same time, the N.Y.S. county District Attorney's Offices confirmed the location of 2 Baxstrom patients who had been incarcerated in N.Y.S. correctional facilities during the fall of 1970.

Three weeks later, we mailed a third wave of 52 letters based on information gathered from hospital visitor sheets and correspondence in files. Also, some letters were sent as certified mail and some others were mailed based on information from telephone books from other cities where our Baxstrom subjects were thought to be living. The letters sent this group were cautiously worded so that any person who was mistakenly contacted would not feel threatened. The results were extremely poor. Only 1 certified letter acceptance was returned. However, 13 other respondents did give some information. Of these 13, 2 called.

In sum, 170 letters were mailed in three waves. In response, some sort of assistance was received from 52 sources with 16 providing complete information. Of the 16, most were written by relatives. Nineteen percent of unknown Baxstroms were located by letters. Of all the letters, only 31 percent produced any data and only 9 percent of all attempts produced acceptable information. One reason why this may have occcurred is indicated by remarks of patients whom we later contacted:

Patient A: "I was afraid that you were looking for me."
Patient B: "What have I done wrong?"
Patient C: "I was scared that you wanted me back."
Patient D: "I remember being a young man. Then my life was cut off of me. Now I am an old man and I don't want to go back."

With the poor success of letters, we began using the telephone.

Telephone. With the minimal success of our mailings, we turned next to the telephone as a tool of intermediate cost, but of expected marginal utility because of the few individuals for whom we had firm telephone leads. However, we were very surprised with the high level of success we experienced with this method. Using the leads from patient records, we called possible informants. Expectedly, some informants at first expressed some hostility and/or fear towards us. However, after spending a great amount of time carefully identifying our affiliation and capacity as researchers with no power to rehospitalize, most hostility or fear disappeared. Many cooperated freely, but could offer little information. Other non-patient informants asked us to call back in a few days in order for them to check with others about the patient.

In addition, we contacted agencies in 8 other states by telephone. Particular success and cooperation was obtained from other states' hospitals. In one case, the director of a Virginia outpatient clinic asked a member of her clerical staff to record our questionnaire in order to administer it to the Baxstrom patient during his next appointment. She did and three days later called back with the information.

Some other telephone contacts, which proved fruitful, were with New York civil hospitals and clinics. A number of criminal justice agencies, such as district attorneys' offices, county jails, county criminal records department, and the legal unit of the Department of Correction also aided us.

Social agencies cooperated considerably. The Social Services Department of New York City (Welfare) rendered continuous help. We called individual neighborhood welfare centers that we thought a Baxstrom patient might be presently using or had been using in the fall of 1971. In each case, we contacted the records department where files were searched while we waited. In this manner, we obtained complete information for 4 patients and received substantial leads for 4 others. The local units were more useful than the central records office where information was regarded more confidentially.

In sum, we completed 129 telephone calls. Ninety-four resulted in some information with 41 of these providing complete information. Thus, 48 percent of the lost Baxstroms were located via telephone contacts. The telephone was our most productive tool.

Field Investigations. Direct field investigation was used only in the final stages of the follow-up. The costs would have been prohibitive if this approach had been utilized earlier for the larger group. Consequently, 23 visits were made searching for 23 unlocated Baxstrom patients. Community visits were limited to possible informants who had received, but not responded to our letters, who were inaccessible by telephone, and who were living in the New York City metropolitan area. Responses were obtained at all addresses except at those places where the buildings were demolished. When the building was there, but the informant's name could no longer be found among the post office boxes in the building lobby, we sometimes received information from landlords. For the amount of time spent, the payoff of the field work was very high, 14 completed responses for the 23 unlocated subjects sought.

Summary of Follow-Up Techniques

The three follow-up techniques produced adequate information for 71 of the 85 (83.5 percent) lost Baxstrom cases. Of these 71, completed data were obtained for 41 (58 percent) by using the telephone, 16 (22 percent) were located by using letters, and 14 (20.1 percent) from field investigations.

Contacts that proved least wasteful (wasteful in the sense of resulting in neither information nor cooperation) were field investigations, followed by telephone calls. The use of the telephone in prodding responses from resistant informants was the most successful. Three out of every 10 calls produced an adequate response. This is particularly favorable when measured against the fact that letters elicited less than 1 complete response for every 10 mailed.

An analysis of the information available on these patients indicated that there were some factors that differentiated the non-contacted community sample from the total Baxstrom population. These 14 were all men. They were about 7 years younger, arrested more often, yet had fewer previous violent crime convictions than the Baxstrom patients located. But there were no other distinctive features beyond these characteristics. Nevertheless, we completed our community follow-up of the Baxstrom patients in September 1971—eight months after it began—and had located and obtained information for 71 of the 85 people sought.

Conclusions

In elaborating our research techniques, we have spent considerable time on our community follow-up of the Baxstrom patients. This may appear as a disproportionate amount of time, especially given the amount of data that resulted and the small amount of it included in Chapter 8. Certainly such things as the rationale, preliminary planning, data sources, modes of data collection, coding procedures, and sample selection of the total project are important and must be spelled out in sufficient detail for the research to be evaluated and to aid those who might find it relevant in the formulation of new research. However, while the community follow-up of our subjects was not the main thrust of the research, no segment of our work had less help from the existing literature. Thus, we have elaborated on it in great detail along with the other techniques employed in the earlier portions of the project.

This chapter completes the background sections of this book. In the next four chapters, we present an analysis of the data that resulted from our research. In these upcoming chapters, we examine the questions of who the Baxstrom and pre-Baxstrom patients were, how these two groups differed in demographic and criminal background characteristics, the criteria apparently employed by psychiatrists in the hospitals for the criminally insane to determine which patients were released and which were detained, how these factors relate to estimations of dangerousness, what happened when the Supreme Court decision resulted in the mass transfer of the "dangerous" Baxstrom patients, how the Baxstrom and pre-Baxstrom patients fared in the civil hospitals, what trouble these patients did cause in the civil hospitals, and how these related to their community releases, and finally, how both groups functioned when they finally returned to the community. The first of these questions is exactly who were the Baxstrom patients?

5 The Baxstrom Patients

Introduction

The next four chapters are concerned with reporting our findings on the careers of the Baxstrom patients. In this chapter, we describe the Baxstrom patients and explore the question of why some individuals were transferred with psychiatric approval (the pre-Baxstrom patients) while others (the Baxstrom patients) had been evaluated as too dangerous to be housed in civil hospitals and were transferred only as a result of the U.S. Supreme Court decision. The next chapter examines the logistics of moving the 967 Baxstrom patients into the civil hospitals in the face of the strong reluctance of the hospitals' staff members to accept these patients, and it also evaluates the behavior problems actually presented by these patients in the civil hospitals. Chapter 7 discusses the release of patients from the civil state hospitals to the community and attempts to determine the factors related to their release. In the last of these chapters devoted to reporting our findings, Chapter 8, the questions of who remained in the community after release and what factors were associated with community success are examined. Thus, emerging from the next four chapters will be a picture of what happened to these criminally insane individuals, as they moved through the criminal justice and mental health systems.

These four chapters and the questions they raise are related in several ways. First, as a whole, they examine chronologically the inpatient and postpatient phases of the Baxstrom patient careers beginning with their transfer from the criminally insane hospitals to the civil hospitals through their release to the community. The final consideration is why some of the released patients remained in the community while others returned to the mental health or criminal justice systems.

These four chapters can also be grouped into two pairs according to their substantive issues. Chapters 5 and 6 are related in that the first probes the criteria used to assess the suitability of patients for transfer to civil hospitals, while the second examines the accuracy of these assessments. In a similar way, Chapter 7 attempts to discover the reasons why patients were or were not released from the civil hospitals to the community, while Chapter 8 looks at the relationships between release criteria and success in the community.

The third way these chapters are intertwined is in the questions they

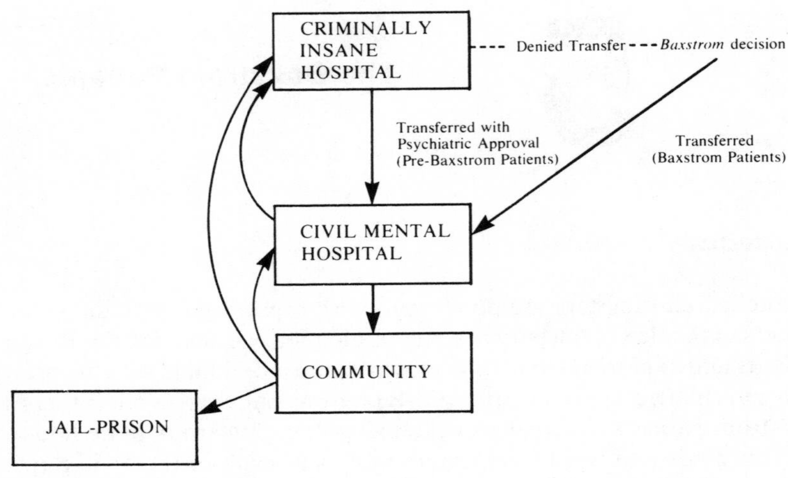

Figure 5-1. Career Movements of Patients under Study.

raise. Chapters 5 and 7, although focusing on different institutions —criminally insane hospitals and civil state hospitals, respectively—ask the same question. What factors distinguished for the psychiatrists those patients no longer in need of institutionalization from those still in need? Chapters 6 and 8 also parallel one another in the main questions they raise. Basically, how successful were these patients? Are the criteria for release employed by psychiatrists in fact related to subsequent success? Are there other or additional factors which better explain patient success? In Chapter 6, we raise these questions for the Baxstrom and pre-Baxstrom patients relative to their behavior in the civil hospitals following transfer. In Chapter 8, we compare the released Baxstrom patients who successfully remained in the community with those who were less successful and were reinstitutionalized.

The basic movements and pathways experienced by the Baxstrom and pre-Baxstrom patients during these stages of their careers, as they will be discussed in these next four chapters, are presented in Figure 5-1.

Comparing the Baxstrom and Pre-Baxstrom Samples

As noted in Chapter 2, there are severe gaps in our knowledge of the criminally insane. Most investigators who have turned their attention to this group have focused on legal or medical questions and have not described in any detail the relevant characteristics of the patients themselves. As a step toward filling this knowledge gap, we attempted to develop a comprehensive picture of the social-psychiatric-criminal backgrounds of these patients.

The second aim of this chapter is to compare the social-psychiatric-criminal characteristics of the Baxstrom patients with those of the pre-Baxstrom group, the 312 male patients transferred from the same two criminally insane hospitals to civil hospitals during the two years immediately preceeding the *Baxstrom* decision. This analysis is undertaken in an effort to discover the factors that may account for the differential evaluation of these patients. Both groups of patients had been institutionalized in the same two criminally insane hospitals. Both groups of patients were legally eligible for transfer. Both groups had undergone psychiatric evaluations. Yet during the years 1964 and 1965, some of these patients were judged by the psychiatrists at the correctional hospitals to be no longer dangerously mentally ill and in need of the special security provided by the criminally insane hospitals. They, therefore, could be and were transferred to civil hospitals. Others, the Baxstrom patients, were passed over as too dangerous and were eventually transferred only as a result of the efforts of Johnnie Baxstrom and the Supreme Court decision. What factors differentiated these two groups of patients? Which patient characteristics were related to the psychiatrists' decision to transfer? Because of the Baxstrom decision, its consequences, and our research, we were provided with the rare opportunity to examine these issues.

In order to accomplish this chapter's two aims of describing the Baxstrom patients and of analyzing how they differ from those patients transferred with psychiatric approval, we examined a large number of variables reflecting their prepatient and inpatient experiences.

These variables are grouped into three major categories. The first two reflect the two sides of the dual label—that is, factors related to their mental illness and factors related to their criminality. The third category or set of variables and the one to be examined first includes their social and demographic characteristics. All of this information, for both patient groups, is presented in Table 5-1.

In the first portion of each of the following sections we delineate the characteristics of the Baxstrom patients. Subsequently, we proceed to the more analytic and interpretive task of determining which characteristics distinguished the Baxstrom from the pre-Baxstrom patients. From these findings we draw some inferences concerning psychiatric decision-making and its effects on the careers of these criminally insane patients.

Social and Demographic Characteristics

Overall, the impression one arrives at from the data on these patients is that

Table 5-1
Characteristics of Baxstrom and Pre-Baxstrom Patients

Characteristics	*Baxstrom (N = 199)*	*Pre-Baxstrom (N = 312)*
Social and Demographic variables		
Place of Birth		
New York State	40.2%	40.3%
South	23.1%	17.0%
Other U.S.	16.6%	12.2%
Foreign born	12.1%	26.0%
Unknown	8.0%	4.5%
Median Grade of Education	7th	7th
Marital History		
Never married	61.3%	58.3%
Previously married	24.1%	37.8%
Still married	9.0%	3.2%
Unknown	5.5%	0.7%
History of Work		
Skilled or semi-skilled	13.1%	11.5%
Unskilled	74.4%	78.9%
Unknown	12.6%	9.6%
Ethnicity		
Black	48.2%	29.8%
White	47.2%	64.4%
Puerto Rican	4.5%	5.8%
Mean Age	51.6 yrs.	62.4 yrs.
Hospitalization and Mental Status		
Mean Age at Admission to Hospital for the Criminally Insane	28.4 yrs.	35.6 yrs.
Mean Number of Years Hospitalized Prior to Civil Hospital Transfer	14.7 yrs.	21.7 yrs.
Reason for Admission to Hospital for the Criminally Insane		
Incompetent	19.6%	53.2%
Mentally ill inmate	67.3%	40.4%
Dangerously mentally ill	0.0%	1.6%
NGRI	0.0%	1.0%
Other	13.0%	3.8%
Previous Mental Hospitalizations		
None	75.9%	74.0%
One	11.6%	13.8%
Two or more	12.6%	12.2%
Psychiatric Diagnosis		
Schizophrenic, paranoia	41.2%	35.3%
Schizophrenic, other	14.1%	14.8%
Schizophrenic, catatonic	11.1%	6.4%
Schizophrenic, hebephrenic	10.6%	16.3%
Psychosis, psychopath	9.0%	3.8%

Table 5-1 Continued
Characteristics of Baxstrom and Pre-Baxstrom Patients

Characteristics	*Baxstrom (N = 199)*	*Pre-Baxstrom (N = 312)*
Psychosis, mental deficiency	7.5%	3.8%
Other	6.5%	19.6%
History of Criminal Activity		
Offense Leading to Current Hospitalization		
Against person	47.7%	40.4%
Against property	33.2%	31.4%
Sexual	5.0%	7.7%
Other	14.1%	20.5%
Sex Crime Convictions		
None	91.5%	95.8%
One or more	8.5%	4.2%
Violent Crime Convictions		
None	48.7%	77.9%
Single	31.7%	16.3%
Multiple	19.6%	5.8%
Number of Previous Arrests		
Mean	4.3	2.7
Median	3.8	1.6
Number of Previous Incarcerations		
Mean	2.4	1.4
Median	2.2	0.8

they are a group who, in almost every way, are marginal to the mainstream of society. For example, of the 199 men in our Baxstrom sample, 61 percent never married, almost 75 percent never held a job above the unskilled level and over 90 percent of them never graduated from high school.

With regard to these three characteristics, as well as place of birth, there was very little difference between the Baxstrom and pre-Baxstrom patients. Baxstrom patients born in New York State accounted for 40.2 percent of the group, while an almost identical 40.3 percent of the pre-Baxstrom patients were born in New York State. For both groups, the median grade of education was the seventh while 6.0 percent of the Baxstrom patients as compared to 4.5 percent of the pre-Baxstrom patients graduated from high school. And just as high a proportion of the pre-Baxstrom patients never married, nor held occupations past the unskilled level. Thus, both groups are remarkedly alike in their marginality and in their lack of integration and achievement in the social system.

The two groups are not, however, equally indistinguishable on other characteristics. The patients judged by the psychiatrists to be suitable for transfer and moved to civil hospitals before the *Baxstrom* decision were older and were more likely to be white than those released by the *Baxstrom* decision. The percentage of blacks among the pre-Baxstrom group was 30 as compared to 48 for the Baxstroms. The mean age of the pre-Baxstrom patients was 62.4 at the time of the study compared to 51.6 for the Baxstrom. Both of these differences proved to be statistically significant and indicate a relationship between these two variables and the decision to transfer.

In order to analyze further the exact meaning and significance of these relationships, we examined each while controlling for the other. This additional analysis revealed that race was evidently not a major criterion in the psychiatric decision to transfer individuals out of criminally insane hospital. Table 5-2 shows that when age is controlled, the significant relationship between race and having been transferred prior to the court decision disappears. The reverse is not true. Controlling for race the two groups are still significantly different in terms of age. Looking at Table 5-2 one can see that for both the black and non-black patients, age is consistently and strongly related to transfer, as indicated by the sharp increase in percent transferred (pre-Baxstrom) as age increases. Thus, the original importance of the variable race seems to be but an artifact of the unequal distribution of blacks in the age groupings—that is, there were proportionately more blacks in the younger age groups, and it was their age and not their race that was related to their being judged unsuitable for transfer prior to the *Baxstrom* decision. In deciding who was safe and well enough for transfer to a civil hospital, the age of the patient appears to have been crucial. The data indicate that of those judged transferable, almost 40 percent were over the age of 70. Of those passed over and only later transferred because of the *Baxstrom* decision, only 9 percent were over 70. To put it differently, if a patient were under 40 his chances for transfer were about 4 out of 10 while if he were over 70 his chances would increase to almost 9 out of 10.

The patients' ages, at the time of the study, were a result of two factors—how old they were when they entered the criminally insane hospital and how long they had been in these two institutions. How old they were when they were admitted is, of course, related to how old the patients were at the time of the study and both are therefore related to whether patients were in the pre-Baxstrom or Baxstrom group. More importantly, however, length of hospitalization was also significantly related to both age and whether or not patients were seen as suitable for transfer. This relationship, which is displayed in Table 5-3, suggested the possibility that the importance of the variable age might be dependent on the fact that older patients tended to be hospitalized for longer periods of time and that the important factor for the psychiatrists and those responsible for making the transfer

Table 5-2
Transfer, by Race, Controlling for Age

	Age					
	Under 40		*40 to 49*		*50 to 59*	
Transfer	*Black* % (N)	*Non-Black* % (N)	*Black* % (N)	*Non-Black* % (N)	*Black* % (N)	*Non-Black* % (N)
Pre-Baxstrom	30.8 (12)	47.1 (16)	39.6 (19)	54.0 (27)	44.7 (21)	55.2 (32)
Baxstrom	69.2 (27)	52.9 (18)	60.4 (29)	46.0 (23)	55.3 (26)	44.8 (26)
Total	100.0 (39)	100.0 (34)	100.0 (48)	100.0 (50)	100.0 (47)	100.0 (58)
	$\chi^2 = 2.04$ N.S. $\phi = .17$		$\chi^2 = 2.04$ N.S. $\phi = .14$		$\chi^2 = 1.14$ N.S. $\phi = .10$	

	Age			
	60 to 69		*70 or Over*	
Transfer	*Black* % (N)	*Non-Black* % (N)	*Black* % (N)	*Non-Black* % (N)
Pre-Baxstrom	66.7 (18)	67.2 (45)	85.2 (23)	87.5 (98)
Baxstrom	33.3 (9)	32.8 (22)	14.8 (5)	12.5 (14)
Total	100.0 (27)	100.0 (67)	100.0 (28)	100.0 (112)
	$\chi^2 = 0.00$ N.S. $\phi = .00$		$\chi^2 = 0.55$ N.S. $\phi = .06$	

Table 5-3
Transfer, by Length of Hospitalization

	Length of Hospitalization			
Transfer	*0 to 10 Years* *% (N)*	*11 to 20 Years* *% (N)*	*21 to 30 Years* *% (N)*	*31 or More Years* *% (N)*
Pre-Baxstrom	49.0 (71)	53.6 (82)	66.7 (72)	82.9 (87)
Baxstrom	51.0 (74)	46.4 (71)	33.3 (36)	17.1 (18)
Total	100.0 (145)	100.0 (153)	100.0 (108)	100.0 (105)

$\chi^2 = 34.91$
$P < .001$
$\phi = .26$

decisions was not how old they were but how long the patients had been continuously hospitalized.

To examine this possibility, age was held constant while relating length of hospitalization to time of transfer. Once again the age of the patients proved to be the more important consideration. As with race, no significant relationships remained between length of hospitalization and time of transfer when age was controlled. Therefore, what determined the transferability of a patient was not how long he had been hospitalized but how old he was. For example, while more than half of the patients over 70 years of age had been hospitalized more than 30 years, the length of hospitalization made no difference for the group as a whole with regard to transfer. Of those aged 70 or more who had been in Matteawan or Dannemora for more than 30 years, 87 percent were transferred, as pre-Baxstrom patients, with psychiatric approval. Astonishingly, there was practically no variation between these patients and others of a similar age who had been hospitalized for shorter periods of time. Of those hospitalized 21 to 30 years, 87 percent were transferred with approval; of those hospitalized 11 to 20 years, 88 percent; and of those hospitalized 10 years or less, 86 percent were released from the two criminally insane hospitals prior to the *Baxstrom* decision. It made no difference whatsoever whether patients were institutionalized for 5 years or 35 years. If they were old, they were no longer seen as dangerous enough to require the special security measures of a criminally insane hospital.

However, the importance of patient age for transfer cannot be seen simply as a reflection of their physical health. By abstracting medical information from patients' hospital progress notes, we developed three categories for analysis: chronic conditions (e.g., diabetes, epilepsy, or arteriosclerosis): acute conditions (e.g. broken bones or appendicitis); and healthy (including handicapping abnormalities not requiring special care or medication). While more of the pre-Baxstrom patients were chronically ill, more of the Baxstrom patients were in an acute condition with the result that an almost equal proportion of both groups and also the majority of both groups (64 percent and 68 percent, respectively) were physically healthy. Thus, it was not the case that just old, dying, inactive patients were being given approval for transfer by the psychiatrist.

Of the factors examined thus far, there is little doubt that the one which made the most difference for these patients was age. The younger the patients were, the more likely they were seen as dangerous and in need of the maximum security offered by the two state hospitals for the criminally insane. The older they were, the more likely they were to be evaluated as suitable for transfer to civil hospitals and therefore had been so moved prior to the Baxstrom decision.

The dynamics of this decision-making process seem to be somewhat analogous to the phenomenon of retirement age in the working world, at which individuals are usually seen as no longer efficient and productive. Similarly, in the world of the criminally insane, once patients reach old age they apparently are no longer seen as dangerous or threatening enough to warrant security hospitalization. The age of retirement, 65, is also the approximate age that seems to make the largest difference for these patients. Referring back to Table 5-2, we find that up to age 60, patients experience, at best, an even chance of psychiatrically approved transfer, while patients 60 and over have an increasingly better chance. This tendency peaks at ages over 70, with almost every 9 out of 10 patients being transferred as no longer dangerous. Thus, as people in their 60s and 70s are seen as no longer capable of working effectively, so these patients are apparently seen as no longer capable of or inclined toward crime and violence.

Before attempting to arrive at any final conclusions, the other two groups of factors must be examined. Factors associated with the study patients' mental illness are discussed next.

History and Type of Psychiatric Disorders

Half of the label applied to these individuals marks them as insane. This portion of their label suggests that they were unpredictable and dangerous as well as criminal. How they came to be labelled insane, their previous experience with mental hospitals, and the psychiatric diagnosis of their illness are the principal topics to be addressed in this section.

Over two-thirds, 134 of the 199, of the Baxstrom patients were convicted inmates who became mentally disordered while serving a sentence.

The other major group in our sample includes the 39 individuals institutionalized in a criminally insane hospital because they had been judicially determined to be incompetent to stand trial. Of the remaining 26 patients, about half were transferred from an institution for mentally defective delinquents. The others were patients transferred from civil hospitals under a statute declared unconstitutional in 1965. This provision had permitted the administrative transfer of civil patients who were troublesome or dangerous to correctional hospitals if they had ever been incarcerated.

There was a large difference between the pre-Baxstrom and Baxstrom patients in their manner of entry into the criminally insane hospitals. While in both groups the two statuses of incompetent to stand trial and convicted mentally ill inmate accounted for around 90 percent of the total group, most of the Baxstroms (67 percent) were mentally ill convicts, while only 40 percent of the pre-Baxstroms were so designated, as shown in Table 5-4. The reason is primarily a legal one. Prior to the *Baxstrom* decision an almost equal number of incompetent defendants and mentally ill inmates were being transferred (166 and 126 of the total 312 pre-Baxstrom patients). Following the decision, most patients transferred as a direct result of that decision were mentally ill convicts because this is the group to which the decision specifically applied. Johnnie Baxstrom fell into this category and while, as discussed in Chapter 3, the principles of the decision were extended to other statuses not specifically affected by it, the majority of those transferred were of this group. The differences between the two groups on reasons for admission to the criminally insane hospitals results primarily from the legal decision and not apparently from any discrimination on this factor by the psychiatrists in their transfer decisions.

Turning to psychiatric diagnosis, we find that diagnostically most of the Baxstrom patients were classified as schizophrenic. The largest proportion of patients were of the paranoid type (41 percent). Other types of schizophrenia accounted for another 36 percent. These others were fairly evenly distributed among hebephrenic, catatonic, and mixed types. Two other diagnostic categories accounted for substantial portions of the group: psychosis with psychopathic personality (9 percent) and psychosis with mental deficiency (7.5 percent). The remaining patients were scattered over 13 other diagnoses.

Psychiatric diagnosis failed to differentiate the Baxstrom from the pre-Baxstrom patients. There was little variation in the percent of patients transferred with approval when the most frequent diagnosis, schizophrenia, paranoid type, was compared to other types of schizophrenia, and no variation when the diagnosis of schizophrenia of all types was compared to all other diagnoses. Of the major diagnostic types found among these patients, schizophrenia, hebephrenic tended to be overrepresented, while psychosis, psychopath tended to be underrepresented in the group trans-

Table 5-4
Reason for Admission to Criminally Insane Hospital for Pre-Baxstrom and Baxstrom Patients

Transfer	*Incompetent* *% (N)*	*Mentally Ill Inmate* *% (N)*	*Other* *% (N)*	*Total* *% (N)*
Pre-Baxstrom	53.2 (166)	40.4 (126)	6.4 (20)	100.0 (312)
Baxstrom	19.6 (39)	67.3 (134)	13.1 (26)	100.0 (199)

ferred with psychiatric consent. The latter group, however, accounted for only 30 of the total 511 patients. Overall, then, the diagnostic label attached to these patients tended to make little difference in their chances for transfer prior to the *Baxstrom* decision.

The next variable examined was the patients' histories of mental hospitalization. It was found, somewhat surprisingly, that few of these patients had ever been previously hospitalized for a mental disorder. Of the 199 Baxstrom patients, 151 (75.9 percent) had no prior reported mental hospitalization, and of the 48 who did, almost half had only one previous admission.

One possible explanation for this low percentage of previous mental hospitalizations is that most of these men were removed from the population at risk by virtue of their lengthy hospitalization—that is, the earlier in life they were hospitalized and the longer they were hospitalized the less opportunity there would have been for their being hospitalized at any other time. This argument is supported, to some extent, by the data. Of those patients who had been housed at Dannemora and Matteawan for more than 20 years, it was found that only 7 percent of them had any previous admissions, as compared to almost 25 percent for the whole group. Further examination revealed that this group was composed primarily of individuals who were 25 years of age or less at the time of their offense and who were, at the time of this study, over 50 years old. Since these individuals were hospitalized at such a young age and never released, their chances of ever generating a history of mental hospitalizations were extremely small. While this group accounts somewhat for the lack of mental hospitalizations among the total group, it does not drastically alter the finding. For with this group of 54 patients removed, the percent of the remaining patients with any history of hospital admissions is increased only by 6 percent to 30 percent. Even among these patients who had a greater chance of experiencing other mental hospitalizations, most—7 out of every 10—still lacked any history of previous hospitalization for a mental disorder.

The pre-Baxstrom patients were found to be very similar and therefore previous mental hospitalizations appeared to have no effect on whether patients were released with psychiatric consent before the *Baxstrom* decision. In the pre-Baxstrom, as in the Baxstrom group, about 75 percent of the patients had no history of previous hospitalizations for mental disorders. Of those who had no previous admissions, 60 percent were transferred with psychiatric approval, of those with one prior hospitalization, 65 percent fell in the pre-Baxstrom group, and of those who had two or more previous admissions, 60 percent were seen as suitable for transfer to civil hospitals before the *Baxstrom* decision. Thus, approximately the same proportion were transferred with consent in all three groups.

In sum, then, the Baxstrom patients differed from the pre-Baxstrom patients in that the majority of the former were mentally ill inmates, while most of the latter group were incompetent defendants. This overrepresentation of mentally ill inmates was not unexpected since the *Baxstrom* decision most directly affected this group. An additional consequence of this decision was that the Baxstrom patients were released as a whole earlier than they would have been. This is reflected in the fact that on the average the Baxstrom patients were hospitalized 7 fewer years than the pre-Baxstrom patients (14.7 and 21.7 years, respectively) before being transferred to civil hospitals.

Both groups of patients were extremely similar in their psychiatric diagnoses and in their lack of prior hospitalizations. This last finding plus the inability of any of the variables examined in this section to clearly answer the question of why some patients were transferred with psychiatric approval, would seem to indicate that, at least at this stage of their careers, the insane portion of the dual label was the weaker of the two. Few had been previously hospitalized, and this factor, plus the others examined in this section, apparently did not influence the decision to transfer. As we shall see next, the same is not true of the criminal half of their label.

Histories of Criminal Activity

Part of the popular stereotype of special security institutions for the criminally insane, and to some extent mental hospitals in general, is that they are fortresses barricading the public from a population of violent patients. Furthermore, these patients are often pictured as hypersexual, with extensive histories of sexual crimes. Our data indicate that neither of these images accurately describes these patients as a whole. This is not to say that this group was not criminally active. They were. Of the 199 Baxstrom patients, all but 25 had been arrested at some time prior to the current offense. The median number of arrests was 3.8. Also, more than 70 percent of them had been previously incarcerated with a mean age at first incarceration of 23 years. It is clear from these figures that these individuals were not strangers to the criminal justice system. However, their crimes appear to be less violent and much less sexually oriented than one would expect.

Looking first at the Baxstrom patients, the figures on violent crime convictions reveal that almost half of them were never convicted of a violent crime.[a] This statistic includes both previous offenses as well as their Baxstrom offense (i.e., the one which led to their being placed in the criminally insane hospital). Of those with violent crime convictions, only 8.5 percent were ever convicted of a sex crime. As a group, these men, as evidenced by their criminal histories, were not all violent criminals or child molesters. They were people who had been frequently arrested and incarcerated and in about half of the cases found guilty of committing a violent crime.

When the data on the criminal activity of the Baxstrom and pre-Baxstrom patients were compared, it was found that on two factors—type of offense leading to current hospitalization and sex crime convictions—there was no significant variation. The type of offense that led to their hospitalizations in the two institutions for the criminally insane made little difference in the proportion of patients transferred with psychiatric approval. So few of the patients had any sex crime convictions—less than 6 percent of the total group—that this factor was insignificant in its effect on transfer.

The other three factors examined were all significantly related to pre-Baxstrom/Baxstrom transfer status. The higher the number of violent crime convictions, arrests, and incarcerations experienced by patients, the more likely it was that they would have been denied transfer prior to the *Baxstrom* decision. Of the pre-Baxstrom patients, 22 percent had a violent crime conviction. The median number of previous arrests and incarcerations for this group were 1.6 and 0.8, respectively. For the Baxstrom patients the figures are, at least, twice as high. Fifty-one percent of them had been convicted of a violent crime and their median number of arrests and incarcerations were 3.8 and 2.2. Because of the highly skewed distributions of these variables, the data were reduced to a nominal type scale and a chi-square test of significance was performed. All three differences were found to be statistically significant at the .001 level. Thus, the absence of a long and serious criminal record appears to be characteristic of the patients transferred with psychiatric approval.

[a]Violent crimes are offenses against or potentially against a person involving injury, restraint, and intimidation. Included in this category are manslaughter, arson, assault, robbery first or second degree, and burglary first and second degree. There are no individuals either convicted of or charged with murder among the Baxstrom patients, since the maximum sentence of life for this offense could not have expired, and the *Baxstrom* decision directly related only to maximum-time-expired cases.

These three variables were also all related to one another and to whether the patients had entered as incompetent defendants or mentally ill inmates. It was possible, therefore, that some or all of the initial three relationships were spurious ones. This possibility was examined and proved to be accurate for two of the variables—number of arrests and number of incarcerations prior to entering the criminally insane hospitals. When reason for admission and violent crime convictions were controlled, neither previous arrests nor previous incarcerations still discriminated between the two groups of patients. Thus, their original relationship was due primarily to their association with the other two variables.

The same was not true for violent crime convictions. Even when arrests and incarcerations were held constant, violent crime convictions continued to be significantly related to transfer with psychiatric consent. Patients who had been convicted of a violent crime were less likely to have been transferred to a civil hospital with psychiatric consent.

This relationship was modified with the introduction of the reason for admission to Dannemora or Matteawan as seem in Table 5-5. Of those who were admitted because of their incompetency to stand trial, almost 90 percent (180 of 205) had no violent crime conviction, and therefore, not surprisingly, there was little relationship between violent crime conviction and transfer with psychiatric consent. This group also tended to have fewer arrests and incarcerations. Among those who entered as mentally ill inmates, the relationship persisted. In this group, those with no violent crime convictions were almost twice as likely to have been evaluated by the psychiatrist as suitable for transfer to a civil hospital as compared to those with a violent crime conviction.

For the incompetent defendant, then, none of the factors related to criminal activity appears to be important in accounting for why some were transferred prior to the *Baxstrom* decision. For the mentally ill inmate, while arrests and incarcerations were more frequent, what apparently was most important in influencing the psychiatrist's decision was whether or not the patient had ever been convicted of a violent crime. If a patient had been convicted of a violent crime, this fact was apparently taken as evidence by the psychiatrist that the patient would be too dangerous to be sent to a civil hospital and the patient would therefore be passed over.

Age and Violent Crime Convictions

Who are the patients judged to be too disturbed or potentially dangerous to be removed from the special security criminally insane hospitals? What criteria are used by psychiatrists in their evaluations of patients to decide whether to deny or grant transfer to civil hospitals?

Table 5-5
Transfer, by Violent Crime Convictions, Controlling for Reason for Admission to Criminally Insane Hospital

	Reason for Admission			
	Incompetent		*Mentally Ill Inmate*	
	Violent Crime Convictions		*Violent Crime Convictions*	
Transfer	*None* *% (N)*	*Some* *% (N)*	*None* *% (N)*	*Some* *% (N)*
Pre-Baxstrom	82.2 (148)	72.0 (18)	61.8 (81)	34.9 (45)
Baxstrom	17.8 (32)	28.0 (7)	38.2 (50)	65.1 (84)
Total	100.0 (180)	100.0 (25)	100.0 (131)	100.0 (129)
	$\chi^2 = 1.49$ N.S. $\phi = .09$		$\chi^2 = 18.90$ $P < .001$ $\phi = .27$	

Our analysis would seem to indicate that the answers to these questions revolve around two factors—the age of the patients and the presence or absence of a conviction for a violent crime. Older age and the absence of a violent crime conviction are the two characteristics that most seem to differentiate those transferred to civil hospitals with psychiatric consent from those passed over because of their potential dangerousness. Actually, the relationship between these two factors and transfer is not quite that simple; yet both remain important.

Since age and violent crime convictions were not only highly related to transfer but also to each other, it was possible that only one of the two was, in fact, important in distinguishing the pre-Baxstrom from the Baxstrom patients. Analysis, however, showed that both remained critical variables but under certain conditions set by the other.

Controlling for the presence or absence of violent crime convictions, there still remained a significant association between age and transfer as shown in Table 5-6. For the group with some violent crime convictions, the association between age and transfer was substantially weakened and actually there was little difference among all the age groupings except for those aged 70 or more. A similar pattern emerged when the relationship was examined controlling for reason for admission to the criminally insane hospitals. However, since the relationship between age and transfer was stronger for those with no violent crime convictions than for incompetent defendants and weaker for those with some such convictions than for mentally ill inmates, it would appear that violent crime conviction is the more important of the two, although there is certainly much overlap.

Table 5-6
Transfer, by Age, Controlling for Violent Crime Conviction

	Violent Crime Convictions				
	None				
	Age				
	Under 40	*40 to 49*	*50 to 59*	*60 to 69*	*70 or Over*
Transfer	*% (N)*	*% (N)*	*% (N)*	*% (N)*	*% (N)*
Pre-Baxstrom	39.5 (17)	60.4 (29)	63.3 (38)	76.1 (54)	89.0 (105)
Baxstrom	60.5 (26)	39.6 (19)	36.7 (22)	23.9 (17)	11.0 (13)
Total	100.0 (43)	100.0 (48)	100.0 (60)	100.0 (71)	100.0 (118)

$\chi^2 = 44.81$
$P < .001$

	Violent Crime Convictions				
	Some				
	Age				
	Under 40	*40 to 49*	*50 to 59*	*60 to 69*	*70 or Over*
Transfer	*% (N)*	*% (N)*	*% (N)*	*% (N)*	*% (N)*
Pre-Baxstrom	36.7 (11)	34.0 (17)	33.3 (15)	39.1 (9)	73.9 (17)
Baxstrom	63.3 (19)	66.0 (33)	66.7 (30)	60.9 (14)	26.1 (6)
Total	100.0 (30)	100.0 (50)	100.0 (45)	100.0 (23)	100.0 (23)

$\chi^2 = 12.71$
$P < .05$

Table 5-7
Transfer, by Violent Crime Convictions, Controlling for Age

	Age					
	Under 40		*40 to 49*		*50 to 59*	
	Violent Crime Convictions					
Transfer	*None* *% (N)*	*Some* *% (N)*	*None* *% (N)*	*Some* *% (N)*	*None* *% (N)*	*Some* *% (N)*
Pre-Baxstrom	39.5 (17)	36.7 (11)	60.4 (29)	34.0 (17)	63.3 (38)	33.3 (15)
Baxstrom	60.5 (26)	63.3 (19)	39.6 (19)	66.0 (33)	36.7 (22)	66.7 (30)
Total	100.0 (43)	100.0 (30)	100.0 (48)	100.0 (50)	100.0 (60)	100.0 (45)
	N.S.		$\chi^2 = 6.86$ $P < .01$		$\chi^2 = 9.26$ $P < .01$	

	Age			
	60 to 69		*70 or Over*	
	Violent Crime Convictions			
Transfer	*None* *% (N)*	*Some* *% (N)*	*None* *% (N)*	*Some* *% (N)*
Pre-Baxstrom	76.1 (54)	39.1 (9)	89.0 (105)	73.9 (17)
Baxstrom	23.9 (17)	60.9 (14)	11.0 (13)	26.1 (6)
Total	100.0 (71)	100.0 (23)	100.0 (118)	100.0 (23)
	$\chi^2 = 10.72$ $P < .01$		*N.S.*	

The relationship between age, violent crime convictions and transfer became much clearer when age was held constant. Table 5-7 shows that there was no significant relationship between violent crime conviction and transfer for those patients under 40 or those 70 and over. On the other hand, patients between 40 and 69 were significantly more likely to be transferred with psychiatric consent if they had never been convicted of a violent crime than if they had.

Thus, it would appear that from a psychiatrist's point of view a patient under 40 is practically always dangerous and a patient over 69 is no longer dangerous, regardless of any other factors including a history of violent crime convictions. For those aged 40 to 69, while age is still somewhat important, the decision as to whether or not they are too dangerous to be transferred to civil hospitals seems to depend primarily on the presence or absence of a record of violent crime convictions.

Discussion

One of the two major aims of this chapter was the attempt to discover characteristics that distinguished the two groups of patients, the comparison group of pre-Baxstrom patients, and the study group of Baxstrom patients. The first group contained those transferred with psychiatric approval; the second, those transferred without psychiatric approval as a result of the *Baxstrom* decision. What was there about the group of Baxstrom patients that led to their being seen as too dangerous for residence in a civil hospital? Our analysis indicates two factors were highly related to psychiatric evaluation of suitability for transfer. These were age and a record of convictions for violent crimes. Thus, while less than a quarter of the pre-Baxstrom patients were under 50 and almost 40 percent were 70 or over, almost half of the Baxstrom patients were under 50 and less than 10 percent were 70 or over. Also, while less than a fourth of the pre-Baxstrom patients had never been convicted of a violent crime, over half of the Baxstrom patients had been.

The age factor dominates within certain ranges. For those patients under 40 or over 69, it makes little difference that they have or have not been involved in major violent crimes. Being in the youngest age grouping means for the patients that they are very likely to be seen as dangerous and in need of continued confinement in special security hospitals for the criminally insane. On the other hand, being 70 or more seems to mean that patients are no longer of potential danger and therefore safe to transfer to civil hospitals, regardless of their past criminal record.

For those patients who fall between these two extremes in age, how old they are becomes a much less important consideration than what they have done. If they are between 40 and 69, their age appears to be only of slight interest. Rather, what matters more is whether they have been involved in violent crimes in the past. Those who have been involved in violent crimes are the ones who are more likely to be evaluated as potentially dangerous. In sum, it would appear that the patients most likely to be seen as dangerous in the future are those who have been dangerous in the past.

Actually, the notion of using past behavior to predict future dangerous behavior and the use of violent crimes as an indicator of such behavior receive some support from the existing literature. Dangerousness itself tends to be a vague and unspecified concept. While most people in the field would agree that it somehow refers to the potential for inflicting serious bodily harm on another (and sometimes oneself), little else is known or agreed upon.

Katz and Goldstein (1960), as mentioned in Chapter 1, in a comprehensive review of dangerousness and mental illness found at least nine different types of behavior plus a tenth that consisted of any combination of the other nine that had been construed as dangerous behavior. Others such as Halleck (1967) and Rubin (1972) have pointed to the lack of adequate empirical data on the concept and the need for much additional research. Our own work on dangerousness presented elsewhere (Steadman 1973) has empirically supported these conclusions.

In much of the work that has been done, the variable used to measure or predict dangerous behavior has been similar to the variable found to be so important here. Rappeport and Lassen (1965, 1966) operationalize dangerousness as the arrest rates of ex-mental patients for murder, manslaughter, rape, robbery, and aggravated assaults. Tong and MacKay (1959) use violent incidents after release as their measure of dangerousness. Rubin (1972) in an extensive review on the prediction of dangerousness in mentally ill criminals concludes that he would limit the concept to violence towards others as operationalized to include the four crimes of criminal homicide, forcible rape, robbery, and aggravated assault. Others such as Kozol et al. (1972), while employing a more clinical approach to the measurement and prediction of dangerousness, place violent assaultiveness at the core of the diagnostic problem. Finally Wenk and his coworkers (1972) have found that the single factor most highly related to violent behavior is a history of actual violence.

Thus, there is some support in the literature for the apparent use of violent behavior and violent crime convictions by psychiatrists at these criminally insane hospitals in their transfer decisions. The support is not, however, very strong. Even in those studies where a direct relationship between past violent behavior and future violence has been established, the result has been far from satisfactory. For example, in the Wenk et al. study while half of the subjects who later became violent had a history of actual violence, for every 1 subject in this group who later became violent, there were 19 similarly designated who did not. The usefulness of this factor as an indicator of dangerousness and its relationship to later violent behavior by the patients under study is examined in later chapters. At this point, it is important to note that for many, including evidently the psychiatrists responsible for this group of criminally insane patients, a critical factor in evaluating patients' dangerousness was their past behavior. Here patients with previous incidents of violent crimes were likely to be seen as dangerous and therefore unsuitable for transfer.

This was only one of the two important factors. For while violent crime convictions was most important in distinguishing the pre-Baxstrom from the Baxstrom transferees, it was so only for those between the ages of 40 and 69. Those under or over these ages appeared to be evaluated not on their previous violent behavior but rather on their age alone. Of those under 40, the majority—over 60 percent—were seen as too dangerous for transfer to the less secure civil hospitals, while of those over 69, less than 15 percent were seen as unsafe risks. Why was age of these patients such an important factor in the psychiatrists' evaluation? Why is it that the principle for the most part seems to be if the patient is young, he is dangerous; if the patient is old, there is nothing to fear?

As with violent crime convictions, there is some support for using age as a criterion for predicting patient dangerousness. While the empirical base for using past violent behavior as an indicator is weak, the relationship between age and criminal activity, including acts of violence, is well documented. Age has been found to be so strongly related to criminal behavior that crime has been referred to as a "young man's occupation" (Vedder and Keller 1968). This association has been found to hold through time and across nations.

An example of the reduction of criminal behavior as age advances can be seen in the arrest data presented in the Uniform Crime Reports (1972, Table 32, pp. 126-27). Those aged 60 to 64 account for only 1.7 percent of all arrests, and those 65 and over account for even less, 1.5 percent. Furthermore, both groups contribute less than 1 percent (0.7 percent) each to arrests made for violent crimes. The only age group that contributes less in total arrest or arrests for violent crimes is the one containing those 10 years old and under. Thus, as age increased from 11 on, there is a general decrease in the incidence of crime, especially in violent crimes against persons (Carlie 1970). A similar pattern has been found with sociopathic behavior. Thus, Robbins (1966) reports a "burning out" or marked dimunition of antisocial symptoms occuring in later life.

While there are many explanations for this reduction in criminal behavior as age advances, there is little confirming evidence (c.f. Sutherland and Cressey 1966; Reckless 1950; Moberg 1953; Keller and Vedder 1965).

Among the main reasons suggested are the following: declining physical strength; greater toleration by others of crime committed by the aged; increased skill of older criminals, enabling them to avoid detection; and increased conformity by the aged to the norms and rules of society. There is little agreement as to which one or ones of these and other suggested reasons account for the impact of age on criminal behavior. There is little disagreement, however, over the fact that the relationship exists.

At the conclusion of one article on age and criminal activity the authors state: "There seems to be some justification for the observation that the chief rehabilitation of those in criminal activity is old age" (Vedder and Keller 1968, p. 16). In a very real sense this appears to have been the approach of those responsible for the patients housed at these institutions for the criminally insane. For patients who lack a history of violent crimes, transfer to civil hospitals increased gradually as they got older. For patients with a record of serious crimes, the guideline seems to have been that until they reached the age of 70, they were to be considered dangerous (Table 5-6). In either case, the data would appear to indicate that in order to assure their prediction that transferred patients were no longer dangerous, the psychiatrists were "rehabilitating" them by letting them grow old in the institution.

Summary

Because one of the aims of this chapter was analytical rather than descriptive, we have spent much more time on examining what distinguished the Baxstrom patients from those released prior to the decision than on describing the characteristics of the Baxstrom patients. Both aims are, however, important.

With regard to the first, we have summarized the data on who these patients were and provided detailed information on their social and demographic characteristics, their prior criminal activity, and their experiences with mental disorders. Our analyses of the second issue enabled us to discover the criteria being used by the psychiatrists in distinguishing dangerous patients from patients not dangerous and suitable for transfer.

The Supreme Court decision in the Johnnie K. Baxstrom case led to the transfer of many patients who did not meet psychiatric criteria. Many of the Baxstrom patients were young, and many had been involved in violent offenses. The decision, then, resulted in the transfer to civil state hospitals of patients evaluated by the psychiatrists as too dangerous to be housed in civil hospitals. The procedures employed to transfer these 967 patients, the behavior of the patients in the civil hospital, and the accuracy of the psychiatrists recommendations implied by their hesitancy to transfer the Baxstrom patients are examined next.

6 The Baxstrom Patients in Civil Hospitals

We have seen in the last chapter that the criminally insane patients most likely to be evaluated as unsuitable for transfer to civil hospitals were those who were younger and who had been involved in violent crimes. These were the characteristics that best set apart the Baxstrom patients from the pre-Baxstrom patients who had previously been judged to be no longer in need of the special security afforded by the criminally insane hospitals. Yet, as a result of the *Baxstrom v. Herold* decision, as detailed in Chapter 3, the state of New York and the civil mental hospitals within the state were faced with the task of transferring and receiving almost a thousand Baxstrom patients. Just the large number of patients involved would be enough to raise the level of anxiety, but this coupled with the fact that these were patients being transferred without psychiatric approval made the task even more precarious.

The actual movement of these patients to the civil hospitals was called Operation Baxstrom. The procedures and problems related to Operation Baxstrom are the first concern of this chapter. Next, we describe the reactions of the civil hospitals to the prospect of receiving these patients. Lastly, we examine, in several ways, the inpatient behavior of these individuals once in the civil hospitals.

Much of the descriptive information to be presented in this chapter is drawn from two earlier studies of the Baxstrom patients mentioned previously. Both Hunt and Wiley's "Operation Baxstrom After One Year" (1968) and White et al.'s, "The Adjustment of Criminally Insane Patients to a Civil Mental Hospital" (1969) provided useful details from which we have reconstructed the following summary of the consequences of the Baxstrom decision during the first few years. Letters from the directors of the 18 civil state hospitals to which the Baxstrom patients were transferred provided an additional source of information. These letters were written in response to a letter of inquiry sent by us in March of 1971, in which we requested the following information: (1) whether their hospitals had any choice as to the type of patients they would accept; (2) whether the Baxstrom patients received any special treatment once they had arrived; and (3) any impressions they had of these patients as a group.

Operation Baxstrom

As described in Chapter 3, the total number of Baxstrom patients to be transferred swelled to 967. The Department of Mental Hygiene with the help of the Correction Department was responsible for the removal, transfer, and allocation of these patients to 18 civil hospitals throughout the state of New York. The *Baxstrom* decision was handed down on February 23, 1966. On March 8, 1966 a conference was held in Albany and the broad procedures to be used were outlined.

According to Hunt and Wiley (1968, p. 975), personnel of the Correction Department were given the responsibility of identifying Baxstrom cases, screening them as to the need for further hospital care, completing records and other paper work, and having the patients examined, certified, and transported. The Department of Mental Hygiene was responsible for allocating each patient to one of the 18 civil hospitals and making preparations for the reception, care, and treatment of the patients. By March 23, 1966 an initial group of 652 identified Baxstrom patients were surveyed and allocated to civil hospitals, which were notified of the imminent transferral of the patients.

The allocation of patients was based on the patient's district of residence (also referred to as catchment area), but numerous problems were encountered in this attempt. Some of the residences on record were actually the patient's place of arrest and not his actual home; some patients' residences were unknown, while for others, their residence was outside the state. A major problem in distribution was the fact that three-fourths of the patients were from New York City where hospitals were most crowded. As a result, 5 of the 8 hospitals serving the city could take only token numbers while the other 3 hospitals received 50 percent of all the patients transferred. As one hospital director put it, the allocation of these patients, "started with geography and ended with reality."

Despite these problems, by March 15, patients had begun to be moved to the civil hospitals. In March, 388 patients were transferred; in April, 323 more. The transportation of patients continued until the end of August, by which time all 967 of the designated Baxstrom patients had reached the civil hospitals.

The Civil Hospitals React

Because these patients were being transferred as a direct result of legal action rather than as a result of psychiatric judgement, because they were considered to be among the most dangerous patients housed in the two criminally insane hospitals, and because of their large numbers—as many as 150 at a single hospital—it was not surprising that Operation Baxstrom generated fear and anxiety among the staff members and psychiatrists at the civil hospitals.

Hunt and Wiley report that when the Baxstrom operation was first announced, there was considerable anxiety among hospital staff at all levels. The move was seen as so potentially dangerous by officials of an employee union that they demanded special training and pay for employees who would be working with the Baxstrom patients. Some officials estimated that as many as one-fourth of the patients would prove to be too dangerous for civil hospitals. Others felt even this figure was optimistic.

In addition to the hospitals' staffs, members of the communities surrounding the civil hospitals were also concerned. "In the neighborhoods surrounding the civil hospitals there were also some flurries of anxiety. With one exception, these died down with explanation and reassurance. Serious public reaction occurred in just one town as a reaction of panic from an event that had occurred eight years before. This also subsided in time but only after a great deal of difficult educational work with the community" (Hunt and Wiley 1968, p. 976).

The Baxstrom patients were now civil cases, and as such, the civil hospitals were reminded that there was nothing in their legal status requiring special security measures. Nonetheless, because of the manner of their transfer, the question of whether the Baxstrom patients would be perceived and treated as just other civil patients remained open. Similarly, regardless of their legal status, they were patients purposely retained in the criminally insane hospitals and therefore the question of their potential dangerousness in the civil hospital remained an important consideration. The hospitals were assured by central office administrators, that most of the patients should prove no more difficult than other patients and that any who did could be recommitted to the criminally insane hospitals following a judicial determination of dangerousness. Evidently these assurances were convincing since few of the receiving hospitals instituted special precautionary measures.

Of the 18 hospitals in the state, only 2 (both in New York City) set up special wards for the processing and care of the Baxstrom patients. At one of these hospitals, according to White et al. (1969, p. 36) interviews with attendants on the special ward revealed that there was mutual distrust between patients and staff. For a few weeks, for example, all recreational equipment was locked away for fear it might be used as weapons by the patients. Despite the fact that at least one hospital had intended to maintain the Baxstrom patients in this special unit indefinitely, both units, reportedly, were disbanded within 60 days. At most of the other hospitals, patients were not treated in any special manner; routine procedures were followed.

Patients were typically received in a closed admissions ward. Following a period of observation, the patients were distributed among the general hospital population on various wards. A few hospitals made a concerted effort to speed the dispersion of patients among the regular patients. For example, the director of one hospital wrote: "We felt it to be in the best interest of these cases to promptly mix them in with other patients on our open wards to be cared for with existing ongoing treatment programs. We did not want to type them from the onset as special cases . . ."

The preceding description does not necessarily imply that the fact that these were Baxstrom patients was completely forgotten nor that they were treated by all as just other civil patients. Indications of the above were at least occasionally encountered in the patients' records. For instance, the psychiatrist heading one unit passed on a directive to his staff that "no patient transferred from Matteawan or Dannemora could receive an Honor Card." In other cases, particularly when the question of release or voluntary status was raised, that they were Baxstrom patients was seen as a relevant although not conclusive factor as exemplified in the following quotation: "This patient is from Matteawan State Hospital and for this reason and his present behavior and his mood and affect, he had to be retained on a court retention." Overall, however, few of the hospitals reacted to the influx of Baxstrom patients in any extraordinary way or found it necessary to treat these patients differently than others.

Inpatient Behavior

Given the initial fear that developed at the prospect of receiving large numbers of these supposedly dangerous patients, the fact that few extraordinary measures were instituted and even less were maintained was somewhat surprising. What appears to account for these developments is that the Baxstrom patients presented much fewer problems than expected. Because they had been passed over as unsuitable for civil hospitals, the expectation was that many of them would prove to be too disruptive and violent for the civil hospital environment. All of the information available on the Baxstrom patients' behavior in the civil hospitals suggests that these "dangerous" patients were not very dangerous at all.

Data on patient behavior were drawn from several sources. The first two were the previous research reporting the experiences of the Baxstrom patients during their first year in the civil hospitals and the information gathered from the letters of the hospital directors. The third source was the data we abstracted and coded from the patients records described in Chapter 4. Of the three, the last is the most important. Unlike the first source, it contained information over a period of 4 years and unlike the directors' letters was not merely impressionistic. All of the data taken together provide a fairly clear and comprehensive picture of how well the Baxstrom patients fared in the civil hospitals.

One Year Later

Both Baxstrom patient follow-up articles reached similar conclusions: "After one year there have been no significant problems with the patients" (Hunt and Wiley 1968, p. 978), and "the information gathered in this study confirms the previously reported findings of Hunt and Wiley that so-called 'criminally insane' patients have presented no unique problems for the staff of a civil mental hospital" (White et al. 1969, p. 38). The data presented in each article clearly supported these conclusions. Not only had none of the hospitals had any particular problems to report, but also within the year, 176 of the 967 patients had been discharged and only 7 patients had proved to be so dangerous that they were recommitted to the criminally insane hospitals.

The research by White et al. examined more closely the treatment and adjustment of the Baxstrom patients by focusing on a single hospital. They found that at the end of a year, most of the patients originally placed on a special security ward had been transferred to other wards. Only one patient who had been moved to an open ward was subsequently returned because of disruptive behavior. Of the 72 patients on which the report is based, 7 were returned to the community within the year, over a third of them had been granted honor cards enabling the patients to move freely about the hospital grounds, and 12 were engaged in some type of work within the hospital area. Furthermore, of the Baxstrom patients transferred to this hospital, there were only 5 for whom formal reports of aggressive behavior were recorded. A few other patients were described as having occasional episodes of threatening, aggressive behavior or as being verbally abusive.

In both studies, then, little evidence was discovered during the first year to justify the fear surrounding these patients or to justify their lengthy retention in the special security hospitals for the criminally insane. This description of the Baxstrom patients in the civil hospitals is reinforced by the retrospective summaries given by the civil hospital directors of their experiences with these patients.

Impressions of the Civil Hospitals Directors

In March of 1971, 5 years after the initial transfers of the Baxstrom patients, we requested and received from the directors of the 18 civil hospitals, letters detailing, in addition to the other information discussed above, their impressions of how the Baxstrom patients had done in their hospitals. In their responses, all 18 directors used similar phrases to describe these patients: "no obvious differences from other patients," "easily handled and caused no management problem," "no particular problems," "behaved well,'' ''adjusted fairly well.'' For each hospital, the response was the same—no special problem and not any different from other patients. Even the one director who stated in his letter that he objected ''to receiving patients who were classified as being so disturbed as being obviously unsuited for a civil hospital'' concludes, ''we had no special difficulties with any of these patients''.

There were only two exceptions to the directors' positive statements on the Baxstrom patients. First, mention is made of those individuals (usually referred to as isolated or special cases) who were returned to the hospitals for the criminally insane because of their behavior. As we will see later, however, less than 3 percent of the 967 patients were so readmitted. In view of the fact that these were patients who were supposedly violent and aggressive and who were denied transfer to civil hospitals because of their dangerousness, the second exception is astonishing. The other problem mentioned by a number of the hospital directors was the difficulty encountered in working with such a docile group. In some ways, this was seen as a positive characteristic. For example, one director reported that ''most of them were good workers and were so highly regarded as helpers by the ward staff that some of the nurses actually came to me and asked for 'their share' of the Dannemora patients.'' The same director, however, also felt: ''The most serious rehabilitation problem we had in trying to resocialize the patient was that we found them oversubmissive and regimented. When they were addressed by an employee they immediately rose and replied with 'Yes, sir' and 'No, sir' and generally bowed and scraped in a rather embarrassing way.'' This is hardly the description one would expect of a group of dangerous patients.

Four Years Later

While the findings presented above are extremely clear in their implications for the adjustment of the Baxstrom patients in the civil hospitals, they remain somewhat inconclusive. First of all, the findings from the studies that provide specific data are limited to the first year following the Baxstrom transfers, and it is possible that although initially successful, the Baxstrom patients' behavior in the civil hospitals may have worsened as the years passed. Secondly, while the information from the hospital directors did not share this limitation in that it represented retrospective overviews 5 years after Operation Baxstrom, it was primarily impressionistic and therefore lacked the specific details necessary to adequately evaluate the Baxstrom experience.

In order to more conclusively answer the question of how well the Baxstrom patients did in the civil hospitals, in our research, we concentrated on a few critical measures of their in-hospital behavior over the entire 4 years of the study. These data we felt would both supplement as well as improve the other existing information.

Were these patients unsuitable for the civil hospitals? Were they dangerous? If the answer to these questions were in the affirmative we would expect among other consequences that (1) a large number of patients would have been returned to the criminally insane hospitals as dangerously mentally ill, and (2) a large number of these patients would display assaultive, violent tendencies in the civil hospitals.

Baxstrom Patients Returned to Hospitals for the Criminally Insane. Patients who proved to be unsuitable for the less secure environment of the civil hospitals could be returned to the criminally insane hospital under Section 85 of the New York State Mental Hygiene Law as "dangerously mentally ill." Under this civil procedure, patients could be returned if their behavior in the hospital was seen as dangerous to the staff, to other patients, or to the community if the patients were to escape. It will be recalled that this provision was one of the reassurances given the civil hospitals to assuage their anxiety over the prospect of receiving the Baxstrom patients. It will also be recalled that it was estimated that a fourth of these patients would prove to be so dangerous as to require reinstitutionalization in the hospitals for the criminally insane.

One-fourth of our sample of 199 is 50 patients. In fact, 4 were returned. Of the 199 patients under study, only 2 percent proved to be too dangerous for the civil hospital and were accordingly returned to the criminally insane hospital.

Two questions can be raised concerning the adequacy of this figure on returnees. It is possible that our sample was biased and as a result underrepresented the proportion of patients actually returned from the total group of 920 male patients. Secondly, it could be argued that the figure is so low because it reflects only those patients returned to the criminally insane hospitals directly from the civil hospitals while it should include all returnees including those returned following their release from the civil hospitals. Some patients may have been released quickly or were able to refrain from the type of behavior indicating a need for reinstitutionalization until they were released back to the community. Both of these possibilities were examined.

Because of the importance of the questions we obtained and coded information on all patient returnees. We found that in addition to the 4 patients from our sample, 9 others were returned to the criminally insane hospitals as dangerously mentally ill. Of the entire male Baxstrom group, a total of 13 of the 920 were returned. These 13 represent 1.4 percent of the total group. If anything, then, our sample overrepresents the proportion of patients found unsuitable for the civil hospitals.

The behavior of these 13 patients which led to their return varied as seen in Table 6-1. For the 6 returnees with assaults against persons, there was a single serious incident that precipitated the return. For the 4 with threatening behavior only, there was a series of incidents culminating in their return to the criminally insane hospital.

The remaining 4 patients who returned under Section 85 (classified as "Other" in Table 6-1) did nothing after their transfers to civil hospitals that specifically led to their return. One was described in a letter requesting Section 85 proceedings as "the most violent and dangerous patient in Dannemora State Hospital" before his transfer. However, during his 5 weeks in the civil hospital before being returned, there was no report of any incident while he was kept in maximum security with a special security attendant assigned to him 24 hours a day. The records of the other 3 patients offered only vague reasons for their return. One patient, who was transferred under a "forthwith" Section 85 order after one day in a civil hospital, had his order recinded three weeks later when his hearing took place. Another patient was sent to Matteawan apparently because his wife read in the newspaper about "Operation Baxstrom" and wrote the hospital director that she was afraid her husband would escape and harm her, although the patient had given no indication of dangerous behavior after his transfer. The last patient in the "Other" category was returned, according to hospital records, because of his criminal history before his Baxstrom detainment; there were no reported behavioral problems after his initial transfer.

If we include in our figure not only those returned from the civil hospitals as dangerous but also those patients who were released from the civil hospitals only to be readmitted to the hospitals for the criminally insane under criminal procedures following an arrest, the figure is necessarily increased. There were 11 patients returned in this way; 3 from our sample and 8 from the remaining groups. Six of the 11 were found incompetent to stand trial after their arrest and were returned to Matteawan. The other 5 were convicted, incarcerated, and then transferred to Dannemora as psychiatrically disordered criminals. The charges and institutionalizations leading to the return of these 11 patients are shown in Table 6-2. With the exception of one unspecified parole violation, all the charges for which these patients were returned were felonies.

Even if we combine these two groups, those returned as dangerously mentally ill and those returned under criminal proceedings, they total only 24 patients or 2.6 percent of the total Baxstrom group. Over 97 percent of the patients transferred out of the criminally insane hospital as a result of the *Baxstrom* decision were never returned during our four-year follow-up. Thus, these patients with few exceptions proved to be suitable for the civil hospital environment and not in need of the continued institutionalization in special security hospitals that they were experiencing until the *Baxstrom* decision.

Table 6-1
Behavior Leading to Return of Baxstrom Patients from Civil Hospitals

Behavior	*Number (N) = 13*	*Percent*
Threats only	4	30.8
Assaults against persons		
With no injury or minor injury	3	23.1
With major injury	1	7.7
Resulting in death	1	7.7
Other (e.g., wife's request, criminal history)	4	30.8

Table 6-2
Incident Precipitating Return of Baxstrom Patients through Criminal Procedures

Charge	*Procedures and Institutionalizations Leading to Return*[a]
Second Degree Assault and Possession of a Dangerous Weapon	10-Year Sentence, Prison, Dannemora
Third Degree Burglary and Unlawful Use of a Motor Vehicle	5-Year Sentence, Prison, Dannemora
Second Degree Manslaughter	3-to-6 Year Sentence, Prison, Dannemora, Prison
Second Degree Larceny	5-Year Sentence, Prison, Dannemora
Parole Violation	Prison, Dannemora, Civil Mental Hospital
Second Degree Robbery	Incompetent, Matteawan
Burglary	Incompetent, Matteawan
Attempted Second Degree Robbery	Incompetent, Matteawan
Second Degree Robbery	Incompetent, Matteawan
Attempted First Degree Robbery	Incompetent, Matteawan, Court, Four-Year Sentence for First Degree Robbery
Homocide, Grand Larceny, and Burglary	Incompetent, Matteawan (malingerer), Court, 10-to-20-Year Sentence for First Degree Manslaughter

(N = 11)

[a]The last notation in each history indicates the patient's location at the end of the follow-up period.

Patient Assaultiveness within the Hospital. The last set of data to be presented on the in-hospital behavior of the Baxstrom patients focuses on their assaultiveness. Perhaps these patients did prove to be assaultive and violent in the civil hospitals, but for various reasons (e.g., the time and work involved in having a patient returned as dangerously mentally ill) the hospital themselves chose to deal with such problems. Available to us among the data we abstracted from the patients' records were any reports that detailed incidents of serious acting out among the patients. Descriptions of individual patient behavior were grouped into two categories: assaultive (reported assaultive behavior against persons) and non-assaultive. While the reporting of less serious acts probably reflect as much the whims of staff members as actual acting out, it is unlikely that serious assaultiveness would not be recorded. Thus, we are fairly confident the hospital records on assaultiveness of these patients neither over- nor underrepresent to any significant degree the amount of such activity as actually occurred.

Over the 4 years, 30 of the 199 Baxstrom patients were assaultive while in the hospital. This represents about 15 percent of the total group. When we compare the Baxstrom patients to our comparison group of pre-Baxstrom patients, we find that two and a half times more of the Baxstrom patients were assaultive than the group transferred with psychiatric consent. Only 6 percent, 18 of 312, of the pre-Baxstrom patients were assaultive.

To some extent this difference is due to the fact that the pre-Baxstrom patients were, on the average, more than 10 years older and experienced a higher death rate while in the civil hospitals than the Baxstrom patients. Nonetheless, those patients transferred to the civil hospitals as a result of psychiatric approval were less likely to be assaultive than those transferred as a result of the *Baxstrom* decision.

More important than the relative differences between the two groups are absolute findings on both groups. Eighty-five percent of the Baxstrom patients and almost 95 percent of the pre-Baxstrom group were not assaultive while in the hospital. The majority of both groups simply did not conform to the image held of these patients. They were not all dangerous, violent, or assaultive patients. And even though the psychiatrically approved transfers were less assaultive, the level of failure by the Baxstrom patients on the success criteria appear insufficient to support the psychiatric decision not to approve transfer.

Our two indicators of patient success in the hospital firmly support the conclusions previously reached from their first year in the civil hospitals and those reported by the directors of the civil hospitals. The Baxstrom patients were not very dangerous. While they represented a group of patients widely feared, once in the hospitals, few were so dangerous as to require readmission to the special security hospitals and few were assaultive.

Before concluding this chapter there is one other question to be examined. We found in the last chapter that the two characteristics that best distinguished the Baxstrom from the pre-Baxstrom patients were age and a history of convictions for violent crimes. The psychiatrists at the hospitals for the criminally insane were much more likely to evaluate patients as not dangerous and suitable for transfer if they were older and lacked any convictions for violent crimes. The last question raised is whether these criteria were related to patient success in the hospital.

Psychiatric Criteria for Transfer and Inpatient Behavior

Our analysis of the data on this question indicated that one of the two criteria influencing the psychiatrist's decision to grant or deny transfer was, in fact, related to patient success as measured by our two indicators, patients returned to the correctional hospitals and assaultive behavior. Let us first look at the findings on patients returnees.

The average age of the entire Baxstrom sample at the time of transfer was 47. The 24 patients who were returned to the criminally insane hospitals were much younger. Their average age was 34. Those returned directly from the civil hospitals as dangerously mentally ill were older than the criminal returnees—36 compared to 30—but both groups differed from the larger group in age.

Neither violent crime convictions nor any other single factor successfully distinguished between Baxstrom returnees and other Baxstrom patients. The only other factor that proved to be somewhat related was a composite measure we developed and referred to as the Legal Dangerousness Scale (LDS) score. This Guttman-type scale summarized information on the criminal history of the Baxstrom patients prior to institutionalization. The following four items were used: (1) presence or absence of a juvenile record; (2) number of previous incarcerations; (3) presence or absence of a violent crime conviction, and (4) severity of Baxstrom offense (against person or property). This scale had a Coefficient of Reproducibility of 90.6 and met all other criteria for scaling. The score ranges from 0 to 15, with the higher the score, the more serious the criminal history. The average score for the returnees was 9.2. (8.1 for the dangerously mentally ill returnees and 10.4 for the criminal returnees). This compares with an average score of 6.0 for the other Baxstrom patients. Younger patients with more serious criminal histories were the group most likely to be returned to the correctional mental hospitals as criminally insane.

With regard to assaultiveness in the civil hospital, the LDS score and most of the other variables examined proved to be unimportant. The factor that was most highly related to patient assaultiveness was age. The 30 patients who were assaultive had an average age of 46, while non-assaultive patients were on the average 55 years of age. Thus, the two groups were significantly different in age ($t = 3.6$, $p < .001$). This relationship between age and assaultiveness existed for both the Baxstrom and pre-Baxstrom group as shown in Table 6-3. As can be seen from this table, while there is some variation in the trend at the 70 and over age level, on the whole the pattern is consistent. Younger patients are much more likely to be assaultive.

Discussion

The psychiatrist at the criminally insane hospitals were at least somewhat correct in their criteria for patient transfers. The absence or presence of violent crime convictions was unrelated to our indicators of patient success although a summary scale reflecting the seriousness of patients' previous criminal activity did distinguish returnees from those Baxstrom patients not returned to the correctional hospitals. Age, however, did significantly distinguish between returnees and non-returnees and between assaultive and non-assaultive patients. The apparent use of patients' age by the psychiatrists seems to be somewhat justified. The older, pre-Baxstroms were less assaultive than the Baxstrom patients, and in both groups the less dangerous, as reflected by our two indicators, were the older patients.

A second conclusion is that the Baxstrom patients were not very dangerous and in general were very successful in the civil hospitals—that is, among the Baxstrom patients (even among the Baxstrom patients who were young), few were returned to correctional hospitals and few were assaultive. For example, we have seen that the Baxstrom patients had an assault rate two and a half times greater than the pre-Baxstrom patients, 15 percent as compared to 6 percent. If the patterns we have found remained constant, and if the *Baxstrom* decision had not occurred, the Baxstrom patients would have been retained until they reached the average age of the pre-Baxstroms and the following would have occurred: (l) the number of assaultive patients would have decreased from 30 to 12, or 6 percent of the total group, and (2) 199 men would have spent 10 more years of their lives in the criminally insane hospitals.

Another example of this can be seen by referring back to Table 6-3. If the psychiatrist had designated all patients under 50 as high risks for transferral to the civil hospitals and had retained the 97 patients who met this criteria in the correctional hospitals, they would have succeeded in reducing the assaultive behavior by over 73 percent. Twenty-two of the 30 assaultive Baxstrom patients were under the age of 50. At the same time, however, they would have been misclassifying 75 patients. Of those under 50, only 22 of the 97 patients in this age group were ever assaultive. Our

Table 6-3
Relationships between Age and Patient Assaultiveness for Baxstrom and Pre-Baxstrom Patients

	Baxstrom Patients				
	Under 40	*40 to 49*	*50 to 59*	*60 to 69*	*70 or Over*
Assaultiveness	*% (N)*	*% (N)*	*% (N)*	*% (N)*	*% (N)*
Assaultive	28.9 (13)	17.3 (9)	5.8 (3)	6.5 (2)	15.8 (3)
Non-assaultive	71.1 (32)	82.7 (43)	94.2 (49)	93.5 (29)	84.2 (16)
Total	100.0 (45)	100.0 (52)	100.0 (52)	100.0 (31)	100.0 (19)

	Pre-Baxstrom Patients				
	Under 40	*40 to 49*	*50 to 59*	*60 to 69*	*70 or Over*
Assaultiveness	*% (N)*	*% (N)*	*% (N)*	*% (N)*	*% (N)*
Assaultive	14.3 (4)	13.0 (6)	5.7 (3)	1.6 (1)	3:3 (4)
Non-assaultive	85.7 (24)	87.0 (40)	94.3 (50)	98.4 (62)	96.7 (118)
Total	100.0 (28)	100.0 (46)	100.0 (53)	100.0 (63)	100.0 (122)

analysis of the data indicated that the Baxstrom patients, as a whole, were passed over for transfer at least partially because of their young age; yet, as we have seen in 85 percent of the cases this decision was inappropriate since that many were never assaultive. Using behavior necessitating readmission to the criminally insane hospital as our indicator, the finding is even more dramatic. Over 97 percent of those who were being retained later failed to behave in a way which would justify such retention. This tendency to institutionalize many in order to prevent the actions of a few leads directly to the issue of psychiatric conservatism.

The medical model as a whole has been described as conservative, inclined toward overprediction. Judging a healthy person sick (a type 2 error, a false positive) is seen as preferable to judging a sick person well (a type 1 error, a false negative). While this bias is reasonable when applied to physical illness, its appropriateness for mental illness and for the prediction of dangerousness is questionable. That this bias is carried over to psychiatry and that it may lead to negative personal, legal and social consequences have been discussed and documented by others (Scheff 1966; Rosenhan 1973).

Similarly, this general medical conservatism has been found by others to extend to the question of dangerousness. Dershowitz (1970, p. 46) notes:

> Even more significant for legal purposes: it seems that psychiatrists are particularly prone to one type of error—overprediction. In other words, they tend to predict anti-social conduct in many instances where it would not, in fact, occur. Indeed, our research suggests that for every correct psychiatric prediction of violence, there are numerous erroneous predictions. That is, among every group of inmates presently confined on the basis of psychiatric predictions of violence, there are only a few who would, and many more who would not, actually engage in such conduct if released.

There are many good reasons available to explain this overprediction. One we have mentioned is the perspective of the medical model itself. Another is the fact that violent behavior is a rare event, and as several authors (Rosen 1954, Meehl 1954; von Hirsch 1972; Wenk et al. 1972) have demonstrated, any attempt to predict a rare event necessarily results in a high number of false positives. Furthermore, psychiatry is intimately connected with the political forces of social control and is influenced by political pressures from legislators and local communities (McGrath 1968; Steadman 1973).

On the one hand, these reasons make the psychiatrists' acts understandable. For example, that they would hesitate transferring patients who might injure or kill someone in the civil hospital is reasonable. On the other hand, as we have seen, although the criteria of age used by the psychiatrists was related to patients' behavior, so few of the transferred patients proved to be assaultive or in need of the special security afforded by the criminally insane hospitals that it is hard to perceive their retention as justifiable. As von Hirch (1972, p. 731) states, "We can afford little tolerance, indeed, of prediction methods that show a high yield of false positives. Here mistakenly predicting non-dangerous individuals to be dangerous is gravely damaging—for it can lead to their prolonged incarceration." While von Hirsch expresses it as a possibility, prolonged incarceration resulting from psychiatric conservatism was a reality for the patients included in this study.

Summary

We began this chapter by describing the procedures used to transfer the Baxstrom patients and the reactions of the civil hospital staffs to the prospect of receiving these patients. The two main issues examined in this chapter were the extent to which the Baxstrom patients proved to be dangerous and unsuitable for the civil hospitals and the extent to which the criteria shown by our analysis to influence the psychiatrists' decisions to deny or grant transfer were related to patient success in the civil hospitals. We found through an analysis of our data and other available information that the Baxstrom patients were not very dangerous and most had little difficulty adjusting to the less secure setting of the civil hospitals. At the same time it was found that at least one of the criteria employed by psychiatrists in the correctional hospitals was associated with post-transfer behavior. The patients most likely to be denied transfer were the same patients who, when transferred as a result of the *Baxstrom* decision, were the most likely to be assaultive in the civil hospital and to require readmission to the hospitals for the criminally insane. These were the youngest patients.

Because of the high level of success of the Baxstrom patients as a whole, the actions of psychiatrists were seen as further evidence of the observed tendency of psychiatrists toward conservatism and overprediction. Continued retention of younger patients would drastically reduce the amount of assaultive behavior. However, in order to attain such a reduction a large number of patients would have to be institutionalized, most of whom would be incorrectly identified as unsuitable for the civil hospital —that is, most of these men, even those in the high risk group of younger patients, were simply not very dangerous.

The immediate focus of the decisions made by the psychiatrists at the correctional hospitals was the patient's suitability for transfer to the civil hospitals. However, the level of success of the Baxstrom patients and, by extension, the degree of accuracy of the psychiatrists' decisions can be more fully evaluated by enlarging the focus. Not only how they behaved in the civil hospitals, but also how many adjusted well enough to be released to the community, and how successful the released patients were in the community are questions that need to be examined to complete our picture of the Baxstrom patients. The first step in extending our focus is the examination, in the next chapter, of our information on patient release and an analysis of factors related to it. In Chapter 8, we explore the subsequent issue of postpatient behavior of the individuals released to the community.

7 The Patients Get Out: Factors Related to Community Release

Over half of the Baxstrom patients in our sample were released from the civil hospitals to the community during the four and a half years of our follow-up study. In this chapter and the next, we examine which patients got out, which ones returned, and what factors related to these experiences. In this section, we have eliminated from our original sample 22 patients who died during our follow-up.

In addition to these 22, we have omitted one other patient. Johnnie K. Baxstrom is excluded from the following analysis primarily because of the atypical circumstances surrounding his release. A short time after his transfer to a civil hospital in March 1966, Baxstrom reinstituted his legal maneuverings. Under the 1966 revision of the state's Mental Hygiene Law, all patients in civil hospitals were entitled to a jury trial on the question of their mental illness as a reason for involuntary hospitalization. Through his own legal expertise and other people's interest in his case, Baxstrom received a trial on this issue. The jury decided that he was without mental illness and therefore should not be involuntarily detained in a mental hospital. Thus, in May 1966, Johnnie Baxstrom was released to the community.

This avenue for release to the community was not the usual one taken by the other Baxstrom patients. Their route involved the same type of psychiatric decision-making associated with estimations of mental illness and dangerousness that was encountered while in hospitals for the criminally insane.

Of the 176 living Baxstrom patients, 98 (56 percent) were, in fact, released to the community under these more regular procedures. The timing of their releases is shown in Table 7-1. The table shows that the release of many patients occurred quite rapidly. Over 17 percent were released in the first 3 months, almost 30 percent within 6 months, and over 45 percent of the patients ever released were back in the community within a year. An additional 30 percent were released in the second year, 15 percent in the third year, and the remaining 9 percent after 3 years.

In order to evaluate the relative level of success indicated by these release statistics, we compared the Baxstrom patients' experiences to those of the pre-Baxstrom patients. Were the patients seen by the psychiatrists at the correctional hospitals as more suitable for transfer to the civil hospital also seen as more suitable for release by the psychiatrists in the civil hospital? The data indicate that the opposite was true.

Table 7-1
Timing of Release from Civil Hospitals for 98 Baxstrom Patients Released to the Community

Length of Time Hospitalized Prior to Release	*Number of Patients Released*	*Percentage of Patients Released (N = 98)*	*Cumulative Percentage*
0 to 3 months	17	17.4	17.4
4 to 6 months	12	11.2	28.6
7 to 9 months	11	11.2	39.8
10 to 12 months	6	6.1	45.9
13 to 18 months	18	19.4	65.3
19 to 24 months	10	10.2	75.5
25 to 36 months	15	15.3	90.8
37 or more	9	9.2	100.0

Of the pre-Baxstrom patients, 116 were released. If we eliminate the 73 patients who died during our follow-up, we find that 49 percent of the living pre-Baxstrom patients were released. This rate is less than the 56 percent rate for the Baxstrom patients. Thus, a higher percentage of Baxstrom patients were released to the community.

This somewhat surprising finding leads to the two main questions to be addressed in this chapter. What criteria were used in release decisions by the civil hospital psychiatrists and what are the relationships between the criteria for release from the civil hospital and criteria for transfer from the correctional mental hospitals?

With our data, not only can we arrive at some notion of the factors considered important by psychiatrists in civil hospitals for release, but we can also examine the relationship between their criteria and the criteria we have found to be considered important by the psychiatrists in criminally insane hospitals for transfer. For example, as we have seen, older patients are more likely to be transferred with psychiatric approval to civil hospitals. Are older patients also more likely to be approved for release from civil hospitals, or do the criteria differ or even conflict? While the two systems comprising the criminally insane hospitals and the civil hospitals remain separate, the patient who passes through both does not. Is what is seen as an advantage in one system a drawback in the other, which thus hinders the movement of the patients through the two, or is there agreement between the two systems, which thus facilitates patient movement? We have already seen that of the many factors considered, two—age and violent crime convictions— appeared to be important criteria in the decision to transfer. Here, we examine the impact of these two and other variables on the release decision and then use this information to evaluate the relationship between the criteria for success in the two settings.

Dangerousness and Patient Release

There are two main reasons justifying the involuntary commitment and continued confinement of individuals in mental hospitals. First, the individual is so severely impaired as to require care and treatment, and second, the individual is potentially dangerous and is therefore committed to protect the community from harm. Conversely, the individual is released when recovered or when the illness is in a state of remission and the individual is not considered to present a danger to the members of the community. We discuss the first of these areas for psychiatric decision-making in the section on psychiatric disorders; here, we look at dangerousness.

Dangerousness is alleged to be a major criterion in the release decision made by psychiatrists (Weinstein 1964; Leifer 1969). Whether it is or not is uncertain. The only careful piece of research conducted on this question was reported recently by Greenley (1972). He found that dangerousness was, in fact, unrelated to length of hospitalization prior to release. A major difficulty, which we have already discussed, is that dangerousness is neither clearly defined nor operationalized in the literature. Greenley measured patients' dangerousness to others by referring to hospital records in which, on the basis of behavior both during and before hospitalization, each patient was listed as either being or not being "assaultive," "destructive," or "homicidal." This, however, is only one of many different variables employed by researchers as an indicator of dangerousness.

We began by first examining the relationship between violent crime convictions and the release of these patients from the civil hospitals. This variable was of particular importance for two reasons. First, as discussed earlier, it critically affected the patients' chances of transfer out of the criminally insane hospitals and was therefore evidently seen as an extremely important criteria of dangerousness by the psychiatrists at those hospitals. Secondly, of the several variables suggested and used as indicators of dangerousness, it is the one that seems to make most sense, a conclusion also reached by Rubin (1972).

Were those who had been convicted of committing a violent crime less likely to be released to the community? The answer is no. Those convicted of one or more violent crimes were not more likely to be still in the hospital at the time of our study. In fact, the data revealed that those who had been involved in violent crimes were released at a slightly higher rate than those with no convictions. Of those Baxstrom patients without a record of violent crimes, 48.6 percent were released; of those with one conviction, 62.3

percent were released; and of those who had several times been convicted of violent crimes, 57.6 percent were released. Thus, while this characteristic was so important to the psychiatrists in the criminally insane hospital, those in the civil hospital actually seemed to pay little attention to it in their release decisions.

In addition to a history of violent crime convictions, five other factors were examined. These were number of arrests prior to the Baxstrom offense, number of incarcerations prior to the Baxstrom offense, the nature of the Baxstrom offense, sex crime convictions, and the Legal Dangerousness Scale score. None of these factors strongly or significantly related to patient release. For example, while 64 percent of the patients who had never been arrested were released, almost 60 percent of those who were arrested 8 or more times were also released.

Thus, none of the major indicators of previous criminal activity employed were significantly related to the release status of the Baxstrom patients. Partially, the lack of association may be due to problems specific to the indicators. With regard to arrests, it is possible that the more dangerous criminals have the fewer arrests since the more serious the crime, the longer the sentence. This argument is supported by Glaser's (1964) conclusion that the lowest recidivism rates among felons are for murder and rape, while the highest rates are for economic offenses not involving violence. The violent crime conviction indicator may reflect more a defense attorney's ability at plea bargaining than actual behavior (Zimroth 1972). And lastly, the dangerousness scale also depends on official crime data with all their problems.

Possibly more important than these specific problems is a characteristic common to them all. All of these measures refer to alleged or actual behavior in the past. The median number of continuous years of hospitalization interrrupted by the *Baxstrom* decision for these patients was 15 years. Only about 20 percent of the patients had been institutionalized for less than 6 years, while more than 60 percent had been for more than 10 years. Thus, in most cases our indicators refer to behavior that occurred 10 or 20 years previous to our study.

If this argument has some validity, we would expect some more immediate indicator of dangerousness to better discriminate between those who are and are not released into the community. When we turn to in-hospital patient assaultiveness as our indicator, the data somewhat support the contention that the immediate behavior of the Baxstrom patients in the civil hospitals is a more important factor in release consideration than any of the others examined. Table 7-2 shows that the less assaultive their behavior in the hospital, the more likely they were to have been released. Of those who were not assaultive, almost 60 percent were subsequently released into the community. Of those who were assaultive, less than 40

Table 7-2
Release, By Assaultive Behavior in Civil Hospitals

Release Status	*Non-Assaultive* % (N)	*Assaultive* % (N)
Never Released	41.3 (62)	61.5 (16)
Ever Released	58.7 (88)	38.5 (10)
Total	100.0 (150)	100.0 (26)

$\chi^2 = 3.67$
N.S.
$\phi = .14$

percent were released. While this relationship is the strongest one found between any of our indicators of dangerousness and patient's release status, the relationship is a non-significant one. Also while assaultive patients were less likely to be released, there were only 26 patients in this group who were assaultive. Thus, while assaultive behavior is related, it helps little in our attempt to understand patient release.

This particular indicator of dangerousness, the recording of assaultiveness in hospital files, and the finding that it is not significantly related to release are very similar to the study mentioned earlier by Greenley (1972). He concludes that "these findings are somewhat surprising in the face of consistent claims by psychiatrists that release depends relatively heavily on the patient's dangerousness" (pp. 29-30). The findings just presented would seem even more surprising given the particular group of patients under study. These patients were part of that group known as the Baxstrom patients. This label carried with it many meanings. It meant that they were patients who had been housed in criminally insane hospitals, who had been arrested and in over half of the cases convicted of a violent crime, who had been denied transfer to the civil hospitals because they were too dangerous, who despite the lack of psychiatric approval were transferred to the civil hospitals as a result of the Supreme Court decision, and who because of the transfer caused so much anxiety among the staffs of the receiving civil hospitals. Yet all of this, evidently, made little difference in the actual release of the patients to the community. Our data reveal that none of the indicators of dangerousness, from past behaviors to in-hospital behavior, significantly distinguished between patients who were and were not released.

Apparently, once the initial fear subsided, the Baxstrom patients did lose the criminal part of the label, at least as far as the psychiatrists within the civil hospitals were concerned. Their criminal past was simply not seen as a significant criteria for release. The psychiatrists' decisions to release were influenced by some other factor than the patients' past and present dangerousness. The most likely alternative explanation is that if the decision were not made on the basis of dangerousness, then it must have been based on how well the patient was doing. Since the other major justification for the commitment and retention of individuals in civil hospitals is the care and treatment of patients seriously mentally ill, one would expect that those patients released are the ones who have improved. Before moving on to the examination of this expected relationship, however, we consider first the effect of the social and demographic characteristics of the patients on their release chances. This diversion occurs primarily because one of these characteristics is age.

The Effects of Patients' Social Characteristics on Release

It was evident in our chapter on transfer that the psychiatrists were influenced by the age of the patient in evaluating the suitability of an individual for residence in a civil hospital. Of those patients under the age of 40, about 38 percent had been transferred prior to the *Baxstrom* decision, while over 85 percent of patients aged 70 or more were sent to the civil hospitals with psychiatric approval. The older the patient, the more likely he would be seen as no longer dangerous and as no longer of potential threat to the staff and other patients in the less secure civil hospitals. Defining success for the patient as being allowed to move out of the criminally insane hospital, success was related to being old. Here, we are interested in whether the criteria related to success in the one system is also related to success in the system encompassed by the civil hospital. If the answer is yes, we would expect age to be related to release, with older patients being more likely to be released than the younger ones. Actually, data on regular civil patients indicates the opposite. The highest discharge rate has always been in the youngest age groups (Sall et al. 1966; Israel and Johnson 1956).

Our data revealed that for this group of patients there was very little age difference between those released and those never released. Those patients less than 50 were slightly more likely to be released than those over 50 (60 percent as compared to 50 percent), but the difference is neither large nor statistically significant. While older patients were more likely to be transferred to civil hospitals with psychiatric consent, the age of the patient, evidently, had no direct impact on psychiatrists' decisions to release patients to the community. As we shall see when we discuss the effect of length of hospitalization, age does, however, indirectly influence release.

Not only was age unrelated to release but all other social and demographic characteristics of the patients also failed to clearly distinguish those released from those denied release. The variables examined, in addition to age, were marital status, race, education, place of birth, occupational skills, and also physical condition at time of release. None of these helped to any great extent to explain why patients were or were not released.

Patient's Mental Illness and Release

While the potential dangerousness of the patient and the personal characteristics of the patient were unrelated, it would seem reasonable to assume that release would be related to the patient's mental illness. If he improved or got better while under treatment in the hospital, he would be released. The literature on this almost taken-for-granted relationship displays some contradictions. While some have stated that release depends on the type and severity of the patient's illness (Kaplan and Curtis 1961, pp. 8-12), others feel that this does not explain which patients are released. Robins (1954) has stated that not infrequently "patients are still hospitalized long after psychiatric improvement." Others (Clausen 1956; Greenblatt 1955) have noted that some released patients may be as ill as some of the patients still in the hospital. And while some studies (Barry and Fulkerson 1966; Bullard and Hoffman 1960) have found that patients who tested as more psychiatrically impaired were not released less rapidly, others (Greenley 1972) have found, at least, a slight relationship between impairment and timing of release. Hence, the precise effect of the patient's illness on release is uncertain and unclear.

A number of variables relating to the type and severity of the disorder were available to us. Data was on hand on the number of previous hospitalizations for mental disorders, the reason for admission to the criminally insane hospitals, and the length of time continuously hospitalized before transfer to the civil hospital. Also available was information on the diagnosis and the psychiatric evaluation of patients made by the psychiatrists at the criminally insane hospitals just prior to transfer. Lastly, we have data on factors related to patient performance in the civil hospitals, including whether and when their status was changed from involuntary to voluntary and whether they were granted honor cards. It was found that some of these variables were highly related to patient release. Let us first discuss the ones that were not.

Few of these patients, less than a fourth, had ever been hospitalized for mental disorders prior to their incarcerations in the hospitals for the criminally insane, and whether they had been was unrelated to release. How they entered was also of little importance. Incompetent defendants were slightly more likely to be released than the mentally ill inmates, but only slightly. With regard to diagnosis the only category of patients who differed greatly were those diagnosed as schizophrenic catatonic. They were much less likely to be released. However, only 18 of the 176 patients were so classified, and hence, diagnosis, overall, explained very little of the release decisions.

The other variable found to be unrelated to release was the granting of voluntary status to the patients. All of the Baxstrom patients when transferred to the civil hospital entered under orders of retention that held them in the hospital involuntarily. However, as the orders of retention expired, some patients were changed to voluntary status, while for others the orders were renewed. The changing of a patient's status to voluntary was taken as an indicator that the patient was improving and presented no major problems. This interpretation coincides with the notes accompanying these changes. For example, a psychiatrist writes in the hospital records: "This patient is up and about, clean and tidy in his personal habits and fairly well orientated. . . . He denies delusions and hallucinations. He helps occasionally in the cafeteria. . . . It is the feeling that this patient may be converted to a voluntary status." Almost a third of the patients were placed on voluntary status within the first 3 months. However, these patients were not more likely to be released than those granted voluntary status at a later date (56 percent as compared to 55 percent released). Nor were those ever granted voluntary status much more likely to be released as compared to those under orders of retention (56 percent and 54 percent respectively).

The remaining three variables were significantly related to patient release. These were length of time hospitalized in the criminally insane institutions before transfer, the psychiatric evaluation of their progress at the time of transfer, and the granting of honor cards on the basis of their condition within the civil hospital.

Perhaps the most surprising of the three is length of hospitalization. To a great extent, this variable is not appropriately placed in this set, since in this section we are considering those factors that impinge on the psychopathology of the individual, and while the length of hospitalization reflects partly the mental well-being of the patient, it also relates to the perceived dangerousness of the patients—that is, since their time had expired, if these patients were seen as mentally ill but not dangerous, they could have been transferred to civil hospitals before the *Baxstrom* decision. But they were not. Regardless of the appropriateness of it being included in this section, its relationship to release is unexpected. This is so primarily because we found age to be unimportant and age and length of hospitalization are so highly related.

With regard to length of hospitalization it was found, as shown in Table 7-3, that the longer a patient had remained in the criminally insane hospitals, the less likely he was to ever be released to the community. Of the patients who had been institutionalized for 5 years or less, 80 percent were released; 6 to 10 years, 68 percent; 11 to 20 years, 52 percent; 21 to 30 years,

Table 7-3
Release, by Length of Hospitalization Interrupted by Baxstrom Decision

	Length of Hospitalization				
Release Status	*0 to 5 Years* *% (N)*	*6 to 10 Years* *% (N)*	*11 to 20 Years* *% (N)*	*21 to 30 Years* *% (N)*	*31 or More Years* *% (N)*
Never Released	20.0 (7)	32.4 (11)	48.5 (32)	64.5 (20)	80.0 (8)
Ever Released	80.0 (28)	67.6 (23)	51.5 (34)	35.5 (11)	20.0 (2)
Total	100.0 (35)	100.0 (34)	100.0 (66)	100.0 (31)	100.0 (10)

$\chi^2 = 20.04$
$P < .001$
$\phi = .34$

36 percent; and for those hospitalized for more than 30 years, only 20 percent were ever released. This pattern is both consistent and statistically significant. The chances of someone who had only been retained for a few years were 8 out of 10 that he would be released, while for an individual who had been housed in the criminally insane hospital for more than 30 years, there was an 8 in 10 chance that he would never be released.

Length of hospitalization is also related to age. The relationship is not perfect. There were, for example, some patients over 60 who had been institutionalized for less than 10 years. But in general the relationship is strong. Thus, for example, while 78 percent of those hospitalized for 10 years or less were under 50, 94 percent of those hospitalized for more than 30 years were 60 or over. What this means is that while the age of the patient was not directly related to release, it was certainly related in an indirect way.

These findings have two ramifications. First of all, the longer patients were held in the criminally insane hospital, the less likely they were to be released once they had been transferred to the civil hospitals. Patients seen as too dangerous or too disturbed to be transferred soon after they entered the maximum security hospitals would be handicapped twice, once by being held in these hospitals for longer periods of time and, again because they were in so long, by being more likely to be seen as unsuitable for release to the community by the psychiatrists in the civil hospitals.

The other conclusion would seem to be that, to a great extent, what made a good patient and increased the patient's chances of success (transfer or release) in one setting was contrary to the criteria in the other. One of the two main factors related to whether patients were seen as suitable for transfer to civil hospitals was their age. The older they were, the more likely they were to be transferred. To a large degree, the older patients were those who had become old in the hospital as a result of lengthy hospitalization. But the longer they had been hospitalized in the criminally insane hospital, the less likely they were to be released from the civil hospital. Assuming that a main goal of both institutional systems is to move the patient out (i.e., reduce his dangerousness and/or mental illness to a point where he can return to society and become if not a productive member at least a non-disruptive one), then the two systems work against one another. In the first, the patient succeeds by becoming old; in the second, being old and the associated lengthy hospitalization leads to failure. Rather than the two systems overlapping to facilitate the movement of patients back to the community, they conflict, with the patient being the loser.

Why was the length of hospitalization such an important factor? What was there about being in the criminally insane hospitals for long periods that made patients less suitable for release? Part of the answer is supplied through an examination of another variable, the psychiatric evaluation

Table 7-4
Release, by Psychiatric Evaluation at Time of Transfer

	Psychiatric Evaluation	
Release Status	*Unimproved* *% (N)*	*Improved* *% (N)*
Never Released	53.4 (47)	21.4 (9)
Ever Released	46.6 (41)	78.6 (33)
Total	100.0 (88)	100.0 (42)

$\chi^2 = 11.86$
$P < .001$
$\phi = .30$

made of the patient. At the time of transfer, each patient was evaluated as unimproved, or improved, by the psychiatrists at the correctional hospitals.[a] This information was available in the hospital records for most of the patients in our study group. This data revealed that about two-thirds of the group were evaluated as unimproved, that the other third was improved, and that the evaluation was significantly related to release, as seen in Table 7-4. Of those evaluated as unimproved, less than half were ever released; of those evaluated as improved, almost 80 percent were released. How well they were mentally, as measured by this factor, did influence the release decision of the psychiatrists.

Psychiatric evaluation of patient's mental disorder was also highly correlated with length of hospitalization. While almost half of those who spent 10 years or less in the criminally insane hospital were evaluated as improved, only a fourth of those in for 11 to 20 years and 13 percent of those in 21 years or more were seen as improved. For every 10 years hospitalized, the chances of being seen as improved were almost halved. Hence, the longer a patient was hospitalized, the less likely he was to be seen as in an improved psychiatric condition, but it was those evaluated as improved who were the most likely to be released from the civil hospital. Part of the reason that length of hospitalization is so highly related to release is that it is correlated with psychiatric evaluation of the level of recovery of the patient, which, in turn, affects the release decision.

[a]We choose to use the psychiatric evaluation made at this point primarily because it was such a systematic and clear indicator. All patients just prior to their transfer to the civil hospitals were evaluated with regard to their overall condition and classified as unimproved or improved. Psychiatric evaluations of the patients made within the civil hospitals tended to be sporadic, less precise, and more difficult to summarize in a single meaningful indicator. Evaluations were also made of patients just prior to release from the civil hospitals. However, these were given only for those released and showed very little variation. Almost everyone released was evaluated as improved. Thus, we will rely throughout on the psychiatric evaluation made at the time of transfer.

The other variable examined in this section that played a part in influencing release was the patient's behavior in the civil hospital, as reflected by the granting of an honor card to a patient. An honor card is a pass given to hospital patients on a trust basis that enables them to move freely about the hospital grounds. Whether or not a patient is granted this privilege would seem to depend primarily on how he behaves. The patient characteristics conducive to the granting of an honor card are very similar to those related to patient's being placed on voluntary status. For example, from the hospitals clinical notes we abstracted the following note on a patient being considered for an honor card: "This patient continues to be well behaved, expresses no delusional ideas and wants to cooperate in all programs. He is somewhat quiet and slow but will participate in recreation, church services and probably home visits . . . and at this time the writer plans to give him honor card privileges."

The difference between placing patients on voluntary status and granting them honor cards is that the latter is a more serious and potentially harmful move. When a patient is placed on voluntary status, it does not mean that he can leave whenever he desires. To sign himself out, he must first make his feelings known. If for some reason the staff decides against his release, his status can be changed back to an order of retention before he has the legal right to leave. Honor cards on the other hand allow the patient to wander freely about the premises. Given the relatively low security of civil hospitals, it is not uncommon for patients to wander off or purposely leave the hospital grounds, which thus presents the potential of patients getting involved in problems, which, in turn, reflect back on the hospital. Thus, the granting of an honor card may, of the two, more accurately reflect how well the patient is doing or improving within the hospital. It is quite probable that the granting of an honor card is also indicative of the perceived dangerousness of the patient. The extent to which it indicates dangerousness rather than mental illness is difficult to determine. We consider it here primarily as a measure of illness, the more usual and overt meaning given to it, while at the same time realizing that it also is related, less obviously, but importantly, to the perceived dangerousness of the patient.

Information on the granting of honor cards was available for all but three of the patients in the study group. A few patients were classified in the no honor card group despite their having at one time been granted an honor card. These were individuals who, shortly after receiving their honor cards lost this privilege because of some event and never had it returned.

Of the 176 Baxstrom patients, slightly more than a third were granted honor cards. Over 75 percent of those with honor cards were eventually released, while only 44 percent of those not granted honor cards were ever released. This difference, which is shown in Table 7-5, is statistically

Table 7-5
Release, by Whether Patients Were Granted Honor Cards in Civil Hospitals

Release Status	*Patients Not Granted Honor Cards % (N)*	*Patients Granted Honor Cards % (N)*
Never Released	56.1 (64)	23.7 (14)
Ever Released	43.9 (50)	76.3 (45)
Total	100.0 (114)	100.0 (59)

$\chi^2 = 11.86$
$P < .001$
$\phi = .26$

significant. It was also found that the granting of honor cards was not correlated with the length of time patients had been hospitalized in the criminally insane hospital nor, interestingly, was it related to psychiatric evaluation of their level of mental impairment. Patients evaluated as improved were not significantly more likely to receive honor cards. Both factors were, however, related to release.

Are patients released because they improve or get well? The answer would seem to be yes. Not an unqualified yes, for as we shall see in the next section, there are other factors involved in the release decision. Yet, at least to a certain degree, the patient's mental illness, his behavior, and the perception of him by psychiatrists does play a part in determining whether he is released. As we have seen, some of the factors such as previous mental hospitalization and diagnosis proved to be unimportant. Yet, the psychiatric evaluation of the patient's condition and the granting of honor card privileges did differentiate between those released and those never released. Thus, those patients who were well enough to be judged as improved by the psychiatrists and well enough to be granted honor card privileges were, according to our data, much more likely to be released to the community. Clinical variables reflecting the degree of illness and the progress of the patient are important in determining who gets out.

The Effect of an Interested Family on Release Decisions

What of factors other than those related to the patient's illness and behavior? To what extent do factors external to the individual patient determine the fate of the patient? Many have argued that social contingencies do affect the course of a patient career, in general, and the decision surrounding his release, in particular. The non-clinical factor suggested as most relevant in the release decision is the influence of family members—that is, the release decision may depend not so much on what the patient does as on what other people do, particularly the patient's family. Sall et al. (1966), for example, in their review of findings on release decisions conclude that patients who are and are not released can be distinguished primarily by social variables, particularly the presence of an interested family. The only systematic attempt to test this relationship is the research conducted by Greenley (1972) mentioned earlier. In his study of 125 state mental hospital patients, Greenley found family wishes concerning release to be highly related to length of hospitalization. This relationship held regardless of whether or not the patient was seen as dangerous, highly psychiatrically impaired, or in need of further hospitalization.

Did the presence or absence of interested family members affect the release chances of our sample of Baxstrom patients? Rather than rely on a single measure of family interest, we abstracted from the hospital notes information that allowed us to examine this factor in several ways. First of all, we gathered information for each patient on whether a family member had expressed any interest in the patient, particularly with regard to any expressed desire to have the patient released. In addition to their desires, we were also interested in their actual behavior and therefore collected data on family contact with the patient. This information was grouped into 6-month periods, since while clinical notes were sometimes entered more frequently, they were made for each patient at least once every 6 months. The data abstracted included type of contact, which was divided into no contact, contact that took place with the patient in the hospital (letters, telephone calls, or visits), and contact that indicated that the family was not only willing to see the patient but also willing to care for the patient for short periods of time, usually weekend home visits. Another indicator used was the frequency of contact, defined as the number of 6-month periods in which contact occurred. Because this basic rate could also be affected by the length of time each patient was hospitalized, it was transformed into a ratio of number of 6-month periods in which contact occurred to number of such periods the patient was hospitalized. The last indicator of extent of family interest utilized was the timing of contact on the assumption that families more interested in the patient would tend to seek contact with the patient soon after transfer to the civil hospital rather than allow a year or more to pass before attempting a contact.

When the data were examined for a possible relationship between these indicators of family interest and patient release, it was found that for our sample having an interested family did increase a patient's chance of ever being released. Each of the indicators proved to significantly distinguish between those who were and were not released. Table 7-6 shows that of those patients whose family had expressed interest in the patient and his

Table 7-6
Release, by Expressed Family Interest in Patient

Release Status	*No Expressed Interest % (N)*	*Expressed Family Interest % (N)*
Never Released	56.6 (73)	11.1 (5)
Ever Released	43.4 (56)	88.9 (40)
Total	100.0 (129)	100.0 (45)

$\chi^2 = 27.90$
$P < .001$
$\phi = .40$

release, almost 90 percent were released as compared to 43 percent of those who lacked interested family. Similar patterns were found with the other variables. With regard to contact, for example, it was found that fewer of those with no family contact were released as compared to those who had some contact with family, whether through letters, telephone calls, or visits, and both groups were released at a lower rate than those who had family in the community willing to sponsor them for short home visits. Of this last group, 82 percent were eventually released.

Those patients who had families that were interested enough to contact the patient soon after the patient arrived at the civil hospital and consistently maintained contact with the patient were also much more likely to be released. Thus, 82 percent of those who experienced contact in the first 6 months were released, as compared to 65 percent of those who had no family contact until after they had been hospitalized for 6 months. The ratio of 6-month periods of contact to 6-month periods hospitalized showed that the more consistent the families were in contacting the patients, the more likely the patients' release. As a matter of fact, of the patients whose family contacted them every or almost every period, between 75 and 100 percent were released.

Thus, all of these variables are consistently and strongly related to release. Having a family interested in the patient seems to affect greatly the likelihood of his being released. Not only what the patient does but what others do also seems to influence the release decision.

The Relationship between the Relevant Variables and Release

From the large number of possibly relevant factors examined we have found four to be significantly related to patient release. The four are the length of time patients were housed in the criminally insane hospitals before transferred by the *Baxstrom* decision, the psychiatric evaluation of the patient's illness at transfer, the granting of honor cards in the civil hospital, and the presence of interested family members. Next, we attempt to analyze these factors and their relationship to each other as well as to release in order to further clarify the processes involved.

Table 7-7 shows the relationships of the four factors with release and with each other. First of all, it will be noted that each of the four variables are related to release. All four are significant at the .001 level.

This table can also aid in clarifying the relationship between release and the presence of interested family. One possible explanation for the importance of family interest for release, given that psychiatric evaluation has also been found highly related, is that the latter leads to the former—that is, families are interested in patients who are well, as reflected by the psychiatric evaluation of improved, and families are less likely to be interested in those patients who seem to be doing poorly. If this were the case, the presence of an interested family rather than independently affecting release would actually be related to release only because of its association with an improved psychiatric status. As can be seen in Table 7-7, this is not the case. Psychiatric evaluation and the presence of interested family members are not significantly related and, therefore, influence the release decision independently of one another. Those patients evaluated as improved are not more likely to have family members express interest in them than patients seen as unimproved psychiatrically.

The same line of argument can be used with regard to the granting of honor cards. There is a slightly significant association between this factor and the presence of interested family. Did the patient's mental progress as indicated by the granting of an honor card influence family members to be more willing to express interest in the patient and his release? The data indicates that if there is any major pattern, it is in the opposite direction. Patients with interested family were more likely to receive honor cards than was the opposite to occur. For example, of those who were granted honor cards, 37 percent also had interested family, while of those with interested family, 49 percent were also granted an honor card. Furthermore, in comparing when the first contact occurred with when the honor card was first granted, the indications were once again in the same direction. Approximately, 30 percent of those whose first contact occurred during the 7-to-12-month period had been previously granted an honor card. On the other hand over 45 percent of those who were granted an honor card during the same period had been contacted by relatives in the previous 6-month period. These findings suggest that the slight relationship between these two factors is probably due to the tendency to grant honor cards to patients with interested family and not a tendency of families to be more interested if the patient is doing well.

Table 7-7
Associations between Factors Related to Patient Release

	Associations (φ)				
	Patient Release	*Length of Hosp.*	*Family Interest*	*Psychiatric Evaluation*	*Honor Card*
Length of Hospitalization	.34[c]				
Family Interest	.40[c]	.29[b]			
Psychiatric Evaluation	.30[c]	.29[b]	.16		
Honor Card	.26[c]	.06	.18[a]	.04	

[a]$P < .05$
[b]$P < .01$
[c]$P < .001$

The presence of interested family members does not appear to be influenced by the patient's condition. It is, however, related to the length of time the patient had been institutionalized in the criminally insane hospitals. Looking at those who had been hospitalized for 5 years or less, 6 to 10 years, 11 to 20 years, and 21 years and more, the percentage of patients with interested family were as follows: 49 percent, 32 percent, 20 percent, and 12 percent. Those who were hospitalized for 5 years or less were four times as likely as those hospitalized for more than 20 years to have someone in the community still interested in them. Why such a strong relationship exists between these two variables is not difficult to understand. The longer the period of hospitalization, the more likely it is that relationships with friends and relatives would be discontinued because of death, geographic mobility, waning interest, and so on. Even 5 years is a long time, and what is remarkable is that there were so many interested family members. Length of hospitalization then is important in two ways. First, those hospitalized for longer periods of time are more likely to be unimproved psychiatrically. Secondly, the longer the hospitalization, the more likely that any family or friends the patient may have had would lose interest, forget about the

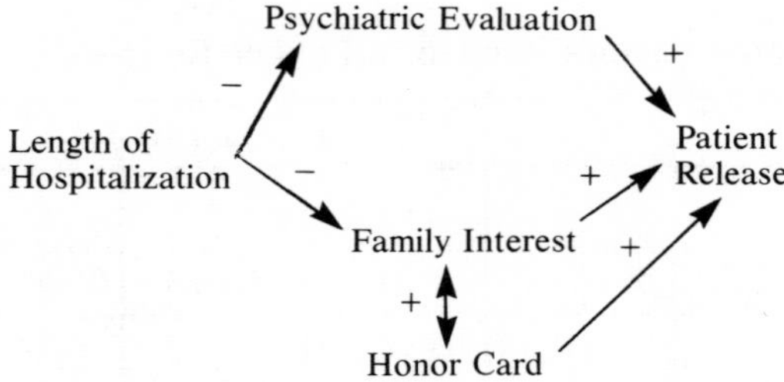

Figure 7-1. Relationships between Relevant Factors and Patient Release.

patient, move away, or die. And an evaluation of unimproved and a lack of interested family members both were highly correlated with never being released from the civil hospital. Graphically, the relationships between these four variables and release as revealed through our analysis are shown in Figure 7-1. In the figure, inverse relationships are designated by a minus sign; direct relationships by a plus sign.

The Relative Importance of the Variables

Which of the four factors was most important in influencing patient release? Were clinical factors relating to the patient's illness more important than the factors external to the patient, such as the interest of his family? To answer these questions, we began by examining the relationship between each variable and release controlling for the other variables one at a time.

The variable that displayed the weakest relationship was the granting of honor cards. Where any of the other three factors were operative, the relationship between having an honor card and being released disappeared. If a patient had been hospitalized for less than 10 years, had been evaluated as improved or had an interested family member, the presence or absence of an honor card made no difference for the patient's release chances. In such cases, the other factor would dominate. Thus, the importance of an honor card was restricted to those patients hospitalized for more than 10 years, who were unimproved and lacked any interested family.

To evaluate the relative importance of the remaining three variables we related each variable to release, while controlling for the other two. This information is presented in Table 7-8. The procedures used to measure their relative effects on release involve comparing the average percentage difference of each variable controlling on the others. This technique, discussed by Rosenberg (1968, pp. 169-178), compares the differential impact of variables and through a comparison of average percentage differences allows one to decide which factor is exerting the greatest influence.

Table 7-8
Relative Influence of Related Factors on Patient Release

	Length of Hospitalization							
	0-10 Years				*11 Years or More*			
Psychiatric Evaluation	*Unimproved*		*Improved*		*Unimproved*		*Improved*	
Expressed Family Interest	*NO E.F.I. (a)*	*E.F.I. (b)*	*NO E.F.I. (c)*	*E.F.I. (d)*	*NO E.F.I. (a¹)*	*E.F.I. (b¹)*	*NO E.F.I. (c¹)*	*E.F.I. (d¹)*
Percentage of Patients Ever Released	47.4	70.0	84.6	100.0	34.0	88.9	50.0	100.0
(Patients Released/ Total Patients)	(9/19)	(7/10)	(11/13)	(11/11)	(17/50)	(8/9)	(6/12)	(4/4)

Of the remaining three variables, the one that displayed the least direct effect is length of hospitalization. It does make some difference. Expecting a higher release rate for those in the 0-to-10-year group, we find that in two cases, (compare cell a with a^1, and c with c^1), the relationship holds; in a third, the rate is the same (d with d^1); and in the last (b with b^1), the relationship is in the opposite direction of what was expected. Thus, its direct impact is neither strong nor consistent. It is, however, important since it indirectly influences the pattern of release through its impact on the remaining two factors.

The length of hospitalization drastically alters the effect of psychiatric evaluation and interested family. The data showed that controlling for length of hospitalization the relationship between psychiatric evaluation and release remained strong for those hospitalized 10 years or less, but was severely weakened for those hospitalized over 10 years. The exact opposite occurred in the relationship between the presence of interested family members and release. For the lesser hospitalized group, psychiatric evaluation is more important. For those hospitalized for more than 10 years, it makes little difference when compared to the effect of having interested family members. This can also be seen in Table 7-8.

In all cases, higher release rates are experienced by patients with interested family. The effect of this variable is lessened, however, for those hospitalized 10 years or less. Comparing cell a with b, and c with d, we find an average difference of 19 percent (47.4 − 70.0 = 22.6; 84.6 − 100.0 = 15.4; average of 22.6 + 15.4 is 19). When we calculate the same figure using cells $a^1 - b^1$ and $c^1 - d^1$, the average percentage difference is found to be 52.5 percent. Thus, controlling for psychiatric evaluation, the presence of interested family is much more important for those who have been hospitalized for longer periods of time.

On the other hand, while in all cases those evaluated as improved were released at a higher rate than those seen as unimproved, psychiatric evaluation was most important for those hospitalized for a shorter period of time. For this group, the average effect of psychiatric evaluation, controlling for family interest is 33.6 percent (47.4 − 84.6 = 37.2; 70.0 − 100.0 = 30.0; average of 37.2 + 30.0 is 33.6). This compares to an average difference of 13.6 percent for those hospitalized longer than 10 years. Thus, the impact of the two main factors, psychiatric evaluation and expressed family interest, is modified by the length of hospitalization experienced by the patients.

Overall, which of these two factors has the greatest impact? If we compare the average percentage difference of each regardless of length of hospitalization, it is found that the presence of interested family has the greater influence on release. The average overall effect of psychiatric evaluation, controlling for family interest is 23.6 percent (the average of

33.6 and 13.6), while the average effect of having an interested family, controlling for psychiatric evaluation, is 35.8 percent (the average of 19.0 and 52.2). Thus, of the two, the presence of interested family members appears to be the more important in accounting for the release of the patients. It more clearly and more strongly differentiated patients who were or were not eventually released.

What of the combined effect of these two factors? As can be seen in Table 7-8, regardless of length of hospitalization, all patients who were evaluated as improved and had interested family members were released (cells d and d[1]). There were *no* exceptions. If a patient had both of these in his favor, he was released. From this level, the release rate decreases for the other groups but never drops lower than 70.0 percent for patients with interested families and never lower than 50.0 percent for those evaluated as improved. The lowest proportion released is found to be experienced by those patients who fall on the negative side of all three factors; they have been hospitalized for more than 10 years, they have been evaluated as unimproved and they have no family interested in them. Within this group (cell a[1]) only 34.0 percent of the patients were ever released. This is also the group in which the granting of an honor card influenced the release decision with 10 of the 17 released having been granted an honor card. Thus, of all the patients released, only 7 did not have at least one of the four factors in their favor.

Summary

There are several important conclusions to be drawn from the findings presented in this chapter. First, despite the fact that these were patients who had been institutionalized in criminally insane hospitals and who had been transferred to civil hospitals without psychiatric approval, many adjusted well enough to be released to the community. Of the 176 living Baxstrom patients, 98 were released to the community during the four and a half years of our study, with almost half of those being released within the first year. When we compared the release rate of these Baxstrom patients to that of the pre-Baxstrom patients, we found that a higher proportion of Baxstrom patients had been released.

The explanation of this finding was related to a second conclusion drawn from this chapter. The criteria used by psychiatrists in one system to evaluate patients conflicted with those employed in the other setting. In Chapter 5, our analysis indicated that age and the presence or absence of a violent crime conviction were the two factors that best distinguished the Baxstrom from the pre-Baxstrom patients. The implication of this was that the psychiatrists in the correctional hospital system were evaluating older, less violent patients as no longer in need of special security and as more likely to succeed in the civil hospitals.

If these same two criteria were used by the psychiatrists in the civil hospitals, more pre-Baxstrom than Baxstrom patients would have been released, since as a group they were both older and had fewer violent crime convictions. In this chapter, we found that they were not and that neither of these two factors were highly related to release. Instead, we found other factors to be related to whether civil hospital psychiatrists saw patients as no longer in need of care and likely to succeed in the community. One of the main characteristics of these patients was that they had been institutionalized in the criminally insane hospitals for fewer years. The longer patients were housed as criminally insane patients, the less likely they were to be released to the community from the civil hospital.

The significance of this finding is that age and length of hospitalization are related. Those patients hospitalized for longer periods of time were more likely to be older, and conversely, older patients were more likely to have been hospitalized longer. Rather than similar criteria, then, the psychiatrists in these two settings were evaluating patients using conflicting criteria. A patient in a correctional hospital would be more likely to be granted a transfer to a civil hospital if he were old. But as an older patient and therefore probably as one who had been hospitalized for a long time, he would be less likely to be seen as someone to be released from the civil hospital. This conflict between these two settings increases the difficulty of patient movement. Younger patients are not likely to be transferred to the civil hospital. Older patients are, but are then not likely to be released from the civil hospital. The *Baxstrom* decision, as we have seen, helped to break this pattern by leading to the transfer of patients from the correctional hospitals when their criminal sentences expired rather than when they got old.

The last major implication of our findings in this chapter is that social contingencies external to the patient may have as much, if not more, influence on what happens to these patients than estimations of the patient's illness or dangerousness. We found that length of hospitalization affected patient release through its impact on two other variables, psychiatric evaluation and the presence of interested family. Patients least hospitalized were the ones most likely to be evaluated as in an improved mental state and were the ones most likely to have family interested in them and their release. In addition, their adjustment within the hospital as indicated by whether or not they were granted an honor card also affected their chances for release.

Of the four factors, psychiatric evaluation and family interest were most directly and strongly related to patient release. Their combined effect was overwhelming. All of the patients who were both seen as improved and had interested family were released regardless of prior criminal histories, age, or assaultiveness in the hospital.

In examining the relative effects of these variables, it was found that the single most important factor for the release of these patients was the presence of an interested family in the community. This finding is very similar to Greenley's (1972) that family desires are closely related to the timing of release. It is also the strongest example encountered in our work of the importance of social factors for understanding what happens to mental patients, an issue we raised in Chapter 1. More important for their release than how well they were mentally, how well they were adjusting within the civil hospital or any other consideration, including those related to their dangerousness, was whether there was an interested family.

There are several possible explanations for the importance of this factor. Many of them revolve around the idea that psychiatrists respond to family desires as a means of coping with their jobs and avoiding potential difficulties and family pressures. Another major explanation is that psychiatrists tend to perceive the patient's chances of succeeding in the community as much better if there is a family available to support and help reintegrate the patient into community life.

A clear example of this view is found in the transcript of the May 1966 trial held to determine whether Johnnie Baxstrom was suffering from mental illness and should be detained in the civil hospital. In the trial, a psychiatrist in response to an expression of concern as to what would happen if Baxstrom were released replied:

> I think one of the outstanding things about him that I noticed in the record is that he has a person who is interested in him and who has maintained contact with him for many years, and has been a tremendous support to him, sent him money and written to him regularly and has offered her home to him. This is his sister in Baltimore. And as he describes the situation to me, his fifty-two or fifty-three year old sister, who happens to be married to an eighty-two year old invalid who owns this property and needs some help, is willing to make a home for him, it seems to me that the record does show that he's got this stable force in the community to go to, and I sincerely believe that this would be a good way to start his rehabilitative return to the community.

With our data, the possibility that patients with interested family adjust better in the community can be examined. In the next chapter, we continue our study of the Baxstrom patients by examining their activity in the community. Of particular interest to us will be two questions. How many patients adjusted well enough in the community to avoid rehospitalization or rearrest and to what extent the availability of interested family and other factors distinguished between those who remained in the community and those who did not?

8 The Patients in the Community

So far, we have traced the careers of the Baxstrom patients from the criminally insane hospitals through their release from the civil hospitals. The last focus of our study concerns their activity in the community. Needless to say, they had little in their favor. They were individuals who had been labelled criminally insane. As a result of the application of this dual stigma, they had been removed from society and housed in correctional hospitals for an average of 15 years and then due to the efforts of Johnnie Baxstrom transferred to civil hospitals. The cumulative effect of all this can partially be seen in the fact that at the end of our study, four and a half years after their being transferred to the civil hospitals, 78 of them —over 40 percent—had never been released from the hospitals.

In the chapter on research methodology, we detailed the procedures used to follow-up released patients. Of the men in our sample, 73 had been released to the community, but complete information as to their whereabouts in October 1970 was lacking. The purpose of the follow-up was to complete our information and to verify already existing information. We were able to locate and obtain information on 61 of these 73 patients. Most of those who had been out of contact were still in the community (49 of the 61 located). Of those no longer in the community 5 had died, 5 had been rehospitalized, and 2 were incarcerated at the end of our study period.

With regard to the 12 unlocated patients, it is quite probable that they were also residing in the community. We were unable to discover any incidents of rehospitalization in New York or 9 other states examined nor any incidents involving criminal activities as reflected by the absence of any information on them in the NYSIIS sheets. Thus, it is likely that all 12 were still in the community. Also, our lack of information of their precise locations at the end of our study does not mean that no information was available on them.

In most cases what is indicated is that at some point after release and before October 1970, we lost contact with them. Actually, in almost half of the cases (5 of 12), we have data on these patients to the year 1969. Overall, information is available on each of them for more than 26 months, almost 12 of which is while in the community. If we assume these 12 are in the community, the location of our entire sample of 199 patients at the end of our study is as shown in Table 8-1. This summary table shows that almost half of the original group were either still in or back in a mental hospital,

Table 8-1
Location of Entire Baxstrom Patient Sample on October 31, 1970

Location	*N*	*%*
Mental Hospital	98	49.2
Community	68	34.2
Dead	28	14.1
Matteawan and Dannemora	3	1.5
Correctional Facility	2	1.0
Total	199	100.0

over a third were living in the community, 28 had died over the four-and-a-half-year period and the remaining 5 were either in prisons or a criminally insane hospital.

More important, for our purposes, than their location at the termination of our study period is what happened to them during these four and a half years. In the last chapter, we presented information on the timing of release for these patients. Those data show that almost half of the released patients could have potentially remained in the community for more than 3 years and over three-fourths of them for more than 2 years. How well did these patients fare during these years in the community? In answering this question, we focus on several related issues—their dangerousness, their overall level of success in remaining in the community, and the relevance of various factors for explaining patient adjustment in the community.

Dangerous Behavior Following Release

Our first question was how dangerous were these patients once placed in the community. We have already seen that their activity in the hospital indicated a low level of violent assaultive behavior. Yet, they did have a history of engaging in criminal activities, some violent. They had displayed non-normative behavior to the extent that they were evaluated as mentally ill. They were the patients housed in the hospitals for the criminally insane who were denied transfer by the psychiatrists. And furthermore, their release to the community for the first time in years removed the constraints and restrictions imposed by institutions and their staffs. Did they live up to the stereotype of those labeled as the criminally insane? Were they dangerous?

In answering these questions, we encounter the same difficulties raised earlier with regard to the definition, measurement, and reliability of the concept of dangerousness. As before, in keeping with other research, we rely on arrests, convictions, and types of crime as indicators of dangerous-

Table 8-2
Offenses of Convicted Released Baxstrom Patients

Type of Conviction	*Number of Counts*
Public Intoxication	3
Disorderly Conduct	3
Vagrancy	3
Possession of Hypodermic Instruments	4
Petit Larceny	1
Driving Stolen Car	1
Grand Larceny	1
Robbery, Second Degree	1
Assault, Third Degree	1
Total	18

(N = 11)

ness. For the 98 released patients, data is available on criminal activity from the NYSIIS and our follow-up. While it is probable that misdemeanors were not regularly reported to NYSIIS, all felonies were.

Looking first at arrest data, it was found that of the 98 patients released from the civil hospitals, 20 were subsequently arrested. For these 20 patients, there was a total of 45 arrests: 11 patients each had 1 arrest; 2 patients, 2 arrests; 4 patients, 3 arrests; and 3 others, 4, 5, and 9 arrests, respectively. These 45 arrests involved 53 charges—31 misdemeanors and 22 felony charges.

Thus, about 20 percent of those released to the community were subsequently arrested and charged with violating the law. Of the 20 individuals arrested, 11 were subsequently convicted of committing the crime. Table 8-2 shows the type of crimes these 11 patients were convicted of and the number of convictions for each crime. In most of the cases, conviction was for minor offenses such as public intoxication, disorderly conduct, or vagrancy. Two of the convictions involved felonies. These were grand larceny and robbery, second degree. Only this last crime and assault would be classified as violent crimes of (potential) danger to others.

Of the 98 patients released, about one-fifth were subsequently arrested, about one-tenth subsequently convicted, and in only 2 of the 98 cases was there a conviction for a violent crime. Clearly, then, these patients were not very dangerous. This conclusion rests not only on this criminal data but on the entire sequence of data collected and presented thus far. While these patients were denied transfer because of their dangerousness, all of their activity following the forced transfer indicates that the label was inappropriate. The Baxstrom patients did not display the assaultive violent behavior expected. Few were assaultive within the hospital. Only a very few behaved in such a way as to necessitate their return to the criminally insane hospitals. The hospitals released many of them. Finally, once in the community, as we have just seen, their behavior reflected by the crime data indicated that few were violent.

The cumulative effect of this information can lead to but one interpretation—the Baxstrom patients were not very dangerous.

Mad or Bad: Confusion Resulting from the Dual Label

The whole body of evidence examined clearly indicates that these patients did not behave in the violent, dangerous way anticipated by many and implied by their label of criminally insane. Yet, the last set of data on arrests and convictions were found to be inadequate. Despite the heavy reliance on them as indicators of dangerousness in the literature, we found that for our sample, these statistics were very poor indicators of dangerous behavior. We suspect that the same holds true for other populations as well, although the extent of distortion may be less.

There are, of course, the well-known and documented problems of official statistics (Doleschal 1972) and the difficulties caused by the impact of plea bargaining on conviction data (Zimroth 1972). These problems were complicated in our study by the apparent confusion as to whether to label a given act a crime or illness. The fact that similar behavior may for some individuals lead to hospitalizations while others are arrested has been noted in the literature (Levine 1970). This confusion was obvious in our work in several ways. As we have seen, there were 20 individuals arrested subsequent to their release from the civil hospitals. *All* 20 were, however, also rehospitalized at some time. There was no patient who was only arrested without also at some point being rehospitalized. In many cases, in fact, rehospitalization was a consequence of an arrest. If we look at the 20 arrestees' first incidents following release, these patterns become apparent. Of the 20, 7 were rehospitalized initially and only later, following a second release, were they arrested. Nine were initially arrested, and their crimes were handled exclusively in the criminal justice system. Later, an unrelated event led to re-entry into a mental hospital for each of these 9 patients. Finally, in 4 cases, individuals moved through both systems as a result of a single incident; their arrests resulted in rehospitalization.

The behavioral event, itself, does not appear to be the critical factor in determining who is rehospitalized, who is arrested first and then rehospitalized, and who is arrested and dealt with without being referred to a mental hospital. For example, an individual who while riding on a subway began breaking windows "to get air" was rehospitalized without ever being arrested. Another individual who walked down the street kicking and smashing cars was arrested and then hospitalized. One individual walking around homeless and confused was charged with vagrancy, fined, and sentenced to 30 days in jail, while another who broke up the house and threatened his family with a knife was rehospitalized without ever being arrested or charged with a crime. Some relatively minor disturbance then might lead to an arrest and conviction. Other more violent incidents, on the other hand, frequently led to rehospitalization.

Our conclusion from these data was that arrest records and other crime statistics are extremely poor indicators of dangerousness. It appears that when an individual is known at the time of his apprehension, or becomes known after the arrest, as an ex-mental patient, he is often rehospitalized rather than booked. At the same time, certain behaviors that might normally be overlooked (such as sleeping on a park bench) are a cause for arrest or rehospitalization when an individual is known as an ex-mental patient. Thus, police statistics concerning the criminal activity of these patients, and perhaps all ex-mental patients, may seriously underestimate the most serious behavior while overestimating the less serious behavior. Quite clearly for our purposes, it is inappropriate to label someone as dangerous who has been arrested and perhaps convicted of a charge of vagrancy, while labelling as non-dangerous someone who is destructive, violent, and threatening because he was rehospitalized for his actions rather than arrested.

In an attempt to correct this problem, we decided to focus on the behavior rather than on the consequences of the behavior. Some support for this strategy already existed in the literature on the dangerousness of the mentally ill. Giovannoni and Gurel (1967) supplement arrest reports by including potential offenses that were not known to the police but conceded by the respondent to the interviewers. Levine (1970) used as his measure of criminal activity the results of an evaluation made by a county attorney as to whether the incident leading to rehospitalization violated the law. Unlike the first study, we are unwilling to rely at all on arrest statistics, and unlike both, we are unwilling to use all violations of the law as our measure. For example, in the Levine study, the crime most frequently claimed to have been committed was disturbing the peace and disorderly conduct. We do not see such acts as dangerous. Rather, in an attempt to determine as accurately as possible the exact incidence of violent and dangerous behavior, we coded all behavior for which information was available. This included both behavior for which patients were arrested and for which they were hospitalized. Of course, some dangerous and law-violating incidents still remain unknown. What we have then is all behavior that became known to the officials in the criminal and mental health systems. And it is this behavior that was then categorized into dangerous or non-dangerous behavior.

Our task in the remainder of the chapter is, therefore, evaluating the success of the Baxstrom patients in the community by examining how many were rehospitalized, how many were rearrested, and how many actually exhibited dangerous behavior.

We first present information related to rehospitalization, including a description of how we classified precipitating incidents. Next, we analyze the characteristics of the patients who were arrested and those not arrested, and we discuss the types of behavior leading to arrest. Then, using the information from the two preceding sections, we address, once again, the issue of dangerousness. From this, we refer back to the issues of rehospitalization and success in remaining in the community. This ordering of our presentation is dictated both by a need to first present the information used in classifying dangerous behavior and by the flow of analysis that proved to most clearly designate the significant variables.

Patients Rehospitalized

Of the 98 Baxstrom patients ever released from the civil hospitals during the four and a half years of our study, 44 were readmitted to a mental hospital. The remaining 54 were never rehospitalized.

The length of time patients remained in the community before being readmitted is reported in Table 8-3. This information is presented in relationship to timing of release. The data indicate that the largest group of rehospitalizations occurred during the first 6 months following release. Overall, approximately 45 percent of patients ever readmitted were rehospitalized within the first 6 months. While this percentage varies with timing of release, regardless of how long they were hospitalized before release, a large proportion of readmissions occurred during this first period.

Table 8-3 also indicates that patients released earlier did not do any better or worse in avoiding rehospitalization. Although a higher proportion of patients released within 6 months were readmitted (65.5 percent), as compared to those released between 7 and 12 months (23.5 percent) or those released after 2 years (16.7 percent), the proportion returning from the group released during the second year is almost as high (60.7 percent). Because of this fluctuation, the data do not support a conclusion with regard to differences between early and late releases relating to successfully remaining in the community.

Furthermore, an analysis of the relationship between various factors and length of stay in the community prior to rehospitalization revealed no significant differences. We classified the 20 patients readmitted within 6 months of their release as the early returnees and the remaining 24 as late returnees and then compared the two groups using the sets of variables

Table 8-3
Length of Time Hospitalized Prior to Release, by Length of Time in the Community Prior to Rehospitalization

Length of Time Hospitalized Prior to Release	*Length of Time in the Community Prior to Rehospitalization*					
	0 to 6 Months	*7 to 12 Months*	*13 to 24 Months*	*25 or More Months*	*Never Rehospitalized*	*Total*
0 to 6 months	8	2	3	6	10	29
7 to 12 months	3	0	1	0	13	17
13 to 24 months	6	2	8	1	11	28
25 or more	3	1	0	0	20	24
Total	20	5	12	7	54	98

already established. These variables included patients' social and demographic characteristics, patients' past criminal behavior, prior mental illness, and such factors associated with the last hospitalization as psychiatric evaluation and family interest. In no instance did the data indicate a significant difference between early and late returnees.

In addition to an initial readmission, 17 of the 44 patients were rehospitalized more than once following their release. Specifically, 27 patients each had 1 readmission; 9 patients had 2 instances of readmission; 4 patients, 3; 2 patients, 4; 1 patient, 6; and 1 patient during our follow-up period was rehospitalized a total of 11 times. From the clinical and readmission notes contained in each patient folder, we were able to abstract information on each of the total 82 readmissions. The type of admission, manner of arrival, and precipitating incident for each was noted.

Type of admission refers to whether the patient was admitted voluntarily or involuntarily. For the most part the former included individuals admitted as voluntary patients, while the latter includes those admitted under involuntary civil orders. In a few cases patients voluntarily admitted themselves to a non-state facility but were transferred under involuntary orders to a state civil hospital. Such cases were defined as voluntary since the initial impetus for rehospitalization clearly stemmed from the individual's desires and not from some external force.

Manner of arrival indicates the individual, individuals, or agency responsible for bringing the patient to the attention of the hospital. The various alternatives were collapsed into the following three categories: (1) the individual himself, (2) the police or courts, and (3) the residual category of "others," including the patient's family, members of the community, and such institutions as hospitals and social service centers.

The third piece of information categorized was the incident precipitat-

Table 8-4
Information on Type of Admission, Manner of Arrival, and Precipitating Incident for 82 Cases of Rehospitalization

	First Readmission (%) (N = 44)	*Subsequent Readmission (%) (N = 38)*
Type of Admission		
Voluntary	37.5	72.2
Involuntary	62.5	27.8
Manner of Arrival		
Self	30.6	59.5
Police	55.6	29.7
Other	13.9	10.8
Precipitating Incident		
Dangerous Behavior	33.3	13.5
Socially Unacceptable Behavior	30.8	24.3
Illness Requires Treatment	35.9	62.2

ing readmission. In coding these data, the categories developed by Smith et al. (1963) were utilized. Thus, the precipitating incident was classified as dangerous behavior, socially unacceptable behavior, or as evidence of mental illness requiring treatment.

The figures presented in Table 8-4 describe the circumstances surrounding the 82 readmissions. Looking at the first readmission following release, we find that over 60 percent of the patients were admitted involuntarily, that more than half of them were brought to the hospital by the police, and that the behavior leading to rehospitalization was almost evenly divided over the three categories. The distribution of patients in the three categories of precipitating incident are extremely similar to those found by Hilles (1970). While Hilles employs different categories in her study, she regroups them in order to compare them with Smith's work, and thus they are also comparable with our figures. For the three categories of dangerous behavior, socially unacceptable behavior, and illness requiring treatment, our figures are 33.3 percent, 30.8 percent, and 35.9 percent, respectively. Hilles reports very similar percentages of 33.8 percent, 36.4 percent, and 29.9 percent.

The three pieces of information presented in Table 8-4 are to a large extent interrelated. Two patterns, in particular, occurred with a high frequency. Many patients voluntarily admitted themselves because of an illness they felt required treatment. On the other hand, another significant group was admitted to the hospital involuntarily after having been picked up by the police for dangerous or socially unacceptable behavior. To a large extent, the repeated readmissions of a few patients is responsible for the variation obvious in the table between first and subsequent readmissions. Three patients alone accounted for 15 similar rehospitalizations in which they voluntarily admitted themselves for illness, which thus inflates these three categories in the data on subsequent readmissions. For our purposes, what is most important about the findings is the fact that at least some of the readmissions involved violent behavior.

Rearrested Patients and Rehospitalized Patients

We have seen thus far, that of the 176 patients in our sample, 98 were released from the civil hospitals during the period of study. Of the 98, 44 were rehospitalized at least once, and of these 44, 20 were also arrested for violating the law. Each of the 20 individuals arrested also experienced rehospitalization. This finding, plus the absence of notable differences between behavior leading to arrest and that leading to rehospitalization, caused us to suspect the value of this distinction. Instead of two distinct types of behavior, it appears that some patients behaved in bizarre, unacceptable ways and depending on such circumstances as who was called or the particular manifestation being displayed by the individual at the moment, patients might either be arrested or rehospitalized. The point is not that these people did not violate the law. Some certainly did. Rather, the point is that some of their behavior was seen as criminal and was handled as such, while in other cases, identical or extremely similar behavior was seen as evidence of illness and led to rehospitalization. To automatically include all behavior leading to arrest, or to automatically exclude behavior leading to rehospitalization, is simply unacceptable in defining dangerousness. At least for those formerly hospitalized, arrest records are totally inadequate as indicators of dangerousness.

While it appears clear that crime statistics do not adequately reflect the degree of seriousness of an act or the actual threat to the members of society, they may reflect differential acts or differential reactions to the individuals committing the acts. If the acts, the individuals, and the reaction of society's control agents were similar for those arrested and for those hospitalized, we would expect to find no significant differences between the two groups of patients. In the main, this is what was found when arrested/never arrested status was examined using our sets of variables. Two factors did, however, successfully distinguish between rehospitalized patients who were or were not also arrested. The two were age and the summary measure of past criminal behavior that we have called the legal dangerousness scale. As can be seen in Tables 8-5 and 8-6 younger patients

Table 8-5
Relationship between Rearrest and Age for Rehospitalized Patients

	Age		
	Under 40 *% (N)*	*40 to 49* *% (N)*	*50 or Over* *% (N)*
Patients Rehospitalized Only	35.3 (6)	46.2 (6)	85.7 (12)
Patients Rearrested	64.7 (11)	53.8 (7)	14.3 (2)
Total	100.0 (17)	100.0 (13)	100.0 (14)

$\chi^2 = 8.40$
$P < .05$
$\phi = .44$

Table 8-6
Relationship between Rearrest and Legal Dangerousness Scale Score for Rehospitalized Patients

	LDS Score		
	0 to 4 *% (N)*	*5 to 10* *% (N)*	*11 to 15* *% (N)*
Patients Rehospitalized Only	84.6 (11)	46.7 (7)	37.5 (6)
Patients Rearrested	15.4 (2)	53.3 (8)	62.5 (10)
Total	100.0 (13)	100.0 (15)	100.0 (16)

$\chi^2 = 6.99$
$P < .05$
$\phi = .40$

and those with a higher score on the scale were significantly more likely to be among those arrested. Of the two, age is slightly more successful in differentiating the two groups. The relationship between age and arrest is interesting given the findings presented in Chapter 4. It will be recalled that in examining the differences between the pre-Baxstrom and the Baxstrom patients, one of the major considerations apparently was age—that is, younger patients were seen as too dangerous for transfer, while older patients with similar criminal and hospital records were viewed as posing no threat to the safety of others in the hospital or the community. The data here would seem to indicate, at least with regard to arrests, that the decision makers at the institutions housing the criminally insane may have been employing relevant criteria.

In addition to age, the other factor found to be significantly related to psychiatric approval for transfer of the criminally insane was the presence

Table 8-7
Arrests, by Age, of Released Baxstrom Patients

	Age		
	Under 40 *% (N)*	*40 to 49* *% (N)*	*50 or Over* *% (N)*
Never Arrested	57.7 (15)	76.7 (23)	95.2 (40)
Arrested	42.3 (11)	23.3 (7)	4.8 (2)
Total	100.0 (26)	100.0 (30)	100.0 (42)

$\chi^2 = 14.17$
$P < .001$
$\phi = .38$

Table 8-8
Arrests, by Legal Dangerousness Scale Score, of Released Baxstrom Patients

	LDS Score		
Released Patients	*0 to 4* *% (N)*	*5 to 10* *% (N)*	*11 to 15* *% (N)*
Never Arrested	95.2 (40)	72.4 (21)	63.0 (17)
Arrested	4.8 (2)	27.6 (8)	37.9 (10)
Total	100.0 (42)	100.0 (29)	100.0 (27)

$\chi^2 = 11.85$
$P < .01$
$\phi = .35$

or absence of a conviction for a violent crime. This variable, nor any other single crime statistic was significantly associated with arrest following release. The best single measure was number of past arrests. Violent crime convictions is, however, one of the four variables used in our legal dangerousness scale. Thus, while not extremely useful by itself, violent crime conviction is also at least somewhat relevant to the criminal activity of these patients once released.

Tables 8-5 and 8-6 show that age and legal dangerousness score do distinguish between those who were or were not arrested from among the 44 patients who did not succeed in remaining in the community. These two variables also distinguish those arrested from all of those released at some time and never arrested. In Tables 8-7 and 8-8 it is apparent that while the differences are not as large as found in the two preceeding tables, young age and a high LDS score are significantly related to arrests following release.

According to this finding, if prior to the release of these 98 patients we had wished to predict which patients would be arrested, the two pieces of information that would have proved most valuable in our task would have been patients' age and their scores on the legal dangerousness scale. This finding also means that the criteria being used by the staffs at the criminally insane hospitals prior to the *Baxstrom* decision reflected, to some extent, the actual outcomes of the patients. Upon analysis, this successful prediction can be seen to have two major flaws, one being the problem discussed earlier of false positives and the other being the problem of using arrest statistics to reflect violence.

Let us illustrate the first problem by referring to Table 8-7. Retrospectively, we see that if we had wished to predict recidivism, our single best indicator would be age. Of the 20 patients subsequently arrested, 18 of them were under the age of 50. If the hospitals had not released these patients, the number of individuals arrested would have been reduced by 90 percent, a drastic decrease. However, by not releasing patients under 50, the hospitals would not only have prevented these 18 from returning to the community but also the 38 individuals who were also under 50 and were not arrested. Any restrictions imposed to decrease criminal activity would, according to these figures, inappropriately detain 2 patients for every 1 who will commit a crime. The number of false positives can be reduced, but only by sacrificing the proportion of arrestees correctly detained. Thus, if we lowered the cut-off age to less than 40, we would be wrong 15 times for every 11 times we are right but the 11 would represent only 55.5 percent of those later arrested.

The best that we can do is to combine both measures of age and legal dangerousness score, as in Table 8-9. Using the information in the previous two tables, we can separate individuals into two groups, those who are less than 50 and who have a LDS score of 5 or more and those who have a score of less than 5 and/or are 50 years or more. Regrouping the data, we find that the first group contains 17 of the 20 people actually rearrested following release to the community. The remaining 3 patients fall in the other group of 62 patients less likely to recidivate. While the 17 patients represent 85 percent of the total arrested, which is slightly less than the 90 percent figure we can attain using just age, we reduce the number of false positives by half. In the likely to recidivate group, for the 17 correctly identified, 19 other patients would also have to be retained. To put it another way, for every patient who would have to be retained in order to reduce the level of incidents leading to arrest by 85 percent, we would also have to retain at least one other individual who if released would not recidivate. Any enthusiasm for success is tempered by the knowledge that these measures, at their best, and assuming that they work equally well on other patient groups, would still mean that any special program or preventive detention established would for every 100 patients classified be inaccurate for over half of them.

Table 8-9
Arrests, by Combined Measure of Age and Legal Dangerousness Scale Score

	Combined Measure	
Released Patients	*< 50 Years Old and LDS ≥ 5 % (N)*	*≥ 50 Years Old and/or LDS < 5 % (N)*
Never Arrested	52.8 (19)	95.2 (59)
Arrested	47.2 (17)	4.8 (3)
Total	100.0 (36)	100.0 (62)

$\chi^2 = 25.19$
$P < .001$
$\phi = .51$

Such a conclusion raises at least two critical questions. The first is what kind of special treatment could or would be given to those identified as likely to be rearrested? The technique used prior to the *Baxstrom* decision at the 2 hospitals for the criminally insane was very simple. If you suspect a patient might be a threat, then keep him institutionalized until he reaches an age of 60 or 70. The old age would then reduce, if not eliminate, any violent and dangerous tendencies. Indefinite confinement without the protection of civil review procedures, however, is what was struck down by the *Baxstrom* decision. Furthermore, such a strategy would seem to result in the complete waste of human lives. For example, the pre-Baxstrom were continuously hospitalized on the average for over 20 years of their lives before they were rehabilitated through old age. While few, if any, are recommending that we simply remove from society anyone evaluated as dangerous for a significant part of their lives, almost any program involves the removal of the individual from society and the restriction of the individual's freedom.

On the other side, society is empowered to protect itself from those who would harm it or its members. This reason and the state's power to care for those incapable of caring for themselves are the only bases for involuntary mental commitment of any type (Ross 1959). The second critical question, then, is how much harm is necessary to justify the institutionalization of patients, at least half of whom would probably never be arrested if simply let go. Let us look at the behavior leading to arrest. We have already seen that of the 11 individuals actually convicted of any crime only two incidents would be classified as violent or potentially violent. This 20 percent figure also holds for all arrests. Of the total 51 incidents leading to arrests after release, only 10 were violent or potentially violent. These 10 charges were brought against 7 people, 3 of whom were arrested 2 times. The 10 charges were as follows: 2 for assault, 2 for assault and robbery, 2 for assault and possession of a dangerous weapon, 1 for rape, 2 for robbery and 1 for robbery and possession of a dangerous weapon.

We find, then, that our success in designating the group of released patients most likely to be arrested is limited. Viewing the process retrospectively, if the high risk group had been identified and been specially handled through retention or treatment, for each patient correctly identified there would be at least one other who would not, following release, ever engage in behavior that would lead to an arrest. Second, any special program that would deprive individuals of their freedom would have to be justified on the basis of preventing these individuals from engaging in behavior that would seriously threaten the members of society. Yet, only 7 of the 20 patients ever arrested allegedly committed acts of a violent or potentially violent nature. If the aim is to restrict or prevent or explain violent dangerous behavior, then such behavior must be the criterion variable examined. Too much of the behavior leading to arrest cannot, except by generalizing the definition to the point where it becomes meaningless, be classified as threatening or violent.

Actual Incidents of Violent Behavior

Arrest statistics are an inadequate measure of dangerousness for two reasons. First, not all arrests are for violent behavior. As we have just seen only 7 of the 20 arrested in our sample were actually violent. They committed 10 violent acts. What was the outcome of this violent behavior for which they were arrested? Examining the disposition of the 10 incidents, we find that in 2 cases the patient was found guilty and sentenced; in 1 case, we lack adequate information; and in the other 7 cases, the arrest resulted not in a trial and criminal sentence but rather in rehospitalization. Thus, most of the arrests for violent crimes led to rehospitalization and *not* imprisonment.

In addition to overestimating dangerous behavior, the use of crime statistics also overlooks violent behavior that is not accompanied by arrests. To rectify this, as described above, we also examined information on the critical incident leading to rehospitalization. Using this information, we found that in addition to the 7 individuals who were arrested and rehospitalized as a result of their violent activity, there were an additional 7 whose behavior led directly to rehospitalization. Together, these 14 account for the one-third of those rehospitalized whose precipitating incident involved dangerous behavior. The 7 patients directly hospitalized were involved in 10 incidents. In all 10 cases, the patient was involuntarily committed to a civil mental hospital. Also, in all cases, the police were involved, although none of the patients were ever arrested or charged with a crime for their act. In 4 of the 10 instances the police were summoned by a member of the patient's family following an incident in which the family member felt threatened. Usually the incident involved violent and argumentative acting out on the patient's part, and in one case, a parent was threatened with a knife. In 3 other cases, the police apparently initiated the process themselves. These 3 were described as violent, and 2 of the 3 had been threatening others with a knife. In the remaining 3 cases, the police were called by non-family members—a bartender, a restaurant owner, and staff from a general hospital—because of their assaultive behavior. All together 14 (15 percent) of the 98 released Baxstrom patients in our sample behaved in a way that was classified as violent or dangerous.

We have seen earlier in this chapter that two variables, age and the legal dangerousness scale score, particularly in combination, are highly related to patient arrests. These variables also distinguish those who became violent while in the community from those for whom no violent incident was ever recorded.

The data on the association between age and violence and LDS score show that the younger patients and those with a higher LDS score are 4 to 6 times as likely to have been involved in a violent incident. Five percent of patients aged 50 or more and 5 percent of those with a low LDS score were violent. Twenty-one percent of those under 50 and 26 percent of those with a LDS score of 11 to 15 were involved in an incident classified as dangerous. Combining these two variables into two categories of those who were older with a low LDS score and those who were younger with a higher LDS score, we arrive at Table 8-10. We find that this combined characteristic not only differentiates those who were arrested from those not arrested, but also those who were violent from those not.

Examining this table, we see that of the 14 violent patients all but 3 fell into the expected group. Of the patients who were to be involved in a violent incident, almost 80 percent were under the age of 50 and had a LDS score of 5 or more. These 11 patients, however, represent less than a third of all the patients who could be placed into the same category—that is, for every 1 patient who was under 50 with a LDS score of 5 or more and who was dangerous, there were at least 2 who were not. Thus, the problem of false positives with our data is more serious when we focus on violent behavior than on arrests.

If we were to attempt to use this information for statistically predicting dangerousness our best strategy would be to assume that none of the patients were dangerous. In this case, we would be wrong in 14 of the 98 cases. *Any other method would increase our error.* If, however, from society's perspective this strategy is unacceptable because of the potential threat posed by these individuals, our findings indicate that almost 80 percent of the violence could be reduced by detaining or treating the group identified by the two variables of age and LDS. Instead of making 14 errors,

Table 8-10
Violent Behavior of Released Patients, by Combined Measure of Age and Legal Dangerousness Scale Score

	Combined Measure	
Incidents of Violent Behavior	*< 50 Years Old and LDS ≥ 5 % (N)*	*≥ 50 Years Old and/or LDS < 5 % (N)*
No Violent Incidents	69.4 (25)	95.2 (59)
Violent	30.6 (11)	4.8 (3)
Total	100.0 (36)	100.0 (62)

$\chi^2 = 12.30$
$P < .001$
$\phi = .35$

however, we now are wrong 28 times out of 98, which includes the 3 patients not expected to be violent who are and the 25 patients expected to be violent who are not. In attempting to distinguish the potentially violent, we double our errors and identify a group of patients for detention and special treatment, two-thirds of whom will not be violent.

Earlier in the chapter we concluded on the bases of arrest and conviction data that these patients were not very dangerous. We criticized these data as inadequate indications of dangerous behavior since some of the behavior that led to arrest could not be classified as dangerous, while some behavior that led to hospitalization should be. Instead, we examined the actual behavior of the patients. Yet, despite our conceptual and empirical clarification of the meaning of dangerousness, our conclusion is identical to the one offered at the beginning of the chapter. The Baxstrom patients were not very dangerous. Only 14 of the 98 released ever displayed behavior that could be classified as dangerous.

Success and Failure in Remaining in the Community

The last question to be addressed in this chapter is that of attempting to understand why some patients were able to successfully remain in the community while others were not. So far, we have found that two variables in particular, age and LDS, have successfully distinguished between those arrested and those not and between those violent and those not. Examined next will be whether these two factors or any others are highly related to rehospitalization. Forty-four patients were readmitted during our study period, while 54 managed to adjust well enough to remain in the community for the entire time. Did the 44 differ significantly in any way from the 54?

Because of their proven importance, we began our analysis with the two

Table 8-11
Rehospitalization, by Combined Measure of Age and Legal Dangerousness Scale Score

	Combined Measure	
Released Patients	*< 50 Years Old and LDS ≥ 5 % (N)*	*≥ 50 Years Old and/or LDS < 5 % (N)*
Never Rehospitalized	36.1 (13)	66.1 (41)
Rehospitalized	63.9 (23)	33.9 (21)
Total	100.0 (36)	100.0 (62)

$\chi^2 = 8.30$
$P < .01$
$\phi = .29$

variables of age and LDS. Both were related to readmission. Almost two-thirds of the patients aged under 40 were rehospitalized while only a third of those 50 and over were. Similarly, those with the highest LDS score were almost twice as likely to be rehospitalized as those with the lowest scores (31 percent as compared to 59 percent). Combining once again these two variables into a single measure, we arrive at Table 8-11. The combined measure is significantly related to readmission. Upon closer examination, the importance of this relationship is diminished. It can be seen that 23 of the 44 patients, slightly more than half, fall into the category containing the younger patients with higher LDS scores. However, from our past analysis, we know that 17 of those 23 are patients who, in addition to being rehospitalized, were also arrested. Thus, it would appear that the combined measure is more appropriately seen as an indicator of behavior leading to arrest than as an indicator of rehospitalization. That it is related to readmission appears to be caused primarily by the fact that those rearrested were also rehospitalized.

Since it appeared that these two factors did not add much specifically to our attempt to understand rehospitalization, we turned to other variables in order to ferret out any significant differences between the two groups. We found two variables that were related to patients' success in remaining in the community. The first and the factor that proved to be most highly related to readmission was the nature of the last criminal act committed by the patient—that is, the offense that led to their being institutionalized in the criminally insane hospital some 15 years previous. We have referred to this as the Baxstrom offense. The type of act, categorized as against person, as property offenses, or as a residual other, significantly differentiated the two groups of patients (Table 8-12). Over 70 percent of those whose offense had been a property crime were rehospitalized as compared to less than 40 percent of those with a crime against person and less than 20

Table 8-12
Rehospitalization, by Type of Baxstrom Offense

	Type of Baxstrom Offense		
Released Patients	*Against Property* *% (N)*	*Against Person* *% (N)*	*Other* *% (N)*
Never Rehospitalized	29.0 (9)	62.0 (31)	82.4 (14)
Rehospitalized	71.0 (22)	38.0 (19)	17.6 (3)
Total	100.0 (31)	100.0 (50)	100.0 (17)

$\chi^2 = 14.58$
$P < .001$
$\phi = .39$

percent of those with other types of offenses. Why this particular variable, out of all the variables examined, was the most important remained unclear until two other associations were discovered. The first was an association with the Baxstrom offense, and the other, with rehospitalization.

The Baxstrom offense was unrelated to many of the factors initially thought to be possible explanations for its relationship to readmission. Factors such as length of hospitalization, age, psychiatric evaluation, and family interest were unrelated not only to success in the community but also to the last offense. The one variable significantly related to Baxstrom offense was the number of arrests experienced by the patient prior to his placement in the criminally insane hospital. This relationship existed for both the entire group of 176 patients in our sample as well as for the group of 98 patients released to the community from the civil mental hospitals. For the entire sample, we found that those patients with a property offense had a median number of arrests equal to 5.8. On the average, this group had over 2 arrests more per person than those with crimes against person or other types of offenses. The median number of arrests for these two groups were 3.1 and 3.4, respectively.

A similar pattern existed for the 98 released. Of those with a property offense, only 3.2 percent had never been arrested, while 64.5 percent had been arrested 4 or more times. On the other hand, 24.0 percent of those whose Baxstrom offense involved a crime against person had never been previously arrested, and only 34.0 percent of them experienced 4 or more arrests. For the group whose offense fell into the residual category, 17.6 percent had no arrests, and 35.3 percent had 4 or more. These data would seem to suggest that the Baxstrom offense is an important indicator of patient rehospitalization primarily because the type of offense appears to reflect the past criminal experiences of the patients. Patients who have repeatedly found themselves in violation of the law are likely to have

Table 8-13
Rehospitalization, by Previous Admissions to Mental Hospitals

	Previous Admissions		
Released Patients	*None* *% (N)*	*One* *% (N)*	*Two or more* *% (N)*
Never Rehospitalized	62.7 (42)	47.1 (8)	28.6 (4)
Rehospitalized	37.7 (25)	52.9 (9)	71.4 (10)
Total	100.0 (67)	100.0 (17)	100.0 (14)

$\chi^2 = 5.99$
$P < .05$
$\phi = .25$

established a pattern of arrests in which they are continually in and out of trouble for relatively minor and usually non-violent crimes. Many of those in this pattern are patients for whom a property offense led to their last institutionalization. This argument is given some support by Glaser's (1964) finding, mentioned earlier, that the lowest recidivism rates among felons are for murder and rape, while the highest rates are for economic offenses not involving violence.

The idea that those whose life history would indicate a pattern of repetitive trouble are those who are most likely to fail in the community, as an extension of the pattern, is also given some support from a different direction. In addition to the type of Baxstrom offense, the other variable that was found to be significantly related to readmission was previous mental hospitalizations. This relationship has been observed by others. For example, Mendel and Rapport (1969) in their analysis showed that patients who had been previously hospitalized were twice as likely to be hospitalized at the time of their study, than those not previously hospitalized. Here, we found, as seen in Table 8-13, that those patients who had never been previously hospitalized were least likely to be readmitted (37.7 percent) followed by those with a single admission (52.9 percent), while those with two or more mental hospital admissions were the most likely (71.4 percent).

That these two factors—Baxstrom offense and previous mental hospitalizations—independently influence readmission can be seen by referring to Table 8-14. This table examines the relationship between the Baxstrom offense and readmission while controlling for previous hospitalization. Both factors are important. If we hold the offense constant, we find that in all three comparisons those previously hospitalized are more likely to be readmitted. For those with a property crime, the comparison is 61.1 percent to 84.6 percent; for those with a crime against person, 32.5 percent

Table 8-14
Rehospitalization, by Type of Baxstrom Offense, Controlling for Previous Hospitalizations

	No Previous Hospitalizations			*Some Previous Hospitalizations*		
	Baxstrom Offense					
	Against Property	*Against Person*	*Other*	*Against Property*	*Against Person*	*Other*
Percentage Rehospitalized	61.1	32.5	11.1	84.6	60.0	25.0
(Patients Rehospitalized/ Patients Released)	(11/18)	(13/40)	(1/9)	(11/13)	(6/10)	(2/8)

to 60.0 percent; and for those with other types of offenses, 11.1 percent to 25.0 percent. Similarly the even stronger relationship between Baxstrom offense and success in the community remains when prior hospitalization is held constant. Looking at both factors simultaneously, we find that those with both a property offense and a prior hospitalization were most likely to be readmitted (almost 85 percent of them were), while those least likely were patients without either of these two characteristics.

The explanation of patient readmissions that seems to emerge from these findings is that individuals who have established a pattern of being unable to remain in the community are likely to continue in this life pattern, even after lengthy detention in correctional mental hospitals, and therefore will be readmitted. Those who have been in and out of institutions, whether they be correctional or mental health facilities, are according to our data the ones most likely to be institutionalized once again.

Why this is so cannot be definitely decided on the basis of our data. However, our experience with these and other criminally insane patients would lead us to favor one of the two most probable explanations. One explanation is that these are patients who are ill and/or bad, and no matter what is done with them or to them by way of care and treatment, they will recidivate. The other explanation is that repeated institutionalizations, whether they stem from criminal- or illness-related behavior, breeds an institutional dependency—that is, the individual spends so much of his life in the institution that it becomes his home while the outside world becomes unfamiliar and alien. Certainly, this phenomenon has been observed by others both in sociological literature by people such as Goffman (1961) as well as in the mass media. For example, the New York Times on December 7, 1973 reported on an individual who has spent all but 16 months of his 39 years in state institutions. The individual has been convicted of 18 crimes, mostly robbery and property damage, and expressing his fears of venturing into the outside world, he requested that the governor of the state sentence him to a life term so he could remain in prison permanently. The story quotes him as saying, "I don't know how to live outside. My home is inside, and I want to stay there the rest of my life."

Such desires were not infrequent among our population. A number of patients, hospitalized for 10 to 20 years, found themselves released from the civil hospitals and back in a New York City that was unlike anything they remembered. In our files, we have reports of some individuals returning to hospitals because, according to them, they are tired and "need to rest for ten or fifteen years" and of others who following short stays in rundown hotels readmit themselves and promise they "won't complain about the wind anymore . . . it's beautiful here . . . the trees and the lawn."

Additional and less impressionistic support for this explanation can be found in Table 8-15, which combines data on the Baxstrom offense and prior hospitalization while controlling for age. Age, it will be remembered, was significantly related to readmission. The younger the patient the more probable was readmission. We find in Table 8-15 that this relationship holds for those with only one, or neither, of the two characteristics of previous mental hospitalizations and a property Baxstrom offense. Thus, the percentage of patients readmitted decreases as age increases. What is unexpected is that for those patients with both characteristics, those who would appear to be most ingrained in a pattern of institutional dependency, the pattern is reversed. In this group, older patients are more likely to be readmitted. This countertrend would appear to support the notion that the high readmission rate of this group is, at least somewhat, influenced by a pattern of institutional dependency that developed and increased through years of being housed in criminal or mental health facilities.

Table 8-15 also shows that this relationship between repeated institutionalization and readmission is almost irrelevant for those under 40, important for those aged 40 to 50, and almost totally determinant for those 50 and over. For this last group, all those with both indicators were readmitted, 42.9 percent of those with one but not the other characteristic, and less than 10 percent of the group with neither.

Summary

This chapter has focused on the community activity of the released Baxstrom patients. We have found that few displayed dangerous behavior in the community and that most of those released succeeded in remaining in the community for the entire period of our study. In our attempt to understand why some patients were able to adjust to community life while others were not, two patterns emerged. The first best characterized those rearrested and those who displayed dangerous behavior. Patients rearrested, as well as those involved in violent incidents, tended to be younger and have a more serious criminal background as reflected by our legal dangerousness scale. Since all 20 patients rearrested were also rehospitalized at some time, these two factors were somewhat relevant in distinguishing the total group of 44 patients who did not remain in the community from the 54 who did. Overall, two other variables were more helpful in this task. These were the type of Baxstrom offense and prior mental hospitalizations. We interpreted these relationships to be indicative of a pattern of continuous difficulty in adjusting to the outside community and of institutional dependency—that is, patients who have over their lives found themselves in and out of mental and correctional institutions were likely to have continued this pattern and be reinstitutionalized.

The findings of this chapter also bear on the issues raised in earlier

Table 8-15
Rehospitalization, by Previous Mental Hospitalizations (PMH) and Type of Baxstrom Offense (TBO), Controlling for Age

	Age								
	Under 40			*40 to 49*			*50 or Over*		
	Both PMH + Property TBO	*Either PMH or Property TBO*	*Neither PMH or Property TBO*	*Both PMH + Property TBO*	*Either PMH or Property TBO*	*Neither PMH or Property TBO*	*Both PMH + Property TBO*	*Either PMH or Property TBO*	*Neither PMH or Property TBO*
Percentage Rehospitalized	66.7	77.8	57.1	75.0	46.2	30.8	100.0	42.9	9.1
(Patients Rehospitalized/ Patients Released	(2/3)	(7/9)	(8/14)	(3/4)	(6/13)	(4/13)	(6/6)	(6/14)	(2/22)

chapters. In Chapter 5, we found that the correctional hospital psychiatrists viewed age as an important criterion for suitability for transfer. Age, in this chapter, proved to be significantly related to posthospital behavior. Younger patients were more likely to engage in behavior resulting in rearrest and in behavior classified as dangerous. Yet, as had been discussed, detaining patients in a criminally insane hospital until they grow old is justifiable only if one is willing to detain many individuals in order to prevent the few who will be violent if released.

In the last chapter, it was found that patients released to the community by the psychiatrists were those who had been hospitalized for a relatively short period of time, who had been evaluated as psychiatrically improved, and who, most importantly, had family in the community interested in their welfare. Somewhat surprising is this chapter's finding that none of these factors were significantly related to patient success in the community. Patients with these characteristics were not any more likely to have remained in the community than patients without them. This finding is particularly important in light of the tendency of psychiatrists to release patients with interested family. Our data indicate that this factor makes little difference in the career of the patient. It does not help in understanding why patients succeed or fail in the community.

Throughout the last four chapters we have raised and addressed many issues concerning the Baxstrom patients through our description and analyses of the data. We have done this by following them from the criminally insane hospitals, to the civil hospitals, into the community and back again. At the beginning of this book we stated that the criminally insane were a group of people who are little known and who suffer because of misunderstandings and ignorance. We have attempted to remedy this situation. Hopefully, this book as a whole, aids by presenting information that reflects more accurately than the stereotype exactly who the criminally insane are, what happens to them as their careers unfold, and why.

As we see in the next chapter, the efforts of Johnnie K. Baxstrom affected not only the patients we have examined here but also many others through the judicial decisions and laws based on the principles of the court decision in his case. Yet, Baxstrom himself, did not benefit greatly from the decision. Two weeks after he was released from the civil hospital, he died in bed during an epileptic seizure. Even after his death, however, controversy surrounded him.

A little more than a year after his death, an editorial comment appeared in the *Psychiatric Quarterly* (October 1967, (p. 766) and used Baxstrom's court-mandated release and ensuing death to illustrate the following point:

> Law persons—judges, lawyers, and "counselors" with no psychiatric expertise —now *do* "second-guess the doctors." They make the decisions as to the nature and extent of treatment (viz. duration of hospitalization), and evaluate the patient's safety and that of others, disdaining medical advice on occasion.

The footnote that accompanied this observation reads as follows:

To the dismay of many, Baxtrom [*sic*] was discharged by a jury under the new law, only to die within two weeks. A deteriorated alcoholic epileptic, he had come from a criminal to a civil hospital, had demonstrated conclusively that he was not yet ready for residence on an open ward in view of his alcoholic habits and the deleterious effect of alcohol on his epilepsy. Encouraged to apply for a court hearing against hospital advice, he was discharged with the predicted result. Incredibly, the jury's verdict was "not guilty" (of mental illness?).

This editorial, plus a copy of an unpublished letter sent in response to it, as well as a post-mortem examination report were brought to our attention by Dr. A. L. Halpern. According to Halpern, the implication that Baxstrom's death resulted from his alcoholic habit was inaccurate. Baxstrom, he reports, was discharged immediately after his trial and was not referred to a clinic or physician. Information obtained from a member of his family and the medical examiner in Baltimore suggested "that he tried to obtain medication at a hospital in Baltimore but treatment was deferred until his Dannemora State Hospital records could be obtained, that he developed status epilepticus and died, and that no alcohol had been consumed by him prior to his death in Baltimore."

That Johnnie K. Baxstrom would die as a direct result of alcohol and indirectly because of being released against the hospital's advice is an interpretation consistent with the stereotype surrounding the criminally insane. Hopefully, our data on Baxstrom and the patients who have been designated by his name tempers this stereotype with fact.

Emerging Trends and Issues in the Custody and Care of the Criminally Insane

This chapter is a statement of what we see as some of the major trends and issues surrounding the treatment of the criminally insane in the United States today. It is a look at what has happened in the custody and care of the criminally insane since 1966, especially in the courts, and a look at current directions of treatment and research. The major trends we examine are (1) the awakened concern for the individual rights of the criminally insane; (2) the increased dependence on the concept of dangerousness for detention; (3) the expansion of psychiatric roles in the criminal justice system; and (4) the growing attention to non-U.S. models for treatment programs.

In line with what we discussed in Chapter 1, our discussions of judicial decisions and legislation is a general one intended particularly to alert various professionals to the most significant decisions and their implications for these areas. For the legal practitioner familiar with the criminally insane, we trust no piece of critical matter will be found wanting, but this is not intended as a detailed study in case law. Simply, these decisions are data that we are using as indicators of major developments in the social sphere.

Individual Rights

As the reader may recall from Chapter 3, the major principle of the *Baxstrom v. Herold* decision was that Johnnie Baxstrom had not received equal protection under the law. He had received neither the protection given civil patients for involuntary commitment nor in the determination of dangerousness. This principle of *equal protection* under the Fourteenth amendment is one of the two dominant concerns for the rights of the criminally insane from 1966 to the present. The second major area of expanded concern under the mantle of individual rights has been the *right to treatment.* This latter principle has been primarily discussed in relation to civil cases, but it has many direct applications and ramifications for patients detained under criminal orders. We first examine some of the developments in equal protection by analyzing how this principle has been applied to both portions of the criminally insane label.

Equal Protection

When Johnnie Baxstrom's sentence expired, he was given a hearing in Surrogate Court with no legal counsel and found to "require mental care and treatment." Although at this time, his custody administratively shifted from the Department of Correction to the Department of Mental Hygiene, he remained in Dannemora, a correctional facility, because the courts determined he required psychiatric treatment. The 1966 U.S. Supreme Court ruling declared that since under New York's Mental Hygiene Law (MHL) a person involuntarily committed under civil proceedings had the right to a jury trial, Baxstrom (and other time-expired mentally ill inmates) should also have this right. Furthermore, since the only mental patients who could be detained in correctional mental hospitals were those found dangerously mentally ill, Baxstrom should have received specific review on the question of dangerousness as he would have under the civil MHL.

The court was giving to patients in Baxstrom's circumstances the same protection afforded mentally ill patients, who were not also labeled criminal. This, however, is only one segment of the equal protections recently accorded the criminally insane. Through a series of court decisions and statutory reforms, the criminally insane also have been given equal protection with criminals in regard to the right to a speedy trial and limits on the length of their commitments. In examining the trends in equal protection, it is useful to look at the equal protection changes for each portion of the criminally insane label separately. First, we look at the stipulations for the equal protections of the "insane" portion of the label.

Equality between Criminal and Civil Commitment Procedures. The Supreme Court decision in Johnnie Baxstrom's case directed that there be equality between the procedures committing individuals to involuntary mental hospitalization whether they be convicted criminals or simply civilians. This type of equal protection actually applied to a very late stage of the mentally ill inmate's patient career. It was relevant only after an individual had been arrested, convicted, incarcerated, administratively transferred to a facility for the criminally insane, had served time in such a hospital, and finally had been recommitted at the expiration of their criminal sentence. An important decision handed down in 1969, *United States ex rel. Schuster v. Herold,* 410 F.2nd 1071, went further back in the patient career of the mentally ill inmate to require equal protection at the point where the inmate was first transferred to a hospital for the criminally insane.

The *Schuster* decision extended the equal protection doctrine to mentally ill inmates at the point of first admission to a hospital for the criminally insane. This case involved Roy Schuster who, at the age of 27, had been convicted in 1931 of second degree murder in the death of his wife. The first 4 years of his 25-years-to-life term were spent in Sing Sing Prison, before his transfer in 1935 to Clinton State Prison. As the court decision related:

> There he made a good adjustment. He taught a "cell-study" course leading to a high school equivalency degree, and even received a letter from the New York State Board of Education commending him for his work. In the normal course of events, Schuster might have expected to serve his time and to be eligible for parole in 1948, when he was still not too old to build a new life. But, in 1941, life took another wrong turn for him. Schuster became convinced of corruption in the prison, particularly on the part of officials in charge of the prison education program. His expression of this belief led to his transfer to Dannemora State Hospital for the Criminally Insane. Although Schuster charges that the state "buried him alive" in Dannemora to prevent him from bringing the corruption to light, the district court was unconvinced the transfer was corruptly motivated. The state contends that there was no corruption, that Schuster was and is a "paranoid" and that his insistence upon the existence of a scandal is prime evidence of his delusion.
>
> Schuster entered Dannemora on September 9, 1941, at the age of 37. Now 64 years old, he still languishes there.

Schuster's petition centered on the question of the lack of access to procedural safeguards at the time of his commitment to Dannemora in 1941. The court agreed with the petitioner that in fact he had received no protections and that he should receive a new hearing on the question of his sanity with the same procedures accorded patients involuntarily committed to civil mental hospitals.

Subsequent to *Schuster* an extension of civil commitment protections for convicted criminals was added by *McNeil v. Director, Patuxent Institution,* 407 U.S. 245 (1972). This decision held that a convicted criminal could not be held for even diagnosis in a mental hospital as a suspected defective delinquent without invoking ordinary civil commitment proceedings.

In addition to such extensions of protection to convicted criminals between the *Baxstrom* and *Schuster* decisions, there had been a number of decisions dealing with equal protection in NGRI cases. These cases also focused on assuring the same procedural checks for purely civil cases and for commitment to mental hospitals after an NGRI determination. There was a series of 3 major cases explicating these rights. The first was a 1967 New York case, *The People v. Lally,* 19 N.Y. 2nd 27 (1967), that concluded that defendants found not guilty by reason of insanity could not be committed directly to Matteawan without receiving the same protections available to involuntarily committed civil patients. This protection provided among other things the right to a jury trial on the questions of insanity and dangerousness, if requested. This *Lally* decision was directly comparable to *Baxstrom,* especially since the civil statutes related to equal protection were exactly the same.

Two other recent equal protection cases dealing with NGRI issues both occurred in the United States Court of Appeals in Washington, D.C. The first was *Cameron v. Mullen,* 128 U.S. App D.C. 235, 387 F.2nd 193 (March 1, 1967). This decision held that upon an acquittal by reason of insanity over a defendant's objection, an additional inquiry—one that embodies the procedural safeguards of civil commitment—is required for commitment. This inquiry, like the one on competency to stand trial, concerns present mental condition, but its purpose is to determine whether the defendant is mentally ill, dangerous, and in need of treatment. A defendant who was insane for the purpose of responsibility at the time of the offense may not be insane for the purpose of civil commitment at the time of the verdict, or (although competent to stand trial) he may be insane, dangerous, and in need of treatment.

The final NGRI case in this series occurred in 1968. This *Bolton v. Harris* case (395 F.2d 642 [1968] carried the theme of equal protection with regular civil commitments for NGRI cases to a conclusion that ruled as follows:

> It is true that persons acquitted by reason of insanity have committed criminal acts and that this fact may tend to show they meet the requirements for commitment, namely, illness and dangerousness. But it does not remove these requirements. Nor does it justify total abandonment of the procedures used in civil commitment proceedings to determine whether these same requirements have been satisfied. Hence persons found not guilty by reason of insanity must be given a judicial hearing with procedures substantially similar to those in civil commitment proceedings.

Thus, through the decisions reviewed in this section so far, equal protection involving review on the questions of mental illness and dangerousness were extended to mentally ill inmates being transferred to a correctional mental hospital, to mentally ill inmates upon expiration of their sentences, and to NGRI cases after this determination by a criminal trial court.

One of the most significant decisions at any time dealing with the criminally insane was *Jackson v. Indiana,* 92 S.Ct. 1845 (1972), which ruled on a number of important equal protection issues related to incompetent defendants. Possibly the most critical of these rulings dealt with the equal protection aspects of the "criminal" portion of the criminally insane label and will be discussed in the following section. However, one portion of the equal protection issues in this case did relate to existing differences between criminal and civil statutes in criteria for admission and discharge.

The Jackson case involved a deaf mute who had been found incompetent to stand trial on two robbery charges involving a total of $9. The alleged incidents occurred in 1968 when Theon Jackson was 27. Because of his pending charges, the criteria under which Jackson was committed and refused release to programs of potential benefit were considerably different from civil guidelines. Thus, the U.S. Supreme Court stated:

> As we noted above, we cannot conclude that pending criminal charges provide a greater justification for different treatment than conviction and sentence. Consequently, we hold that by subjecting Jackson to a more lenient commitment standard and to a more stringent standard of release than those generally applicable to all others not charged with offenses, and by thus condemning him in effect to permanent institutionalization without the showing required for commitment or the opportunity for release afforded by Section 22-1209 or Section 22-1907, Indiana deprived petitioner of equal protection of the laws under the Fourteenth Amendment. Thus, not only must rights such as jury trials be similar in the processing of the criminally insane with the civil laws, but the criteria for admission and discharge in the civil statutes must be applied, since the alleged commission of a criminal offense does not allow more severe restrictions on the question of mental illness.

Another recent U.S. Supreme Court decision was an affirmation without comment on a lower court ruling in New York that an incompetent defendant who had been found dangerously incapacitated by a criminal court was entitled to a jury trial review on the question of dangerousness (*Gomez v. Miller,* 341 F. Supp 323 [1973]. Precisely for the same reasons that Johnnie Baxstrom had been ruled to have the right to such review, Gomez and the other petitioners in this class action suit were granted the right of jury trial because under New York civil statutes for commitment as dangerously mentally ill, the person had this same right. Thus, with the *Gomez* and *Jackson* cases, incompetent defendants have been given, as had mentally ill inmates and NGRI cases previously, equal protection with patients civilly committed as mentally ill and dangerous.

A final group that has received some court attention regarding their rights under these equal protection doctrines is that of psychopathic sex offenders. The two major decisions relating to this class of patients were *Specht v. Patterson*, 386 U.S. 605 (1967), and *Humphrey v. Cady,* 405 U.S. 504, 92 S. Ct. 1048 (1972). In these cases, the Baxstrom principal of equal protection was extended to individuals committed for psychiatric treatment in lieu of sentence after a conviction as a sex offender. These decisions require that such individuals also must receive judicial review for commitment as mentally ill, independent of criminal conviction.

Thus, all classes of the criminally insane have been accorded the rights of equal protection with individuals who are simply called insane. In addition to these changes relating to this half of the criminally insane label, attention has also been paid in court decisions following *Baxstrom* to the "criminal" portion of this label.

Specifications of Detention Limits. The manner in which the recent court decisions have affected the "criminal" segment of the criminally insane label is by establishing some limits on maximum lengths of confinement. These limits reflect equal protection with criminals who after conviction usually have definite limits for detention. Such limits have been absent from the frequently indeterminate institutionalizations of the criminally insane.

The *Baxstrom* decision dealt specifically with procedural safeguards at the termination of the criminal sentence of a mentally ill inmate. However, in the implementation of this decision, the State of New York included among the 967 patients it transferred, 185 patients who were incompetent defendants. The *Baxstrom* decision was interpreted to mean that similar review was necessary for incompetent defendants detained for a period that was equal to or greater than the sentences that they could have received for their pending charges. Thus, although the *Baxstrom* decision did not specify any detention limits for incompetent defendants, the state inferred that the maximum length of time they could be detained was the maximum sentence for their alleged offenses.

An analogous situation is found in the 1969 *Schuster* decision where the opinion of the majority indicated that one of the detrimental aspects of Schuster's confinement in Dannemora was that had he remained in prison from the time of his conviction in 1931, he would have been eligible in 1948 for parole from his 25-years-to-life sentence. Since Dannemora confinement was not counted as "good" time and since even if it were, the policy of the parole board was not to consider parole for any inmates regardless of length of confinement, Schuster could have been detained indefinitely in Dannemora. Although not included as part of the specific directives of the court in *Schuster,* the implication was that there should be equality in the protections afforded insane and non-insane criminals in terms of time off for good behavior, upper limits of sentences, and parole review.

Some of the themes of the criminal protections found in the *Baxstrom* and *Schuster* decisions became explicit in New York through the 1971 revision of its Criminal Procedure Law. Felony defendants who are found incompetent may not be detained under criminal orders for more than two-thirds of the maximum sentence for the crimes with which they are charged. For incompetent misdemeanor defendants, charges are dropped upon a finding of incompetency. Other recent changes in these regards in other state and federal jurisdictions have limited lengths of confinement for incompetent defendants at somewhere between the two-thirds maximum and outright dismissal of charges.

A 1967 revision of Michigan statutes (c.f. Slovenko 1971) set an 18-month limit on the confinement in a mental hospital of an incompetent defendant. After 18 months, if the defendant is still considered mentally ill and in need of treatment, commitment must be under a regular civil commitment order. There was no directive that criminal charges had to be dismissed at the end of 18 months, however. In fact, charges would remain outstanding indefinitely, and the defendant could be rearrested whenever he was discharged from the hospital. This Michigan statute is very similar to the federal statute, which also sets an 18-month limit on the hospitalization of incompetent defendants. The one major difference between the federal and Michigan statutes is that in the former charges are dismissed at the expiration of the 18 months. The basic principle to which both of these latter statutes address themselves is the right of the defendant to bail and speedy trial, both of which are severely restricted by their status as incompetent defendants.

Discussing some of these recent trends, Burt and Morris (1972) present a proposal that would limit to 6 months the hospitalization of incompetent defendants under criminal orders. Their proposal is developed from *Jackson* since one section of its equal protection principles stated that a defendant "who is solely on account of his incapacity to proceed to trial cannot be held more than the *reasonable period of time* necessary to determine whether there is *substantial probability* that he will attain that capacity in the *forseeable future* (italics added). The innovative feature of the Burt and Morris proposal is that a defendant may opt for a trial under special rules at the expiration of the 6-month hospitalization, even if competency is not regained.

Proposals such as these and recent statutory changes are indicative of the growing realization of the right of the criminally insane to the same protections convicted criminals have. Limits for the hospitalization of mentally ill inmates, NGRI patients, and other categories such as sex offenders are only recent developments. Some earlier indications that such maximum limits should be developed are found in the *Baxstrom* and *Schuster* decisions. Both of these decisions strongly implied that "good time" should be accumulated while hospitalized under criminal orders in special security mental hospitals and that review for civil commitment should occur at normal parole time. Thus, the procedural protections of the mentally ill and of the criminal are becoming available to the criminally insane who have the label of both, but traditionally have had the protections of neither.

Right to Treatment

The second major development in the emerging concerns for the individual rights of the criminally insane is the right to treatment. When the *Wyatt v. Stickney* decision, 325 D 781 (MD Ala 1971), was handed down in the spring of 1972, it received widespread media coverage because it stipulated very specifically the components of treatment to which involuntary civil mental patients had a right. This decision was seen as a breakthrough for the 275,000 people then estimated to be in U.S. mental hospitals. While this decision was certainly important, there was little note made in these same media reports that, as McGarry and Kaplan (1973) pointed out, the right to treatment doctrine for mental patients was actually first mandated in NGRI cases, such as *Rouse v. Cameron* 373 F. 2nd 451 (DC Cir 1966). This latter decision concluded that since the mental condition of those found not guilty by reason of insanity and committed for involuntary mental hospitalization indicated an absence of criminal responsibility, punishment and incarceration were precluded. Thus, commitment to a mental hospital was appropriate only for psychiatric care. Such confinement without adequate treatment would be nothing but incarceration and punishment, both of which were unacceptable.

Two years after *Rouse,* the Supreme Court of Massachusetts extended the right to treatment to incompetent defendants. In the case of *Nason v. Superintendent of Bridgewater State Hospital,* 233 N.E. 2d 908 (Mass, 1968), the court ruled that an incompetent defendant charged with murder had the right to challenge the legality of his confinement if the state failed to provide adequate treatment. The rationale of this decision was the same as that of *Rouse.* If treatment were absent, the hospital was only a prison and hospitalization to regain competency was the sole purpose for such confinement.

In the 1969 *Schuster* decision, the court stated that "while we do not pass upon the possibility of such a constitutional right to treat, we are of the view that, in light of the procedural posture of this case, the state may wish to reexamine the validity of its confinement of Schuster in Dannemora without the treatment for which he was originally committed since it is conceded he does not need purely custodial detention in a mental hospital."

In the 1972 *Jackson* case, besides ruling that an incompetent defendant could be detained only for "reasonable period[s] of time to determine whether there is substantial probability that he will regain capacity," the court determined that continued commitment must be justified by "progress towards that goal" (i.e., probability of capacity to stand trial in the forseeable future). Since such progress would imply treatment, the *Jackson* case added further support to the right to treatment for the criminally insane. So, while the right to treatment for the criminally insane has not been as widely publicized as its application to civil mental patients, it has been a major trend in recent court decisions.

In addition to the emerging concerns for individual rights of the criminally insane through equal protection in commitment procedures and in detention limits and through the right to treatment, another equally significant trend has been a rapidly growing reliance on estimations of dangerousness in the custody of the criminally insane.

Dangerousness

Since the *Baxstrom* decision, the idea of dangerousness has become even more important for the detention of the criminally insane through court decisions, revised state stautes, and increased awareness of the implicit role this concept has always played in confinement. In the *Baxstrom* decision, there was considerable discussion of the unsupported contentions of the Department of Mental Hygiene psychiatrists that the Dannemora patients were dangerous and that a determination of dangerousness did not have to be made independently of the question of mental illness. *Baxstrom* strongly implied that criminal conviction did not indicate dangerousness for mentally ill inmates. This latter theme was one of the major conclusions of the 1968 study of the Association of the Bar of the City of New York that considered revisions of New York's procedures and programs for the criminally insane. This group concluded: "The basic and unifying thread which runs throughout our recommendations is a rejection of the notion that the mere fact of a criminal charge or conviction is a proper basis upon which to build other unnecessary, unprofitable, and essentially unfair distinctions among the mentally ill" (ABCNY 1968, p. 1).

The centrality of dangerousness to the custody and treatment of the criminally insane is apparent in two court decisions related to federal incompetency procedures and in a series of CSP cases in the Circuit Court of Appeals in Washington, D.C. In a 1956 case, *Greenwood v. United States,* 350 U.S. 366 (1966), an incompetent defendant challenged his continued commitment on the grounds that his condition was unlikely to respond to treatment and that he would not become competent in the forseeable future. The court rejected his contention by ruling that the federal statutes under which he was confined were constitutional because in addition to a determination of incompetency, one of dangerousness had also been made.

In *United States v. Curry,* 410 F. 2d 1372 (1969), Claude Curry appealed that his commitment as incompetent to face his charge (sending threatening mail to the president) required some limitation; otherwise the statutes were unconstitutional by providing indefinite detainment without due process. The court ruled that Curry should be permitted to apply for a hearing as to his dangerousness, which was the only criterion by which he could continue to be detained. The court added that "in the future, furthermore, after incompetency has been adjudged . . ., we think the trial court should not commit a defendant into custody, unless and until the court shall also have determined that the defendant might, if released, be a public or private danger. The court may, of course, detain him for a reasonable time to observe and otherwise inquire into his propensities, and also to treat him for his illness in the hope of restoring competency."

Slovenko (1971) notes that these federal guidelines are quite similar to the criterion of dangerousness used for indefinite commitments of incompetent defendants in the four states of Idaho, Iowa, Oklahoma, and South Dakota. In addition, he notes that Kansas, Oregon, and Wisconsin permit parole of incompetent defendants while awaiting trial, if there is assurance that the defendant is not dangerous.

Two recent decisions of the District Court of Washington, D.C. similarly accepted dangerousness as a basis for detention, but in his opinions on these two rulings, Judge David Bazelon expertly discussed some of the complexities of conceptualizing and predicting dangerousness, which the federal decisions had glossed over. Both *Millard v. Cameron,* 125 U.S. App. D.C. 383, 373 F.2d 964 (1966), and *Cross v. Harris,* 418 F. 2d 1095 (D'C. Cir. 1969), involved exhibitionists. In addressing these questions, Judge Bazelon concluded that a finding of dangerousness, which was essential to the retention of Millard, "must be based on a high probability of substantial injury" to others.

Bazelon proposed that many problems surrounding the use of dangerousness were results of statutes purposefully leaving this concept undefined to let "the courts . . . refine that unavoidable vague concept of 'dangerousness' on a case-by-case basis, in the traditional common-law fashion."

Having noted thus, Bazelon continued:

> This does not mean, however, that the statutory language may be disregarded. To be *dangerous* for purposes of the Sexual Psychopath Act, one must be likely to attack or otherwise inflict injury, loss, pain, or other evil on the objects of his desire. The focus of the statute is not on expected conduct, but on the harm that may flow from that conduct. Commitment cannot be based simply on the determination that a person is likely to engage in particular acts. The court must also determine the harm, if any, that is likely to flow from these acts. A mere possibility of injury is not enough; the statute requires that the harm be likely.
>
> These determinations must be made on the basis of the record in the particular case before the court. The expert testimony will therefore be relevant to these questions of fact: (1) the likelihood of recurrence of sexual misconduct, (2) the likely frequency of any such behavior, and (3) the magnitude of harm to other persons that is likely to result.
>
> Having found the facts, the court then determines as a matter of law whether those facts provide a legal basis for commitment. Two questions must be answered in making the determination. The first is what magnitude of harm will justify commitment. It is clear that Congress did not intend to authorize indefinite preventive detention for those who have a propensity to behave in a way that is merely offensive or obnoxious to others; the threatened harm must be substantial. Thus, commitment under the Sexual Psychopath Act requires that a person be found likely to engage in sexual misconduct in circumstances where that misconduct will inflict *substantial* injury upon others.
>
> The second quesion is what *likelihood of harm* will justify commitment. It may well be impossible to provide a precise definition of "likely" as the term is used in the

statute. The degree of likelihood necessary to support commitment may depend on many factors. Among the particular relevant considerations are the seriousness of the expected harm, the availability of inpatient and outpatient treatment for the individual concerned, and the expected length of confinement required for inpatient treatment.

It is particularly important that courts not allow this second question to devolve, by default, upon the expert witnesses. Psychiatrists should not be asked to testify, without more, simply whether future behavior or threatened harm is ''likely'' to occur. For the psychiatrist may—in his own mind—be defining ''likely'' to mean anything from virtual certainty to slightly above chance. And his definition will not be reflection of any expertise, but of his own personal preference for safety or ''liberty''. Of course, psychiatrists may be unable or unwilling to provide a precise numerical estimate of probabilities, and we are not attempting to so limit their testimony. But questioning can and should bring out the expert witness's meaning when he testifies that expected harm is or is not ''likely''.

In this statement Bazelon has captured some of the crucial and extremely difficult problems of using dangerousness as a commitment criterion; problems which most often are de-emphasized in favor of using this handy concept for commitment of the criminally insane.

A fairly recent statutory change that reflects the growing use of dangerousness and skims over its difficulties is the New York State Criminal Prodecure Law (CPL), which became effective in September 1971. In the sections of the CPL dealing with incapacitated defendants, there was an attempt to implement procedures so that fewer defendants would be in maximum security facilities and more defendants would more rapidly be returned to trial. The major innovation in these statutes was to first divide defendants into misdemeanor and felony defendants. Misdemeanor defendants found incapacitated were committed to civil hospitals for 90 days and their charges dropped. The second division separated felony defendants into the indicted and unindicted. The unindicted, upon a finding of incapacity, were commited for 90 days in a civil hospital with indictment possible up to 6 months after the expiration of the 90-day commitment.

For the indicted, incapacitated defendant, another distinction was introduced in the CPL. For this group, after a finding of incapacity, the further determination of dangerousness was to be made. If found dangerous, commitment was for one year and could be, and almost always is, in a correctional mental hospital. For the non-dangerous, commitment is also for one year, but must be in a civil mental hospital, which may be maximum security facility, but which must be run by the Department of Mental Hygiene. Thus, with the CPL, for the first time in New York, an explicit determination of dangerousness was introduced for this class of incompetent defendants.

Perhaps of greater impact than the introduction of dangerousness into state statutes and the use of this concept in court decisions will be its relationship to equal protection doctrines necessitating similar criminal and civil commitment procedures and criteria. Burt and Morris (1972) have noted some of the potential negative possibilities of applying such equal protection doctrines: "If equal protection analysis requires equal treatment for the 'insane' and the 'criminally insane,' then states may well be drawn to greater abuses of the mad in order to be sure of ensnaring the bad" (p. 70). Their concern is that there will develop an exploitation of imprecise civil statutes where "substantive standards are vague; fact-finding processes are haphazard; and no effective time limits on commitment are assured" (p. 73).

What makes dangerousness so problematic in the context of equal protection concerns is that in the last 10 years dangerousness has become a major reason for involuntary *civil* commitment of the mentally ill. For example, a recent case in Wisconsin, *Lessard v. Schmidt*, 349 F. Supp. 1078 (1972), concluded that to commit an individual "the state must prove beyond a reasonable doubt all facts necessary to show that an individual is mentally ill and dangerous".

Another example of evolving civil commitment standards is the much discussed 1969 revision of the California Mental Health Law (Lanterman-Petris-Short Act). Under this law's provisions, the only reasons for involuntary mental hospitalization, after a 72-hour period of detention for evaluation, is either dangerousness or grave disability. The guidelines for the determination of dangerousness are unusually precise, although still inadequate. Dangerousness to self involves evidence of an actual threat or attempt to commit suicide. Dangerousness to others involves very similar guidelines to those listed by Bazelon in *Cross*. There must be a threatened or actual attack causing physical harm to another during or leading to hospitalization *and* "an imminent threat of substantial physical harm to others." How imminent and how substantial are left to judicial discretion.

What may be a backlash to California's regulations on dangerousness, which are considered overly restrictive by many psychiatrists, is a tendency for public agencies to criminalize behavior that would have led to civil commitment under easier commitment criteria. Abramson (1972, p. 15) argues:

> From my own vantage point as a psychiatric consultant to a county probation department, I believe that as a result of LPS, mentally disordered persons are being increasingly subjected to arrest and criminal prosecution. They are often charged with crimes such as public drunkenness, disorderly behavior, malicious mischief, or interestingly, possession of marijuana or of dangerous drugs. Frequently, mentally deranged youth come to police attention because of their disorderly public behavior and are found to have some marijuana in their possession. Illegal barbiturates are sometimes found on a comatose or groggy person following a suicide attempt or gesture. On occasion, concerned friends or relatives inform police that a mentally disordered person has a stash of marijuana in his room in order to secure his involuntary detention and treatment.

He goes on to observe: "Police seem to be aware of the more stringent criteria under which mental health professionals are now accepting responsibility for involuntary detention and treatment, and thus regard arrest and booking into jail as a more reliable way of securing involuntary detention of mentally disordered persons." The developments observed by Abramson are serious ones that cannot fully be analyzed without considerably more data. Nevertheless, his views raise a number of issues that researchers must examine.

Another problem encountered by growing reliance on dangerousness for the confinement of the criminally insane is the apparent assumption that such predictions are in fact something psychiatrists are uniquely equipped to do. Judicial decisions continue to emphasize the importance of dangerousness and statutes continue to be developed that rely on psychiatric predictions of dangerousness to dictate the type and/or length of confinements for the criminally insane. With the exception of Bazelon's decisions, attempts at judicial clarification of the meaning of dangerousness are exceedingly rare. Almost totally absent are efforts to define the critical words associated with dangerousness (imminent, substantial, and harm), which disciplines might have shown some ability to ascertain such propensities, and how a witness demonstrates that in fact he/she is expert. Instead one is confronted with unhesitating confidence that dangerousness is a concept with legal meaning and that psychiatrists are appropriate professionals to predict it.

This legislative and judicial confidence is especially unsettling when one examines what psychiatrists themselves say about their abilities to predict dangerous bahavior. In his comprehensive summary of the psychiatric literature on dangerousness, Rubin (1972, p. 397) notes:

> Treatment interventions depend on predictions of the likely consequences of such interventions. Such predictions are unavoidable for the psychiatrist, as indeed they are for anyone who proposes to treat another's illness. There is, however, another type of prediction, that of the likely dangerousness of a patient's future behavior. This prediction is expected of the psychiatrist and psychiatrists acquiesce daily. This belief in the psychiatrist's capacity to make such predictions is firmly held and constantly relied upon, in spite of a lack of empirical support.

One of the few legislative indications of the lack of documentation for psychiatric expertise in predicting dangerousness was the 1972 report of the Task Force studying proposals for the revision of Pennsylvania's Mental Health and Mental Retardation Laws: "The Task Force ascertained to its complete satisfaction that the assumption of this kind of predictive expertise [i.e., predicting dangerousness in the mentally ill] is quite unwarranted and rejected it after extensive deliberations." However, despite such a conclusion and despite the bulk of psychiatric literature on the topic, dangerousness is becoming the most important justification for involuntary civil hospitalization.

As criminal commitment procedures are further likened to civil procedures and as dangerousness is more explicitly introduced into criminal commitment codes themselves, the use of dangerousness to detain the criminally insane is one of the most significant trends since the *Baxstrom* decision. Such developments have occurred despite the extensive literature showing no special psychiatric abilities to predict it and contrary to the data reported in this book on the success of the Baxstrom patients despite the predictions of their dangerousness.

Because of this rapidly growing emphasis on dangerousness, we have begun focusing directly on this concept in our current research. We are currently involved in a series of studies related to the 1971 revision of the New York CPL with its mandate for the courts, on the basis of psychiatric testimony, to separate the dangerous from the non-dangerous incompetent, indicted felony defendants. We are currently collecting data on the manner in which these determinations of dangerousness are being made, the criteria being employed by the psychiatrists and the courts, and, through follow-up data on the defendants, evaluating the predictive validity of these estimations of dangerousness. Within these investigations of dangerousness, we are also probing the questions of this book about who these people are who become designated as incompetent and dangerous, how the institutions that process these defendants structure career contingencies, and how these institutions respond to revised statutory mandates. The movement towards greater dependence on the criterion of dangerousness as a primary rationale for the confinement of the criminally insane has been steady and pervasive, but associated research has not kept abreast. Our current work, developed from these Baxstrom data, is one attempt to respond to the empirical needs of this major emerging issue.

The Expanding Role of Psychiatry

One of the trends that has had a great part to play in the rise of dangerousness as a major criterion for the custody and care of the criminally insane is the recent expansion of the role of psychiatry throughout the criminal justice system. The confidence in psychiatric abilities implicit in recent legislative statutes is also apparent among some correctional administrators.

These movements have not actually expanded what psychiatrists are expected to do relative to the treatment and detention of the criminally insane. Rather, recent indications of greater use of psychiatrists throughout the criminal justice system suggest the possibility of increases in the number of people who may become defined as criminally insane. This could result from the increased activities of psychiatrists in correctional institutions where mental health problems traditionally have gone unattended. By broadening psychiatric roles, there will be more evaluations, diagnoses, and treatment of mental health problems in prisons. Where such intervention occurs within a prison medical service and when such intervention is not associated with transfer to special mental hospitals, expanding psychiatric services probably will have little impact on more people being defined as criminally insane. However, a frequent outcome of increased psychiatric evaluation is treatment in a special security mental hospital for the criminally insane, both because of inadequate treatment facilities in penal institutions and because the conditions in jails and prisons are often sources of the mental problems being treated.

When this expansion of psychiatric services to correctional facilities is viewed in a Szaszian framework (Szasz 1962, 1963, and 1966) it is suspect and detrimental. He views the extension of the medical model to explain and treat behavioral aberrations that have led to incarceration as inappropriate and to the inmate's disadvantage. Kittrie (1972) has also analyzed many of these trends towards increased dependence on medical/psychiatric explanations of deviance and has concluded that such continued expansion without definite checks is counterproductive. The recent analysis of Abramson (1972) discussed above sharply contrasts with the views of Szasz and Kittrie. He suggests that although a medical model with psychiatric evaluation and treatment may be becoming more common within the criminal justice process, that with stricter criteria for admission to civil mental facilities and demands for more precise indications of dangerousness, various behaviors that previously had led to mental hospitalization are now leading to arrest and criminal detention.

Certainly with the extensive documentation of the less than humane conditions in most U.S. penal institutions, there is little question that the medical care of inmates requires improvement. Yet, when the question of medical services focuses on mental health, a conflict develops between the needs for improving all medical services and the contention of Szasz and Kittrie that the introduction of psychiatric services means that specific behaviors that were initially defined as bad and deserving punishment will become defined as sickness. Such shifts in definition, they believe, then require changes in the basic personality structure of the person to demonstrate rehabilitation. Thus, what began as punishment for a specific criminal act, becomes long-term, often indefinite, confinement under psychiatric aegis.

These punishment-sickness issues do not appear to trouble those concerned about the abhorent day-to-day conditions of U.S. prisons as seriously as they do Szasz and Kittrie. Many such medical service personnel feel that mental health programs in penal facilities have had direct success in alleviating some of the most severe inmate medical problems (Resnik and

Scheck 1972). Their confidence in evolving prison mental health services is striking. However, a question that often seems overlooked by those people expressing confidence in additional psychiatric services is the level of demonstratable effectiveness of such programs. This question might best be framed: Could any well-intentioned, concerned individual have similar successes improving decrepit penal conditions or are there some unique psychiatric contributions to be made?

When viewing recommendations such as that of the Health-Law Project of the University of Pennsylvania Law School (1972) for "the immediate development of an effective psychiatric program at every prison," or Matthews (1967) statement that "at present, with exception altogether too rare, the criminal process does not receive the psychiatric consultation that the social, political, and human importance of its work warrants" (p. 1576), and the report of Alabama's Center for Correctional Psychology on minimal Mental Health Standards for the Alabama Correctional System (1972), it appears that there is an *assumption* that psychiatric services are effective. For instance, in the entire Alabama report with its very specific recommendations for staffing patterns and the like, only the consultant report in the appendix by Ralph Shwitzgebel asks about first documenting the previous effectiveness of the proposed programs.

The literature we have discussed throughout this book on previous psychiatric interventions with the criminally insane highlights excessive confinement, strong psychiatric conservatism in decision making, and few or ineffective programs. Yet, despite this, psychiatrists are now being asked to predict the dangerousness of the criminally insane and to determine the type and lengths of their confinements. They are even recommended as participants in the sentencing of offenders through the Model Sentencing Acts' formulae for determining and sentencing the dangerous offender. While there can be little question of the need for better penal medical services, there are serious questions about the effectiveness of additional psychiatric services within prisons that are otherwise unchanged and the more general objections about the appropriateness of applying the models of human behavior that such services have traditionally utilized. The expansion of psychiatric services, nevertheless, remains one of the main trends affecting the custody and care of the criminally insane.

Consideration of Non-U.S. Treatment Programs

As part of the trend towards increasing psychiatric services for the criminally insane, there has been increasing examination of programs of innovative facilities outside the United States. Our aim here is to indicate briefly what some of the most discussed programs are, how their structures and operations relate to U.S. problems and trends, and to indicate where additional material on them may be found.

The facility that may have received the most recent attention in the United States is Herstedvester in Denmark. Much of this attention has resulted from the selection of its superintendent, Dr. George Sturup, as the winner of the 1966 Isaac Ray Award of the American Psychiatric Association for forensic psychiatry. As part of this award, Sturup presented a series of lectures on the philosophy and program of Herstedvester, and these lectures were subsequently published in a book entitled, *Treating The Untreatable* (Sturup 1968). Herstedvester's program, as with most outside the United States, is hard to evaluate in a U.S. context because of numerous differences in the criminal justice and mental health systems that intimately relate to facilities for the criminally insane. At Herstedvester, patients may be committed indefinitely, with provisions for periodic review and opportunities to petition for release. However, the indeterminate sentence is considered a key factor in their treatment program.

Herstedvester is only for psychopathic, chronic criminals. They do not treat individuals who are mentally ill in any other diagnostic category. Their aim is not to cure these psychopaths but to make them understand themselves and avoid subsequent crimes. Their range of resources and the use of aftercare are two of the ways in which this facility diverges most markedly from U.S. programs. Other aspects are also distinctive, such as Sturup's insistence that there be a door on each patient's room so that he can be by himself when he needs to be. This is startling when one sees the usual pattern of patient sleeping and living quarters in U.S. facilities. They are usually large, open dormitory areas that allow the greatest possible view of the largest possible number of patients by the smallest number of staff members.

The successes of Herstedvester are well documented. Although the property offenders have usually been arrested from 3 to 12 times before admission to Herstedvester and the violent crime offenders are considered dangerous, the recidivism rate of patients released after an average of 2.5 years is 50 percent. Thus, of the 50 percent recidivists who are readmitted and then subsequently released after an average of another 2.5 years, another 50 percent recidivate. The same percentage holds for third and subsequent admissions. So, after 10 years there is an overall 10 percent rate of recurring recidivism.

Similar recidivism statistics are reported from the English hospital for the dangerously mentally ill, Broadmoor Hospital. This facility, like Herstedvester and other European and Canadian programs, is a high security institution and makes no pretentions of being otherwise. From its superintendent's reports (passim DeReuck and Porter 1968), its aftercare network appears more limited than Herstedvester's. Yet in the past 50 years, they have released about 140 patients per year and have had a total of only 5 ex-patients murder anyone. Only one previous homicide, a woman who killed her child before admission to Broadmoor, was directly discharged to the community and killed again. Many years later she killed her husband (McGrath 1972). Of all released patients, only 4 percent have been recalled to Broadmoor (deReuck and Porter 1968, p. 128).

Aftercare components similar to the Danish system are also an integral part of the treatment programs in Holland discussed by Kempe (1968). One of the three methods by which an offender can receive psychiatric treatments in these centers, however, is in lieu of sentence or with a conditional suspended sentence. This alternative suggests that primary care rather than aftercare is actually being provided. The other two paths to outpatient treatment are as a result of psychiatric care being required by a criminal sentence, a mix of criminal disposition and medical intervention not ordinarily possible within the U.S. criminal justice system, or after inpatient treatment. The Dutch aftercare system appears to be truly a comprehensive system centering on the therapeutic partnership of a psychiatrist and social worker. This system has developed despite a public attitude that Kempe (1968) characterized as an ". . . irrational demand that the mentally disturbed offender be permanently banished from the community . . . particularly in those cases where the public is shocked by the crime he has committed" (p. 162). Thus, while Holland's program may be different, the public attitudes it confronts are not unlike those of the United States.

Two quite recent programs of note have been developed in Canada. One is the Philippe Pinel Institute in Montreal and the other is Penatang Psychiatric Hospital in Penetanguishene, Ontario. Both of these programs have indeterminately sentenced patients, like the previous three programs described, and also like these other inpatient programs, the two Canadian facilities place a heavy and unveiled emphasis on security. Their theory is that if the institution's perimeter security is unquestioned by the patients, (1) the patients will not spend all their time thinking about how to escape and will more likely consider the treatment being offered and (2) an unquestioned perimeter security allows more flexible internal programs through decreased internal security. Both Canadian facilities have organized active patient governments that do make a variety of meaningful decisions, although there is little hesitancy to remind them that the medical superintendant still runs the facility. To further develop patient responsibility in Penetang, there is a suicide security precaution technique by which a patient threatening suicide has another patient volunteer hand-cuffed to him until the critical period of suicide threat passes. Both parties in this arrangement are thought to profit through less frequent suicide attempts and the mutual concern patients develop for each other.

These, then, are a few of the programs that are being examined for their potential in U.S. situations. Application of programs remains difficult because of the significant differences in the existing criminal justice philosophies and codes such as indeterminate sentencing and the generality with which dangerousness determinations may be made to employ the indeterminate sentence. Although psychiatrists do not have the same level of judicial influence in Europe as in the United States (c.f. deReuck and Porter 1972, p. 179-84), our impression from the literature is that dangerousness may be invoked within the European and Canadian psychopath and sex offender acts with considerably more ease than in the United States. Despite the inherent difficulties in applying such divergent programs to U.S. situations, the success of many of these programs through large numbers of releases and infrequent recidivists suggest some serious consideration for the possible benefits of indeterminate sentences and utilizing maximum security when necessarily coupled with comprehensive inpatient *and* aftercare programs. These aftercare services are conspicuously absent in most U.S. programs.

These are the major trends in the care and custody of the criminally insane in the mid-1970s. Some of these, such as equal protection and the use of dangerousness as a commitment criterion, are directly related to the *Baxstrom* decision, which generated the research we have reported. The others, the increasing role of psychiatry in the criminal justice system and the growing interest in non-U.S. programs for the criminally insane, are independent of the *Baxstrom* decision but are intimately associated with the issues that evolve from the main thrust of this book.

The main aim of this book has been to document empirically the manner in which the mental health and criminal justice systems *actually* process the people we call criminally insane. When it becomes apparent how mental health programs actually operate in treating some people who have been apprehended for crimes, typically excessive, conservative, and obfuscated detention is evident. Accordingly, questions of individual rights, which have taken up much of the discussion of this chapter, logically follow. In turn, when questions of individual rights are raised the corollary issue of society's right to protect itself also must be faced. As such, the trends we have analyzed in this chapter and the data on the Baxstrom patients demonstrate how the role of psychiatry in social control becomes closely linked with the tensions between societal protection and individual rights. The final chapter focuses on the current dilemmas these conflicting interests present in the context of past and present treatment of the criminally insane in the United States.

10 Social Control and Psychiatry: Implications of the Baxstrom Experience

One of the methods of social control that has developed in the United States is involuntary psychiatric treatment. What for some has been beneficial treatment has often functioned for others simply as a mechanism of social control, allegedly to provide some sort of protection for society. The data we have presented in this book about one group of individuals who received psychiatric treatment as criminally insane demonstrate that the Baxstrom patients were not nearly as dangerous as they were expected to be. This is not to say, certainly, that among these 967 people there were not some who were extremely dangerous and after their transfers or community release did violently assault others. As a group, however, their generally positive outcomes point to some extreme societal conservatism in the handling of such deviants.

A central theme in the recent court decisions relating to the criminally insane and involuntary civil mental patients, as detailed in the last chapter, is the conflict between the rights of patients and the need of society to protect its members. Although this is undoubtedly a critical issue, its discussion presupposes that there is an existing, documented need for society to protect itself from all those people called criminally insane. Our findings severely question the validity of this assumption. It is reasonable to discuss the necessity of hospitalization and detention for society's protection when it can be shown that a real threat is presented. But our work and that of the many others reviewed find this fear to be unwarranted except for a very small percent of the criminally insane and involuntary mental patients.

In light of such findings, these systems can be seen as exerting inappropriate and excessive social control. Certainly, there is some awareness that hospitals for the criminally insane and all mental hospitals with involuntary patients are institutions of social control in that through the use of dangerousness as a commitment criterion, they are facilities for preventive detention. However, the ways in which such preventive functions of mental health programs have been extended into criminal justice processes have rarely been explicated empirically. Thus, there is an obfuscation of the actual practices of defining and controlling deviance, and it is this obfuscation that is the central focus of this book.

The critical issue we have attempted to address through the data on the Baxstrom experience, through previous research, and through an analysis of the institutional processing of the criminally insane is how do these systems of social control actually operate (i.e., what are the actual implications of the use of psychiatry in the criminal justice and mental health systems?). In the United States what are the mechanisms of social control that have actually developed under the auspices of mental health treatment?

In such questions, we are faced with the tensions between two systems of social control, the criminal justice and the mental health. The institutions that have developed at the interface of these two systems most frequently have been examples of excessive and inappropriate forms of social control. What has systematically developed is a situation whereby psychiatry has been asked to take over more and more responsibilities in the control of violent, socially disruptive behavior. This shift occurred in the civil realm through the development of mental hospitals in the United States in the eighteenth and nineteenth centuries and in the criminal arena through the statutes on dangerousness that were discussed in Chapter 9. All of these developments related to societal control and treatment for the individual have occurred (1) despite large gaps in documentation that, in fact, psychiatrists can predict future violent behavior and (2) despite the lack of evidence that treatment programs are efficacious either for the individual or society (i.e., by significantly reducing the occurrence of dangerous behavior).

To understand some of these developments, it is useful to recognize some of the societal demands and assumptions that have been associated with the programs for the treatment of the mentally ill since their first appearance in the United States. In these regards, it is interesting to reflect upon current considerations of non-U.S. treatment programs for the criminally insane in light of the history of U.S. programs. When the settlers of America first began developing facilities for the custody and treatment of the mentally ill, they depended on the models of the nations from which they had come. As such, in the late seventeenth century, witchcraft and burnings at the stake were the typical societal responses to aberrant behaviors in the mental realm as were the gallows in the criminal realm. The legacy from the witchhunts of fifteenth-, sixteenth-, and seventeenth-century Europe, in which an estimated 100,000 people had been tortured and killed (Deutsch 1949), was a series of major witch trials and executions in the United States from 1647 to 1663 and, especially in Salem, from 1688 to 1693. With the development of medical ideas and technologies in the early eighteenth century, the idea of mental illness evolved as an explanation for deviant behavior.

As the idea of mental illness evolved, it was used primarily as a means of societal protection. During colonial times, U.S. common-law standards allowed for the arrest of "furiously insane" persons or those deemed too "dangerous to be permitted to be at large" (Deutsch 1949). Such confinement was to be for the duration of the period of dangerousness. There was no intent of therapy. There was simply the requirement of humane treatment. As Deutsch (1949) notes, "insane persons recognized as such (namely, the violent and the dangerous) were dealt with by the police powers" (p. 420). In fact, the only type of insane patients specifically considered in early colonial legislation were those seen as "furiously mad" or "dangerous" to themselves or others. Deutsch reports an example of this legislation in the 1788 New York State provisions which were taken, practically word for word from a 1744 English law:

> Whereas, There are sometimes persons who by lunacy or otherwise are furiously mad, or are so far disordered in their senses that they may be dangerous to be permitted to go abroad; therefore,
>
> Be it enacted, That it shall and may be lawful for any two or more justices of the peace to cause such person to be apprehended and kept safely locked up in some secure place, and, if such justices shall find it necessary, to be there chained.

Thus, for as long as there has been any laws for the involuntary confinement of the mentally ill in the United States, societal protection through estimations of dangerousness has been a primary reason for their detention.

Initially, the mentally ill were detained in whatever type of facilities were available or could be constructed with local resources. Construction was often necessary because jails had yet to replace the gallows, and thus no penal facilities were available in which to detain these people. Deutsch noted that the first known provision in this regard in Pennsylvania was reported in the 1676 records of the Upland Court:

> Jan Vorelissen, of Amesland, Complayning to ye Court that his son Erik is bereft of his naturall Senses and is turned quat madd and yt, he being a poore man is not able to maintain him; Ordered: yt three or four persons bee hired to build a little block-house at Amesland for to put in the said madman.

These facilities were only for detention and public protection. They were in no way intended to benefit the individual confined there.

The first actual hospital treating the insane was the Pennsylvania Hospital opened in 1752. The early record of this facility reflects little that differed from the prisons from which the insane were supposedly being removed. Strict discipline, chains, and cells in the hospital basement were standard features. What seems most significant about Pennsylvania Hospital is that although its practice differentiated it little from prisons, it established the principle of attempting to treat the mentally ill rather than simply detaining them as malefactors. Between the opening of Pennsylvania Hospital in 1752 and the opening of the first hospital for the criminally insane in

Auburn, New York in 1859, the mentally ill were kept in mental hospitals. These were intended to be more humane and treatment oriented institutions than the purely custodial blockhouses of colonial America. However, mental hospitals, in practice, were primarily custodial facilities under the auspices of treatment.

As medical explanations for many types of maladies and behaviors developed, psychiatry, through its efforts to encompass these areas within its purview and through societal interest in designating someone to make predictions of dangerousness through which protection could be afforded, became a primary agent of social control. Concommitant with these control functions, or by some interpretations under its guise, treatment was a stated aim. However, in the rehabilitation of the criminally insane, hospitals especially designated for them have been notoriously unsuccessful in doing anything beyond detention. This fact, however, even when recognized, has not been very disturbing to the public or legislators because such institutions were seen as providing necessary protection for society from some very dangerous mentally ill people whose criminal backgrounds and propensities made them poor risks for freedom. There can be no denying that some very violent, bizarre individuals have been and are being so detained. Some of these violent people have been detained in hospitals for the criminally insane after convictions for murder, assault, or rape. However, what we have found with our data on the Baxstrom patients is that such images of universally violent, threatening individuals, which have become the common stereotype of the criminally insane, represent a distinct minority of the criminally insane.

In following the 967 Baxstrom patients, we found that on the average they had been continuously institutionalized for 14 years. These retentions on the average exceeded the actual or possible sentences they could have received by 8 years. Thus, with most in their late forties and early fifties, they were transferred from maximum security correctional hospitals for the criminally insane following Johnnie Baxstrom's case in the U.S. Supreme Court in 1966. When the New York State Department of Mental Hygiene indicated to its civil hospitals that the *Baxstrom* decision would result in their receiving large numbers of patients en masse, directly from Dannemora and Matteawan and in a 5-month period, there was extreme anxiety among both the hospital staffs and the surrounding communities. They did not want nor, they claimed, were they equipped to handle such dangerous patients.

By following the patient and postpatient careers of the Baxstrom patients for 4 years after their transfers, it is quite evident that such fears were quite unwarranted for the vast majority of these criminally insane patients. While in the civil hospitals, about 15 percent of our sample of these 967 patients exhibited assaultive behavior and about 25 percent were discharged to the community during their first year in state civil facilities. Interestingly enough, even among these Baxstrom patients, who were considered so dangerous, there was no relationship between their assaultiveness in hospitals and their release to the community. Having interested family or friends in the community who expressed concern and willingness to help them led to their release, even when assaultiveness was present. Thus, the supposed protective function for society from assaultive mental patients was not provided by psychiatric decision-making. If there was mental improvement in the patient, combined with some expressed interest by community members in the patients, level of assaultiveness was of negligible concern.

When released to the community, the Baxstrom patients fared well on indicators such as rearrest and conviction, although almost half were rehospitalized. Between 1966 and 1970, 20 percent of the released Baxstrom patients were rearrested. Practically all arrests were for nuisance crimes such as vagrancy and intoxication. Conviction for a felony occurred in less than 5 percent of the cases. Similarly, of the 967 patients, only 27—24 males and 3 females—were returned to hospitals for the criminally insane at any time during our four-year follow-up. The factors that, not surprisingly, were most associated with recidivism and rehospitalization (all those rearrested were also rehospitalized at some time) were age and a summary scale of severity of criminal history. By using these two factors together, it was possible to designate those who were rearrested and those who displayed dangerous behavior, whether or not it led to rearrest, with a false positive rate of 2 to 1. However, the age break that best discriminated for this patient population was 50 and older. For similar groups of people in traditional state hospitals for the criminally insane, such a finding does have some usefulness. However, since the average age of those passing through the interfaces of the criminal justice and mental health systems today is about 30, additional research is required to test the ultimate applicability of such indicators for practical use.

In sum, the experiences of the *Baxstrom* patients as shown in our data certainly indicate that society through institutions for the criminally insane exercised considerably more social control than was warranted by their subsequent behaviors.

Although assaultive, violent behavior in any group is infrequent, in any large groups, at some time, there will be some. It is assumed that among the criminally insane, the incidence of violent behavior is greatly increased and that because such behavior is no longer low-base rate behavior, preventive detention is justified for essential societal protection. The difficulty in such a position is that while there is some increased frequency, it is still considerably lower than is usually assumed and the behavior remains confined to a minority of the group. Thus, to release most individuals in hospitals for the criminally insane would surely result in some very severe cases of bizarre, violent behavior. However, to support recent practices of detention results in the preventive detention of about four or five times as many individuals as will actually display such behaviors.

Unfortunately, there are no easy solutions to such tensions. Current clinical acumen is so limited that neither psychiatrists nor behavioral scientists can select persons who will become dangerous without designating many times more who will not be dangerous. In addition, any such selection process can expect to indicate only about half of those who will be assaultive. With advances in medical technology, such as psychotropic drugs, it is possible for many people to function in the community who in the past might have required detention. However, such technological advances do not answer the more fundamental issues that the Baxstrom data raise. What risks are the community willing to take to alter the inappropriate preventive confinement of the criminally insane? Should the mental health system function as an agent of social control? Is such control the primary intent of such institutions or has their development into such mechanisms been masked by ideological facades?

With current and foreseeable tools, it is impossible to designate those who will be dangerous without making many times more errors than accurate predictions. Because of this, there are numerous insoluble dilemmas surrounding psychiatry's role in social control. As society considers shifts away from a total emphasis on its protection needs to a recognition of individual rights, it is imperative that the situations made clear by the Baxstrom data about the actual functioning of the mental health system at its interfaces with the criminal justice system become known. In order to develop acceptable policies, to design appropriate research, and to adequately understand how society functions and changes, it is necessary first to understand the manner in which such systems actually operate. Before society can decide on the level of risks it is willing to accept to lessen excessive preventive detention, it first must recognize how some of its therapeutic systems are functioning to preventively detain many non-dangerous individuals under the aegis of mental health treatment.

There are few answers to these critical questions, and we certainly can propose no perfect one. Instead, what we have attempted to do within the framework of this book and through the Baxstrom patient data is to point out (1) how the mental health system has worked in the past, (2) how many of its current arrangements in concert with the criminal justice systems are based on inaccurate ideas about how dangerous these people are, and (3) how the mental health system in unseen ways offers excessive social control of non-dangerous, but deviant individuals. For analyses to proceed and for appropriate policy to develop, the actual operations of these systems must be understood by many more people (the public, the lawmaker, and the researcher) than have expressed interest in them in the past. The careers of the Baxstrom patients provide a firm step towards such understanding.

Bibliography

Abramson, Marc F. 1972. "The Criminalization of Mentally Disordered Behavior: Possible Side-Effect of a New Mental Health Law." *Hospital and Community Psychiatry* 23 (April): 101-5.

Alabama's Center for Correctional Psychology. 1972. *Minimal Mental Health Standards for the Alabama Correctional System.*

Allen, Harry E., Clifford F. Simmonsen, and Marshall S. Gordon. 1973. "Operational Research in Criminology: An Examination of the Decision-Making Process for Commitment under Sexual Psychopath Statute for Apparently Unrelated Offenses." Paper presented at Annual Meeting of the American Society of Criminology. New York.

Angrist, Shirley, Mark Lefton, Simon Dinitz, and Benjamin Pasamanick. 1968. *Women After Treatment: A Study of Former Mental Patients and Their Normal Neighbors*. New York: Appleton Century Crofts.

Arens, Richard. 1969. *Make Mad the Guilty: The Insanity Defense in the District of Columbia*. Springfield, Ill.: C. C. Thomas.

Association of the Bar of the City of New York. 1968. *Mental Illness, Due Process and the Criminal Defendant*. New York: Fordham University Press.

Barry, John R. and Samuel C. Fulkerson. 1966. "Chronicity and the Prediction of Duration and Outcome of Hospitalization from Capacity Measures." *Psychiatric Quarterly* 40 (January): 104-21.

Becker, Howard, ed. 1963. *Outsiders*. New York: The Free Press.

Bullard, Dexter Jr. and Barbara R. Hoffman. 1960. "Factors Influencing the Discharge of Chronic Schizophrenia Patients," p. 215-28, in Research Conference on Therapeutic Community, Manhattan State Hospital, Wards Island, New York, 1959. Springfield, Ill.: C. C. Thomas.

Burt, Robert A. and Norval Morris. 1972. "A Proposal for the Abolition of the Incompetency Plea." *The University of Chicago Law Review* 40: 66-95.

Carlie, Michael Kaye. 1970. "The Older Arrestee: Crime in the Later Years of Life." Unpublished Ph.D. Dissertation. St. Louis, Mo.: Washington University.

Clausen, J. A. 1956. *Sociology and the Field of Mental Health*. New York: Russell Sage.

Colorado State Hospital. 1966. *The Criminally Insane: A Follow-Up Study*. Research and Program Evaluation Series.

Cooke, Gerald. 1969. "The Court Study Unit: Patient Characteristics and Differences between Patients Judged Competent and Incompetent." *Journal of Clinical Psychology* (April): 140-3.

Cooke, Gerald, Norman Johnston, and Eric Pogany. 1973. "Factors Affecting Referral to Determine Competency to Stand Trial." *American Journal of Psychiatry* 130 (August): 870-5.

Crittenden, Kathleen S. and Richard J. Hill. 1971. "Coding Reliability and Validity of Interview Data." *American Sociological Review* 36 (December): 1073-80.

Cunningham, Murray K. 1969. "Community Placement of Released Mental Patients: A 5 Year Study." *Social Work* (January): 54-61.

de Reuck, A. V. S. and Ruth Porter, eds. 1968. *The Mentally Abnormal Offender*. Boston: Little, Brown & Co.

Dershowitz, A. M. 1970. "The Law of Dangerousness: Some Fictions about Predictions." *Journal of Legal Education* 23: 24-56.

Deutsch, Albert. 1949. *Mentally Ill in America*. New York: Columbia University Press.

Doleschal, Eugene. 1972. "Criminal Statistics." Rockville, Md.: National Institute of Mental Health, Center for Studies of Crime and Delinquency.

Eckland, Bruce K. 1968. "Retrieving Mobile Cases in Longitudinal Surveys." *Public Opinion Quarterly* 32: 51-64.

Erickson, Kai. 1962. "Notes on the Sociology of Deviance." *Social Problems* 9 (Spring): 307-14.

Faris, Robert E. L. and H. Warren Dunham. 1939. *Mental Disorders in Urban Areas*. Chicago: University of Chicago Press.

Freeman, Howard E. and Ozzie G. Simmons. 1963. *The Mental Patients Comes Home*. New York: John Wiley and Sons, Inc.

Gathercole, G. E., M. J. Craff, J. McDougall, H. M. Barnes, and D. F. Peck. 1968. "A Review of 100 Discharges from a Special Hospital." *British Journal of Criminology* 87: 419-25.

Gibbs, Jack P. 1966. "Conceptions of Deviant Behavior: The Old and the New." *Pacific Sociological Review* 9 (Spring): 9-14.

Giovannoni, J. M. and L. Gurel. 1967. "Socially Disruptive Behavior of Ex-Mental Patients." *Archives of General Psychiatry* 17: 146-53.

Glaser, Daniel. 1964. *The Effectiveness of a Prison and Parole System*. Indianapolis: Bobbs-Merrill Company, Inc.

Goffman, Erving. 1961. *Asylums: Essays on the Social Situation of Mental Patients and Other Inmates*. Garden City, N.Y.: Doubleday.

Gove, Walter. 1970a. "Societal Reaction as an Explanation of Mental Illness: An Evaluation." *American Sociological Review* 35 (October): 873-84.

———. 1970b. "Who Is Hospitalized: A Critical Review of Some

Sociological Studies of Mental Illness.'' *Journal of Health and Social Behavior* 11 (December): 294-303.

Gove, Walter R. and Patrick Howell. 1974. ''Individual Resources and Mental Hospitalization: A Comparison and Evaluation of the Societal Reaction and Psychiatric Perspectives.'' *American Sociological Review* 39 (February): 86-100.

Greenblatt, M., R. York, and E. L. Brown. 1955. *From Custodial to Therapeutic Patient Care in Mental Hospitals*. New York: Russell Sage.

Greenley, J. R. 1972. ''The Psychiatric Patient's Family and Length of Hospitalization.'' *Journal of Health and Social Behavior* 13 (March): 25-37.

Halfon, Arlene, Marcia David, and Henry Steadman. 1971. ''The Baxstrom Women: A Four Year Follow-Up of Behavior Patterns.'' *The Psychiatric Quarterly* 45: 518-27.

Hall, Oswald. 1948. ''The Stages of a Medical Career.'' *American Journal of Sociology* 53: 327-36.

Halleck, Seymore. 1967. *Psychiatry and the Dilemmas of Crime*. New York: Harper & Row.

Hess, John H. Jr. and Herbert E. Thomas. 1963. ''Incompetency to Stand Trial: Procedures, Results, and Problems.'' *American Journal of Psychiatry* 119 (February): 713-20.

Hilles, L. 1970. ''Critical Incidents Precipitating Admissions to a Psychiatric Hospital.'' *Bulletin of the Menninger Clinic* 34: 89-102.

Hollingshead, August B. and Frederick C. Redlich. 1958. *Social Class and Mental Illness*. New York: John Wiley and Sons, Inc.

Hughes, Everett C. 1937. ''Institutional Office and the Person.'' *American Journal of Sociology* 43: 404-13.

Hunt, Robert C., and E. David Wiley. 1968. ''Operation Baxstrom After One Year.'' *American Journal of Psychiatry* 124 (January): 134-8.

Israel, Robert H. and Nelson A. Johnson. 1956. ''Discharge and Readmission Rates in 4,254 Consecutive First Admissions of Schizophrenia.'' *American Journal of Psychiatry*, 112 (May): 903-9.

Kaplan, Stanley M. and George C. Curtis. 1961. ''Reactions of Medical Patients to Discharge or Threat of Discharge from a Psychosomatic Unit of a General Hospital,'' pp. 7-15, in M. Greenblatt, D. Levinson and G. Klerman, eds., *Mental Patients in Transition*. Springfield, Ill.: C. C. Thomas.

Katz, J. and J. Goldstein. 1960. ''Dangerousness and Mental Illness.'' *Journal of Nervous and Mental Disease* 131: 404-13.

Keller, O. J. and C. Vedder. 1965. *The Elderly Offender and Theories of Crime and Cessation*. Chicago: University of Chicago Press.

Kempe, G. T. 1968. "Aftercare for Mentally Abnormal Offenders in the Netherlands," pp. 152-63, in A. V. S. de Reuck and Ruth Porter, eds., *The Mentally Abnormal Offender*. Boston: Little, Brown & Co.

Kitsuse, John. 1962. "Societal Reaction to Deviant Behavior: Problems of Theory and Method." *Social Problems* 9 (Winter): 247-56.

Kittrie, Nicholas N. 1972. *The Right to be Different: Deviance and Enforced Therapy*. Baltimore: The Johns Hopkins Press.

Kozol, Harry L., Richard J. Boucher, and Ralph F. Garofalo. 1972. "The Diagnosis and Treatment of Dangerousness." *Crime and Delinquency* 18 (October): 371-92.

Laczko, Andrew L. et al. 1970. "A Study of Four Hundred and Thirty-Five Court-Referred Cases." *Journal of Forensic Sciences* 15: 311-23.

Lanzkron, John. 1963. "Murder and Insanity: A Survey." *American Journal of Psychiatry* 119 (December): 754-8.

Leifer, Ronald. 1969. *In the Name of Mental Health*. New York: Random House.

Lemert, Edwin. 1967. *Human Deviance, Social Problems and Social Control*. Englewood Cliffs, N. J.: Prentice-Hall.

Levine, D. 1970. "Criminal Behavior and Mental Institutionalization." *Journal of Clinical Psychology* 26: 279-84.

Lewin, Travis. 1968. "Disposition of the Irresponsible: Protection Following Commitment." *Michigan Law Review* 66 (February): 721-36.

Madge, John. 1965. *The Tools of Social Science*. New York: Doubleday.

Maisel, Robert. 1970. "Decision-Making in a Commitment Court." *Psychiatry* 33: 352-61.

Matthews, Arthur R., Jr. 1967. "Mental Illness and the Criminal Law: Is Community Mental Health an Answer?" *American Journal of Public Health* 57: 1571-9.

_______. 1970. *Mental Disability and the Criminal Law*. Chicago: American Bar Association.

McGarry, A. Louis. 1965. "Competency for Trial and Due Process via the State Hospital." *American Journal of Psychiatry* 122 (December): 623-31.

_______. 1971. "The Fate of Psychotic Offenders Returned for Trial." *American Journal of Psychiatry* 127 (March): 101-4.

McGarry, A. Louis and Richard H. Bendt. 1969. "Criminal vs. Civil Commitment of Psychotic Offenders: A Seven-Year Follow-Up." *American Journal of Psychiatry* 125 (April): 93-100.

McGarry, A. Louis and Honora A. Kaplan. 1973. "Overview: Current Trends in Mental Health Law." *American Journal of Psychiatry* 130 (June): 621-30.

McGrath, P. G. 1968. "Custody and Release of Dangerous Offenders," pp. 221-9, in A. V. S. de Reuck and Ruth Porter, eds., *The Mentally Abnormal Offender*. Boston: Little, Brown & Co.

———. 1972. Personal Communication. October 6.

Meehl, Paul E. 1954. *Clinical versus Statistical Prediction*. Minneapolis: University of Minnesota Press.

Mendel, Werner M. and Samuel Rapport. 1969. "Determinants of the Decision for Psychiatric Hospitalization." *Archives of General Psychiatry* 20 (March): 321-8.

Michaux, William W., Martin M. Katz, Albert A. Kurland, and Kathleen H. Gansereit. 1969. *The First Year Out*. Baltimore: The Johns Hopkins Press.

Miller, Dorothy and Michael Schwartz. 1966. "County Lunacy Commission Hearings: Some Observations of Commitments to a State Mental Hospital." *Social Problems* 14 (Summer): 26-35.

Moberg, David O. 1953. "Old Age and Crime." *Journal of Criminal Law, Criminology and Police Science* 43: 764-6.

Morris, Norval. 1968. "Psychiatry and the Dangerous Criminal." *Southern California Law Review* 41: 514-47.

Morrow, William R. and Donald B. Peterson. 1966. "Follow-Up of Discharged Psychiatric Offenders—'Not Guilty by Reason of Insanity' and 'Criminal Sexual Psychopaths'." *The Journal of Criminal Law, Criminology and Police Science* 57: 31-34.

Myers, J. K. and L. L. Bean. 1968. *A Decade Later: A Follow-Up of Social Class and Mental Illness*. New York: John Wiley and Sons, Inc.

Pfeiffer, Eric, Richard Eisenstein, and E. Gerald Bobbs. 1967. "Mental Competency Evaluation for the Federal Courts: 1. Methods and Results." *The Journal of Nervous and Mental Disease* 144: 320-8.

Rappeport, Jonas and George Lassen. 1965. "Dangerousness—Arrest Rate Comparisons of Discharged Patients and the General Population." *American Journal of Psychiatry* 121 (February): 776-83.

———. 1966. "The Dangerousness of Female Patients: A Comparison of the Arrest Rates of Discharged Psychiatric Patients and the General Population." *American Journal of Psychiatry* 123 (October): 413-9.

Reckless, C. 1950. *The Crime Problem*. New York: Appleton Century Crofts.

Resnick, Judith and Robert J. Shack. 1972. *Undelivered Care: The Incapacitated and the Mentally Ill New York City Defendant*. Report to the Mayor's Criminal Justice Coordinating Council, December.

Robbins, Lee N. 1966. *Deviant Children Grown Up*. Baltimore: The Williams and Wilkins Company.

Robins, A. J. 1954. "Prognostic Studies in Mental Disorder." *American Journal of Psychiatry* 3 (December): 434-44.

Rollin, Henry J. 1965. "Unprosecuted Mentally Abnormal Offenders." *British Medical Journal* 1: 831-5.

Rosen, Albert. 1954. "Detection of Suicidal Patients: An Example of Some Limitations in the Prediction of Infrequent Events." *Journal of Consulting Psychology* 18: 397-403.

Rosenberg, Arthur Harris and A. Louis McGarry. 1972. "Competency for Trial: The Making of an Expert." *American Journal of Psychiatry* 128 (March): 82-86.

Rosenberg, Morris. 1968. *The Logic of Survey Analysis*. New York: Basic Books.

Rosenhan, D. L. 1973. "On Being Sane in the Insane Places." *Science* 179: 250-8.

Ross, Hugh Alan. 1959. "Commitment of the Mentally Ill: Problems of Law and Policy." *Michigan Law Review* 57 (May): 945-1018.

Rubin, Bernard. 1972. "The Prediction of Dangerousness in Mentally Ill Criminals." *Archives of General Psychiatry* 77 (September): 397-407.

Rundle, Frank. 1972. "Institution vs. Ethic: The Dilemma of a Prison Doctor." *The Humanist* (May/June): 26-28.

Sall, Joan, William W. Vosburgh, and Abby Silverman. 1966. "Psychiatric Patients and Extended Visit: A Survey of Research Findings." *Journal of Health and Human Behavior* 7 (March): 20-28.

Scheidenmandel, D. and C. Kanno. 1969. "The Mentally Ill Offender: A Survey of Treatment Programs." The APA Joint Information Service. Washington, D.C.

Scheff, Thomas J. 1964. "The Societal Reaction to Deviance: Ascriptive Elements in the Psychiatric Screening of Mental Patients in a Mid-Western State." *Social Problems* (Spring): 401-13.

———. 1966. *Being Mentally Ill*. Chicago: Aldine.

Schur, Edwin. 1969. "Reactions to Deviance: A Critical Assessment." *American Journal of Sociology* 75 (November): 309-22.

Slovenko, Ralph. 1971. "Competency to Stand Trial: The Reality Behind the Fiction." *Wake Forest Law Review* 8 (December): 1.

Smith, K., M. W. Pumphrey, and J. C. Hall. 1963. "The 'Last Straw': The Decisive Incident Resulting in the Request for Hospitalization in 100 Schizophrenic Patients," *American Journal of Psychiatry* 120: 228-32.

Spitzer, Stephen P. and Norman R. Denzin. 1968. *The Mental Patient: Studies in the Sociology of Deviance*. New York: McGraw-Hill.

Srole, Leo et al. 1962. *Mental Health in the Metropolis: The Midtown Manhattan Study*. New York: McGraw-Hill.

Steadman, Henry J. 1973. "Some Evidence on the Inadequacy of the Concept and Determination of Dangerousness in Law and Psychiatry." *Journal of Psychiatry and Law* 1 (Winter): 409-26.

Steadman, Henry J. and Jeraldine Braff. 1973. "Incompetency to Stand Trial: The Easy Way In," in M. Reidel and T. Thornberry, eds., *Crime and Delinquency Dimensions of Deviance*, forthcoming.

Steadman, Henry J. and Gary Keveles. 1972. "The Community Adjustment and Criminal Activity of the Baxstrom Patients: 1966-1970." *American Journal of Psychiatry* 129 (March): 80-86.

Sturup, Georg K. 1968. *Treating the "Untreatable,"* Baltimore: The Johns Hopkins Press.

Sutherland, Edwin H. and Donald R. Cressey. 1966. *Principles of Criminology*. New York and Philadelphia: J. B. Lippincott Company.

Szasz, Thomas S. 1962. "Mind Tapping: Psychiatric Subversion of Constitutional Rights." *American Journal of Psychiatry* 119 (October): 323-7.

———. 1963. *Law, Liberty, and Psychiatry*. New York: Macmillan and Co.

———. 1966. "Whither Psychiatry?" *Social Research* 33: 439-62.

———. 1970. *The Manufacture of Madness: A Comparative Study of the Inquisition and the Mental Health Movement*. New York: Harper & Row.

Tong, John and G. W. MacKay. 1959. "A Statistical Follow-Up of Mental Defectives of Dangerous and Violent Propensities," *British Journal of Delinquency* 9 (October): 276-84.

Tuteur, Werner. 1969. "Incompetency to Stand Trial, A Survey," *Corrective Therapy and Journal of Social Therapy* 15: 73-79.

Uniform Crime Reports. 1972. U.S. Federal Bureau of Investigation.

University of Pennsylvania. 1972. Health-Law Project of University of Pennsylvania Law School.

Vann, Carl R. 1965. "Pre-Trial Determination and Judicial Decision-Making: An Analysis of the Use of Psychiatric Information in the Administration of Criminal Justice," *University of Detroit Law Journal* 43: 13-33.

Vedder, Clyde B. and Oliver J. Keller, Jr. 1968. "The Elderly Offender, Probation and Parole," *Police* 13 (1): 14-16.

VonHirch, A. 1972. "Prediction of Criminal Conduct and Preventive Confinement of Convicted Persons." *Buffalo Law Review* 21: 717-58.

Webb, Eugene J., Donald T. Campbell, Richard D. Schwartz, and Lee Sechrest. 1966. *Unobtrusive Measures*. Chicago: Rand McNally and Co.

Wegner, Dennis L. and C. Richard Fletcher. 1969. "The Effect of Legal Counsel on Admissions to a State Mental Hospital: A Confrontation of Professions." *Journal of Health and Social Behavior* 10 (March): 66-72.

Weinstein, Louis. 1964. "Real and Ideal Discharge Criteria," *Mental Hospitals* 15 (December): 680-3.

Wenk, Ernst, James O. Robinson, and Gerald W. Smith. 1972. "Can Violence Be Predicted?" *Crime and Delinquency* 18 (October): 393-402.

White, Leonard, Wilherlm B. Krumholz, and Ludwig Fink. 1969. "The Adjustment of Criminally Insane Patients to a Civil Mental Hospital," *Mental Hygiene News* 53 (January): 34-40.

Zeidler, J. C., W. H. Haines, V. Tikuisis, and E. J. Uffelman. 1955. "A Follow-Up Study of Patients Discharged from a Hospital for the Criminally Insane." *The Journal of Social Therapy* 11: 21-24.

Zimroth, Peter. 1972. "101,000 Defendants Were Convicted of Misdemeanors Last Year. 98,000 of Them Had Pleaded Guilty—To Get Reduced Sentences," *New York Times Magazine*, May 28, pp. 14, 37, and 42-44.

Zitrin, Arthur, Morris Herman, and Yorihiko Kumasaka. 1969. "New York's Mental Hygiene Law—A Preliminary Evaluation," *Mental Hygiene* 54: 28-36

Indexes

Name Index

Subject Index

About the Authors

Henry J. Steadman is a Senior Research Scientist and Director of the Mental Health Research Unit in the New York State Department of Mental Hygiene. He received the M.A. from Boston College and the Ph.D in sociology from the University of North Carolina, Chapel Hill. He has worked in his current position for the past four years and in this capacity is now director of a project entitled "Dangerousness, Due Process, and the Criminally Insane," continuing his investigations into the institutional networks and organizational processes at the interfaces of the mental health and criminal justice systems which were begun with the research for this book.

Joseph J. Cocozza received the Ph.D from Case Western Reserve University. Formerly Chairman of the Department of Sociology at Ursuline College, he is a Senior Research Scientist with the Mental Health Research Unit. As co-principal investigator with Dr. Steadman of a study of the criminally insane, Dr. Cocozza's main interests are in drawing out the theoretical and methodological implications of the research for the study and understanding of deviance and deviant behavior in general.

DATE DUE		
NOV 25 1980		
DEC 2 1980		
APR 26 1983		
DEC 09 1983		
DEC 8 '88		
APR 25 '90		
OCT 13 1992		
NOV 02 1998		
APR 10 2001		

CARD REMOVED